FORD
ZEPHYR ZODIAC EXECUTIVE MARK III and MARK IV

ISBN 978-1-84155-816-5

CONTENTS

Ford Zodiac Mark III Road Test	4
Ford Zodiac Mark III 2553cc	8
Ford Zodiac Mark III, Zephyr 4 and 6	13
Ford Zodiac Mark III	27
Ford Zephyr 4, Automatic, Road Test	32
Ford Zephyr 6, Zephyr 4	36
Ford Executive Zodiac, Road Test	38
Ford Zephyr 4, Road Test	43
Ford Zephyr 6, Automatic	48
Looking at the Ford Zephyr Six	52
Ford Zephyr 6 and Zodiac Mark IV	56
Ford Zephyr Six Estate	72
New Zodiac and Zephyr, Advert	77
Ford Zephyr 6 Mark IV, Road Test	78
Ford Zodiac/Zephyr MK. IV, Advert	85
Fred Hart discusses Mark IV Fords	86
Zodiac/Zephyr V-6/V-4 Range	90

The Ford Zodiac Mk. III

WITH the new Zodiac Mk. III, a 100 m.p.h. saloon with sports car acceleration, the largest and most expensive British Ford moves into a new performance category although beneath a body/chassis structure of entirely new appearance the mechanical components are substantially similar to the well-tried units of the previous model.

The new car looks bigger and more imposing than its predecessor and yet, in fact, its size is largely an optical illusion; overall plan dimensions remain much the same as before and the height has decreased by some 3 in. giving much more elegant proportions and a lower centre of gravity which reflects very favourably in road behaviour. In external appearance the separate influences of current American, British and Continental fashions are blended harmoniously rather than strikingly; internal trim leans towards traditional British with no untrimmed body metal visible, pile carpets and a walnut-finished metal facia.

Performance & Price

THE six-cylinder o.h.v. engine retains a capacity of 2,553 c.c. but extensive internal changes have raised maximum power by 28%. A maximum torque increase of 3% matches a weight rise of 4% (to 25 cwt. unladen) so that with higher overall gearing the impressive acceleration, of which we shall speak later, owes a great deal to a new and very good four-speed gearbox. No other large saloon available on the British market can offer speed and acceleration of the same order at a price as low as £1070.

A genuine two-way 100 m.p.h. was achieved by our very new test car which had done less than 1,500 miles when the figures were taken. A standing quarter mile took 19.2 sec. and 0-50 m.p.h. was recorded in 9.2 sec.; results which fall within a range normally exclusive to some of the better sports cars and to a few large-engined relatively expensive saloons.

In Brief

Price £778 plus purchase tax £292 15s 3d equals £1070 15s 3d.
Capacity .. .. 2,553 c.c.
Unladen kerb weight 25 cwt.
Acceleration:
 20-40 m.p.h. in top gear .. .. 8.8 sec.
 0-50 m.p.h. through gears .. .. 9.2 sec.
Maximum top-gear gradient .. .. 1 in 8.9
Maximum speed .. 100.7 m.p.h.
"Maximile" speed .. 96.5 m.p.h.
Touring fuel consumption .. .. 22.6 m.p.g.
Gearing: 19.9 m.p.h. in top gear at 1,000 r.p.m.

The increase in power output from the previous 85 to the present 109 b.h.p. (net) has been achieved partly by an increase in compression ratio from 7.8 to 8.5, at which the engine is still perfectly content with Premium grade fuel, but mainly by

Painted metal is now an accepted part of internal finish but the Zodiac has the much greater air of luxury that goes with a fully trimmed interior. Note the curved window frame of the nearside rear door; all the exterior glazing is curved. On the left of the facia is quite a large glove box which drops downwards on hinged links.

induction modifications which include a larger single choke carburetter, larger ports and valves and a twin exhaust system. Top gear acceleration figures show that power at high revs has not been bought at the expense of low speed torque and in spite of gearing which gives nearly 20 m.p.h./1000 r.p.m. an elapsed time of 8.6 sec. from 10 to 30 m.p.h. is the best of all the figures for 20 m.p.h. increments.

However, although on full throttle the Zodiac will pull away strongly and smoothly from below 10 m.p.h. in top gear, a light flywheel permits a rather jerky part throttle response at these speeds and makes it very easy to stall the engine if any attempt is made to trickle away from rest at low r.p.m. High gearing gives easy high-speed cruising with no intrusion of engine noise. Above 80 m.p.h. the only sound of which one is really conscious is wind noise and, although there are quieter cars from this point of view, the background level remains low enough for conversation to be easy and unstrained at maximum speed. Nylon speed tyres are a standard fitting so that fast cruising does not involve special tyre inflation.

Four Speeds

IN changing to a four-speed gearbox for the first time on one of their larger British cars, Fords have elected to fit synchromesh on all the forward gears, a particularly wise decision for a box which has well-chosen and fairly close ratios and lower gears which are intended for use rather than for emergency. Indeed, we found that the near 40 m.p.h. bottom gear was too high for a re-start on the 1 in 3 test hill, high revs producing fade from an otherwise very satisfactory clutch with light operation.

It is not easy to design a gearbox for a large and powerful engine with really effective synchromesh and still retain precision and lightness of control but Fords have succeeded. One can only criticize the Zodiac column gearshift on the grounds of rather a long travel which puts third gear at arm's stretch. Most drivers found, before they were familiar with the car, that it was very easy to think that third gear had been engaged when, in fact, the lever had not been moved sufficiently far.

All the gears are quiet, although certainly not inaudible, and third is used extensively for motoring slowly in traffic, for overtaking on busy roads and for accelerating out of them very rapidly up to 70 m.p.h. with silky smoothness. On Devonshire hills, second gear is often needed for acceleration after a sharp corner. A double exhaust system which emits a deep and slightly sporting note outside the car is heard only remotely and unobtrusively inside.

Very Controllable

WITH 4½ turns from lock to lock, the Zodiac steering may be considered low-geared but freedom from play and a variable ratio mechanism giving higher gearing around the central position make this more obvious on sharp corners than on fast roads. When manœuvring it becomes a little heavy; at other times it is smooth, friction-free and accurate both on corners and on straight roads at speed. On wet roads or dry a noticeable understeer characteristic persists right to the well-balanced breakaway point; the back wheels can be made to slide first if a lot of power is

Independent front suspension is still by Macpherson struts but modifications to the layout have lowered their upper mountings and permitted a much lower bonnet line. The car is some 3 in. lower and longer than its predecessor.

used but the handling is only slightly throttle-sensitive and correction is very easy. Modern tyres do not squeal easily but it was not difficult to produce a loud scrubbing noise from the Zodiac front tyres on sharp corners.

Although photographs revealed the presence of considerable roll in extreme conditions, occupants felt that this Ford had more than average stability and a pleasing ability to change direction without disconcerting lurches. Although occasional bad bumps caused back axle hop and it was possible to generate wheelspin and tramp by full-throttle acceleration in second gear when cornering, the handling was characterized by lack of vice and by first-class controllability which imparted considerable confidence when hurrying over fast main roads.

Front-seat occupants enjoy a soft, well-controlled and generally comfortable ride; there is a certain amount of body shudder on sharp-edged bumps such as tar strips, and appreciable road noise is generated by certain surfaces. Those in the back are more conscious of the up and down movement that relatively soft damping allows and which is most noticeable with a full load.

The Interior

FROM the point of view of width the Zodiac has room inside for six people, but a driver no taller than 5 ft. 10 in. or so will normally have the bench front seat right back on its adjustment slides, and this leaves less than enough legroom for anyone of the same height to sit comfortably in the back. A better compromise might have been achieved by increasing passenger length at the expense of the very long boot which has some 22 cu. ft. of usable space.

Individual front seats adjustable for rake are offered as an extra but our test car had the standard bench seat with roll edges to the cushion and a folding centre arm rest; to compensate for a fairly low seating position the squabs slope back quite a lot and they have the strong profile curvature which characterises current Ford seats and which offers proper spinal support. Most people found them comfortable but a few would have preferred a more upright position. There is first-class visibility in all directions although the sloping bonnet affords little indication of the width of the car. The steering wheel is placed well away from the driver but has an awkward horn ring which is so pivoted that it is easiest to operate in the 6 and 12 o'clock position and most difficult around 3 and 9 o'clock where the hands normally rest.

The imitation walnut of the facia panel offends some people and not others. Speedometer, fuel gauge and thermometer are large and well placed but whereas the first of these is clear and easy to read, the other two are rather vague. Minor controls have been planned with care and thought and therefore lack the confusing symmetry of appearance and position on which some designers insist. The main light switch is well away from the others and headlamp flashing is conveniently arranged by a finger tip button in the end of the direction indicator lever. The foot dipper is less satisfactory in that it needs a downward movement which is natural only to a driver sitting very close to the wheel. To reduce the drain on the battery, a parking switch is provided which cuts out the nearside side and rear lamps and also isolates the starter switch as a deterrent against theft.

Windscreen washers and variable speed wipers are controlled by respectively pushing or twisting the same knob and the wiper blades, which are of the twin rubber type, deserve particular praise for their behaviour at cruising speeds in the nineties where they show no signs of lifting off the glass.

A pull-out handbrake under the facia was found convenient to use and powerful enough to hold the car on a 1 in 3 gradient. The brake pedal is also well placed and near to the floor so that the accelerator foot moves over to it naturally with a minimum of transition lag. Repeated use of these light progressive servo-assisted brakes (disc front) from high speeds failed to disclose any weaknesses.

A cavernous boot is ideal for those who do not believe in travelling light. The lid is spring-loaded open but if the car is standing on a steep up-gradient it will not remain open wide enough for loading.

Coachwork and Equipment

Starting handle	None
Battery mounting	Under bonnet
Jack	Triangular screw type
Jacking points	Two each side under door sills
Standard tool kit	Jack and wheelbrace
Exterior lights:	4 headlamps, 2 side/flashers, 2 tail/stop lamps, 2 rear flashers, number-plate lamp.
Number of electrical fuses	One (plus one if radio fitted)
Direction indicators	Self-cancelling flashers
Windscreen wipers:	Twin-blade, self-parking, variable-speed electric.
Windscreen washers	Manual pump type
Sun visors	Two, universally pivoted
Instruments:	Speedometer (with total mileage recorder and decimal trip), fuel gauge, water thermometer, clock.
Warning lights:	Generator, direction signals, oil pressure, main beam, heater fan.
Locks:	
With ignition key:	Both front doors, glove locker and boot.
With other keys	None
Glove lockers	One in nearside of facia panel
Map pockets	One in each front door
Parcel shelves	One behind rear seat
Ashtrays	One front, one rear
Cigar lighters	One
Interior lights	Two courtesy lights in roof
Interior heater	Standard fitting fresh-air type
Car radio	Optional extra, manual or push-button types
Extras available	Radio and standard accessories
Upholstery material	Hide or cloth
Floor covering	Carpet on felt
Exterior colours standardized	12 single colours
Alternative body styles	None

Maintenance

Sump	6¼ pints, S.A.E. 20W (plus 1¼ pints in filter)
Gearbox	2¼ pints, S.A.E. 80
Rear axle	2¼ pints, S.A.E. 90
Steering gear lubricant	S.A.E. 90 EP oil
Cooling-system capacity	21 pints (2 drain taps)
Chassis lubrication	By grease gun every 5,000 miles to 12 points
Ignition timing	8° b.t.d.c.
Contact-breaker gap	.015 in.
Sparking-plug type	Champion N5
Sparking-plug gap	.030 in.
Valve timing:	Inlet opens 17° before t.d.c. and closes 51° a.b.d.c. Exhaust opens 49° before b.d.c. and closes 19° a.t.d.c.
Tappet clearances (cold):	
Inlet	.014 in.
Exhaust	.014 in.
Front wheel toe-in	$\frac{1}{16}$ to $\frac{3}{16}$ in.
Camber angle	1°-2°
Castor angle	0°-1°
Steering swivel-pin inclination	6° 17' to 7° 17'
Tyre pressures:	
Front	24 lb.
Rear	24 lb.
Brake fluid	Girling
Battery type and capacity	12 v., 57 amp hr. (Optional heavy duty 80 amp hr. available)

For the last few years Fords have been notable for heating systems of excellent power and controllability and the Zodiac is no exception although many people will prefer sliding controls, with easily visible settings, to rotary ones. A feature which should be particularly valuable in summer is a controllable deflector which allows a strong draught of cold air to be projected on the faces of the occupants. The booster fan is very quiet and a warning light has been incorporated in its switch.

It is a tribute not only to the engine but even more to the safety of the chassis that this powerful car was driven at full throttle a great deal during our test. The overall fuel consumption of 19½ m.p.g. is therefore reasonable although it would probably have been worse if secrecy considerations had not prohibited the usual substantial mileage in heavy rush-hour traffic. We see this new Ford as a car which will appeal particularly to the long-distance business motorist by virtue of the outstanding performance and impressive appearance at such a low price. It may have less attraction for the buyer who seeks maximum passenger space inside a car of compact overall dimensions.

The Motor

MAKE: Ford. TYPE: Zodiac Mk. III.

MAKER: Ford Motor Co. Ltd., Dagenham, Essex.

ROAD TEST • No. 15/62

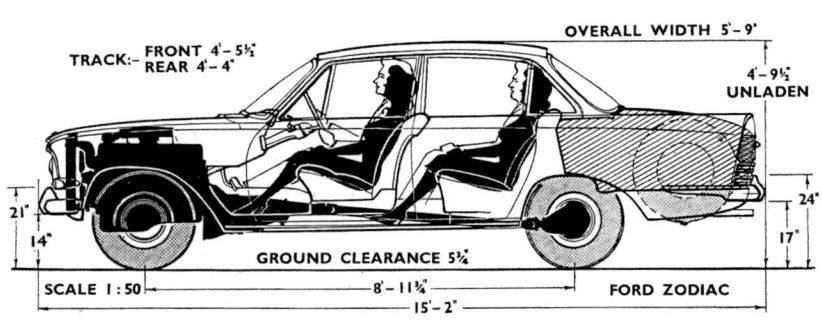

DATA

World copyright reserved; no unauthorized reproduction in whole or in part.

CONDITIONS: Weather: Cold and dry, wind 8-10 m.p.h. (Temperature 35°-44° F., Barometer 29.8 in. Hg.) Surface: Dry tarmacadam. Fuel: Premium grade pump petrol (approx. 97 Octane Rating by Research Method).

INSTRUMENTS
Speedometer at 30 m.p.h.	3% fast
Speedometer at 60 m.p.h.	2% fast
Speedometer at 90 m.p.h.	Accurate
Distance Recorder	1% fast

WEIGHT
Kerb weight (unladen, but with oil, coolant and fuel for approximately 50 miles) ... 25 cwt.
Front/rear distribution of kerb weight 54½/45½
Weight laden as tested ... 28¾ cwt.

MAXIMUM SPEEDS
Flying Mile
Mean of four opposite runs ... 100.7 m.p.h.
Best one-way time equals ... 102.3 m.p.h.
"Maximile" Speed (Timed quarter-mile after one mile accelerating from rest.)
Mean of opposite runs ... 96.5 m.p.h.
Best one-way time equals ... 98.9 m.p.h.
Speed in gears
Max. speed in 3rd gear ... 84 m.p.h.
Max. speed in 2nd gear ... 56 m.p.h.
Max. speed in 1st gear ... 39 m.p.h.

FUEL CONSUMPTION
37.0 m.p.g. ... at constant 30 m.p.h. on level
32.0 m.p.g. ... at constant 40 m.p.h. on level
28.5 m.p.g. ... at constant 50 m.p.h. on level
25.5 m.p.g. ... at constant 60 m.p.h. on level
22.5 m.p.g. ... at constant 70 m.p.h. on level
19.0 m.p.g. ... at constant 80 m.p.h. on level
15.0 m.p.g. ... at constant 90 m.p.h. on level
Overall Fuel Consumption for 1,091 miles, 55.9 gallons, equals 19.5 m.p.g. (14.45 litres/100 km.).
Touring Fuel Consumption (m.p.g. at steady speed midway between 30 m.p.h. and maximum, less 5% allowance for acceleration) ... 22.6 m.p.g.
Fuel tank capacity (maker's figure) 12 gallons

BRAKES from 30 m.p.h.
0.99 g retardation (equivalent to 30½ ft. stopping distance) with 100 lb. pedal pressure.
0.91 g retardation (equivalent to 33 ft. stopping distance) with 75 lb. pedal pressure.
0.62 g retardation (equivalent to 48½ ft. stopping distance) with 50 lb. pedal pressure.
0.30 g retardation (equivalent to 100 ft. stopping distance) with 25 lb. pedal pressure.

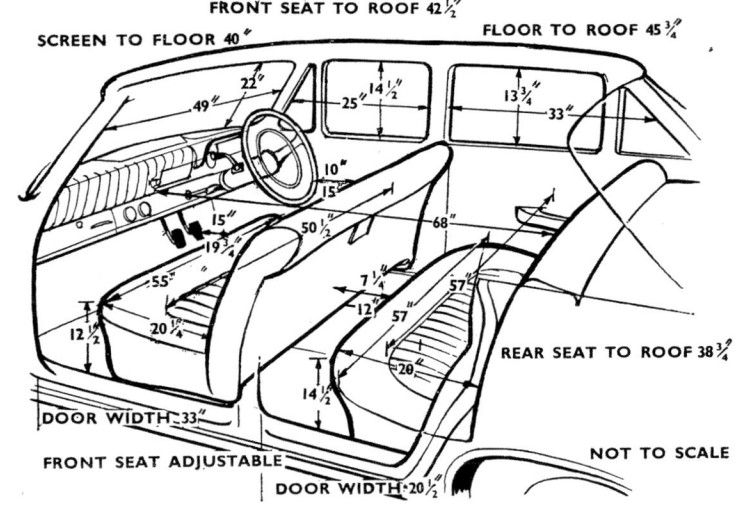

HILL CLIMBING at sustained steady speeds
Max. gradient on top gear ... 1 in 8.9 (Tapley 255 lb./ton)
Max. gradient on 3rd gear ... 1 in 6.0 (Tapley 370 lb./ton)
Max. gradient on 2nd gear ... 1 in 3.8 (Tapley 570 lb./ton)

ACCELERATION TIMES from standstill
0-30 m.p.h.	4.0 sec.
0-40 m.p.h.	6.1 sec.
0-50 m.p.h.	9.2 sec.
0-60 m.p.h.	13.4 sec.
0-70 m.p.h.	18.2 sec.
0-80 m.p.h.	24.2 sec.
0-90 m.p.h.	37.9 sec.
Standing quarter-mile	19.2 sec.

ACCELERATION TIMES on upper ratios
	Top gear	3rd gear
10-30 m.p.h.	8.6 sec.	5.6 sec.
20-40 m.p.h.	8.8 sec.	5.9 sec.
30-50 m.p.h.	9.7 sec.	6.4 sec.
40-60 m.p.h.	10.9 sec.	7.0 sec.
50-70 m.p.h.	12.5 sec.	8.5 sec.
60-80 m.p.h.	13.6 sec.	—
70-90 m.p.h.	18.9 sec.	—

STEERING
Turning circle between kerbs:
Left ... 35½ ft.
Right ... 35½ ft.
Turns of steering wheel from lock to lock 4¼

Specification

Engine
Cylinders	6
Bore	82.55 mm.
Stroke	79.5 mm.
Cubic capacity	2,553 c.c.
Piston area	49.74 sq. in.
Valves	Overhead (pushrods)
Compression ratio	8.3/1
Carburetter	Zenith 42 W.I.A.-2, downdraught
Fuel pump	AC mechanical
Ignition timing control	Centrifugal and vacuum
Oil filter	Full flow
Maximum power (net)	109 b.h.p.
at	4,800 r.p.m.
Piston speed at maximum b.h.p.	2,500 ft./min.

Transmission
Clutch	8¼ in. dia. Ford/Borg & Beck s.d.p.
Top gear (s/m)	3.550
3rd gear (s/m)	5.013
2nd gear (s/m)	7.860
1st gear (s/m)	11.229
Reverse	11.878

Propeller shaft .. Open, Hardy Spicer needle roller
Final drive .. Hypoid bevel
Top gear m.p.h. at 1,000 r.p.m. .. 19.9
Top gear m.p.h. at 1,000 ft./min. piston speed 38.1

Chassis
Brakes .. Girling hydraulic with vacuum servo
Brake dimensions:
Front .. 9¾ in. dia. discs
Rear .. 9 in. dia. drums, 2¼ in. wide
Friction areas: 98 sq. in. of friction lining operating on 330 sq. in. swept disc and drum surface.
Suspension:
Front: Independent by Macpherson coil-spring damper strut and bottom wishbone incorporating anti-roll bar.
Rear: Live axle and semi-elliptic leaf springs.
Shock absorbers:
Front .. Armstrong telescopic
Rear .. Armstrong lever arm
Steering gear .. Ford/Burman recirculating ball
Tyres .. 6.40—13 four-ply nylon sports, tubed or tubeless

Ford Zodiac Mark III 2,553 c.c.

WHENEVER the assembly lines at Dagenham are geared to the production of a completely new model, one can be sure that several years of intense thought and searching experiment lie behind it; for once those lines are moving, the new car will be rolling off in tens of thousands for several years to come. It has to be good right from the start, as well as being so up to date that it should not fall out of fashion before its time is up. Moreover, today's designers have to look farther afield than this country when laying out a new vehicle, in anticipation of taking a much greater share in the European market.

Admirers of the previous Zodiac will surely concede that its replacement is a significant advance in outward appearance and equipment. On the road the improvements in its behaviour and performance are just as marked. Among other assets it is the first British-made Ford to reach and exceed a top speed of 100 m.p.h.

There was a full description of the Zodiac Mark III in *Autocar* on April 13, 1962. Mechanically it is like its predecessor in fundamentals, the most significant innovation being a four-speed gearbox with synchromesh on each forward gear. This can be supplemented by a Borg-Warner overdrive, and B-W automatic transmission remains an alternative. Engine power has been boosted by no less than 28 per cent, from 85 to 109 net b.h.p. Ford-Macpherson telescopic struts, in a more highly developed form, are retained for the front suspension, but the rear axle assembly remains conventional except that the spring leaves are sandwiched with rubber. As with the Mark II Zodiac, there is servo-assisted disc-and-drum braking by Girling.

In the body nothing of the former car remains, and the new Zodiac has an individuality in appearance and equipment which lifts it a rung higher on the ladder of luxury. External distinctions include the four headlamps, a compound curvature screen and rear window, and single-curvature side windows. Frameless, hinged windows in the rear quarters, once quite a common feature of British family cars, make a welcome reappearance on this car.

Within external dimensions virtually unchanged, except that the height has been reduced by 4·5in., and upon the same wheelbase and tracks as before, the new car has inches more in seat width—4in. extra across the rear cushion, for instance—and appreciably more legroom for the driver. The finish and appointment of the interior are immediately attractive, and there are three choices of seat trim material —Cirrus fabric, Bedford cord or leather. The last-named, which costs £33 13s 9d extra in this country, was fitted in the car tested.

One is immediately impressed by the ease and quietness with which the doors close. There are folding centre armrests for front and back seats, as well as small rests attached to the door panels, and the seats are generously dimensioned

PRICES

Basic (with four-door saloon body and manual gearbox)	£778
Purchase Tax	£292 15s 3d
Total (in G.B.)	**£1,070 15s 3d**

Extras (total):

	£ s d
Automatic Transmission	110 0 0
Overdrive	58 8 9
Leather trim	33 13 9
Reclining seats ... ... Price not yet announced	

This view shows the curved door windows, the full quota of arm-rests and leather seat trim. Clearly those travelling in front are much better off for space and ease of entry. The strange pedal pad angles are also obvious here

in cushion length and backrest height. They give good but unexceptional support—a trifle too pronounced at the rolls on the leading edges of the cushions. Three can ride abreast on each seat, but because of the need to allow plenty of clearance above the final drive casing the middle passenger at the back sits on very thin cushioning.

It is, however, in the matter of seating that the new Zodiac displays its one rather considerable shortcoming. With the front seat full back on its runners—and this is where the majority of drivers are likely to find it most comfortable for long-distance motoring—there is precious little space for legs behind it. Indeed, one does not have to be a giant to find one's knees jammed against it, and the base of the seat butting firmly against the shoelaces. Moreover, the combination of thick doors, and centre door pillars of which the bases are unusually far back, is such that even young and agile people find it none too easy to get their feet in or out. On the face of it, one can only express surprise that the manufacturers did not add three or four inches to the wheelbase to ensure adequate passenger space.

From a driver's viewpoint the front seat could well be raised an inch or two, without prejudicing headroom too much, which would also improve the angle of attack on the curiously arranged brake and clutch pedals. As it is, the pads are too nearly horizontal, so that on the brake particularly there is a danger of a wet shoe sliding forward off the pad. The pedals are also too near the floor, and a local depression in that panel would improve matters.

Other controls are well arranged, and so spaced that there is never confusion. There is a full horn ring in the dished steering wheel, and a headlamp flashing button is included in the direction signalling lever. The T-handle for the parking brake is particularly neatly installed in the facia.

The test car had the standard manual transmission (without overdrive) with a somewhat austere-looking black gear lever to the left of the steering column. This has very long vertical movement between first and second, third and top—about 11in. in each case, which calls for excessive exertion and stretch of the arm. Together with a not altogether smooth action, this made the test car's changes somewhat clumsy—not so good, in fact, as on other examples of the new box which we have tried. For our collective taste the lever end would be better if set an inch or two lower.

Especially neat is the full door trim, without metal or other sills at the windows, this trim having a resilient backing. The padded plastic over the upper part of the facia is also neat, but being light in colour and not wholly matt, it creates annoying reflections in the screen, especially in dull weather and, we suspect, in fog.

As a long-distance touring car the Ford is well provided with stowage space for travelling paraphernalia. A drop-down container above the front passenger's legs, spring-loaded upwards so that it should not fall inadvertently, is large enough to carry a handbag as well as a reflex camera. Although it has a lock, on the test car one could easily overcome this with a sharp tug downwards. On the front door panels are well-designed pockets for maps and papers, and behind the back seat is a wide and deep shelf.

Of all the new Ford's virtues, none is more outstanding than the heating and ventilating system. It can give off almost breathtaking quantities of heat within moments of a cold start, and is very easily set by simple, well-engineered controls. In our view the ability to have cool air fed into the upper part of a car, while the lower part is heated, is a major contribution to comfort and safety, for it enables the driver, in particular, to be kept warm without becoming drowsy. Such a system also ensures better heat circulation to the rear compartment and avoids the passengers receiving all the warmth in the face while the feet remain cold. As with so many heaters, downward delivery is concentrated towards the middle of the car, so that one leg receives more benefit than its fellow. Some form of thermostatic (automatic) temperature control would have been appreciated.

Usually extra power is extracted from a given engine with some sacrifice of smoothness and quiet running. Of the new Zodiac the reverse is true, and a deal of thought and application given to sound insulation has, in fact, appreciably reduced the mechanical noise reaching the passengers. The unit remains refined and notably unobtrusive at high engine revolutions, and the car can maintain 80-90 m.p.h. on a motorway with most agreeable ease.

Under-bonnet accessibility is excellent, while the compartment is particularly tidy and neatly finished. Zodiac IIIs have rocker covers and air cleaners painted distinctively in bright yellow

Make · FORD Type · Zodiac Mark III

Manufacturers: The Ford Motor Co. Ltd., Dagenham, Essex

Test Conditions
Weather ......Dry and fine, 7-12 m.p.h. breeze
Temperature ....44 deg. F. (6·7 deg. C.)
Barometer ....29·8in. Hg.
Dry concrete and tarmac surfaces.

Weight
Kerb weight (with oil, water and half-full fuel tank): 25·1cwt (2,814lb, 1,276kg)
Front-rear distribution, per cent: F, 53·7; R, 46·3
Laden as tested .... 28·1cwt (3,150lb, 1,429kg)

Turning Circles
Between kerbs ....L, 38ft 6in.; R, 37ft 2in.
Between walls ....L, 40ft 7in.; R, 39ft 3in.
Turns of steering wheel lock to lock 4

Performance Data
Top gear m.p.h. per 1,000 r.p.m................. 20·3
Mean piston speed at max. power 2,504ft/min
Engine revs at mean max. speed ...... 4,950 r.p.m.
B.h.p. per ton laden .... 77·6

MAXIMUM SPEEDS AND ACCELERATION (mean) TIMES

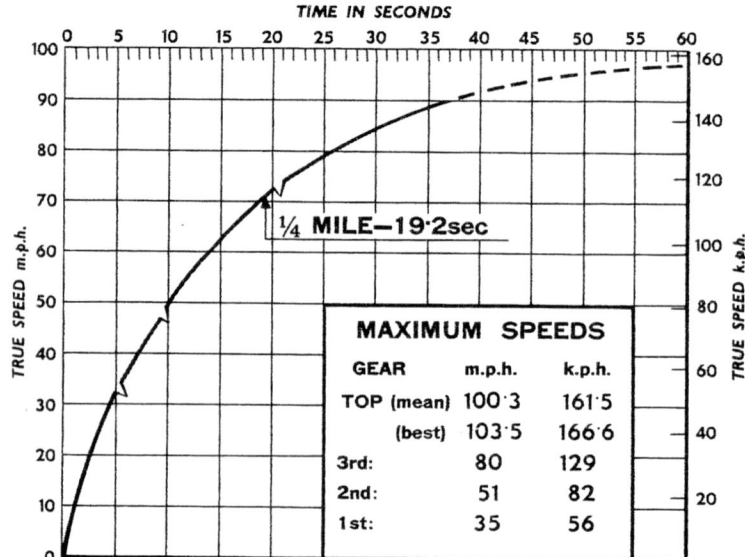

MAXIMUM SPEEDS

GEAR	m.p.h.	k.p.h.
TOP (mean)	100·3	161·5
(best)	103·5	166·6
3rd:	80	129
2nd:	51	82
1st:	35	56

¼ MILE—19·2sec

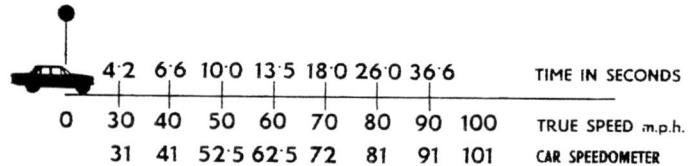

TIME IN SECONDS	4·2	6·6	10·0	13·5	18·0	26·0	36·6
TRUE SPEED m.p.h.	30	40	50	60	70	80	90	100
CAR SPEEDOMETER	31	41	52·5	62·5	72	81	91	101

Speed range and time in seconds

m.p.h.	Top	Third	Second	First
10—30	—	6·8	4·3	3·2
20—40	9·5	6·3	4·5	—
30—50	10·2	6·7	5·0	—
40—60	10·6	7·3	—	—
50—70	11·9	8·0	—	—
60—80	14·7	12·0	—	—
70—90	19·4	—	—	—

FUEL AND OIL CONSUMPTION

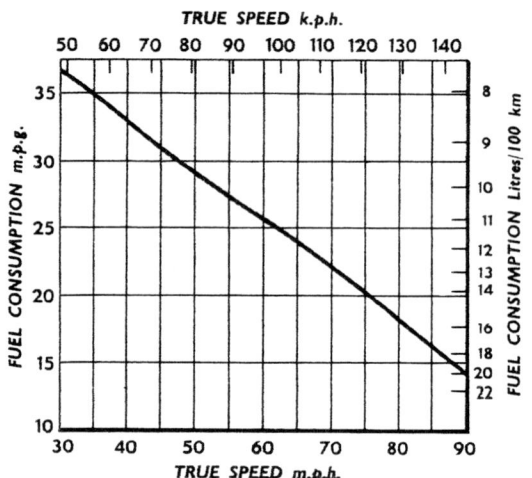

FUEL .... Premium grade (97 octane RM)
Test Distance .... 1,093 miles
Overall consumption ...... 19·1 m.p.g. (14·8 lit/100 km.)
Normal range .... 18-25 m.p.g. (15·7—11·3 lit/100 km.)
OIL: S.A.E. 20 ...... Consumption: 3,500 m.p.g.

BRAKES (from 30 m.p.h. in neutral)	Pedal load	Retardation	Equiv. distance
	25lb	0·21g	144ft
	50lb	0·50g	60ft
	75lb	0·81g	37ft
	100lb	0·98g	30·8ft
	Handbrake	0·40g	75ft

CLUTCH Pedal load and travel—40lb and 5·5in.

HILL CLIMBING AT STEADY SPEEDS

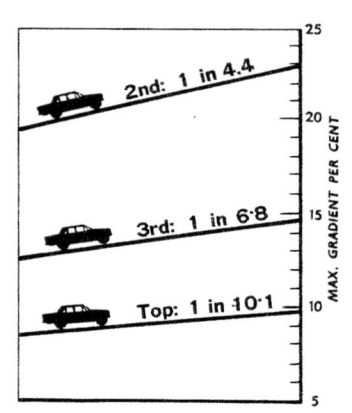

GEAR PULL (lb per ton)	Top	3rd	2nd
	220	325	500
Speed range (m.p.h.)	40–50	35–44	29–34

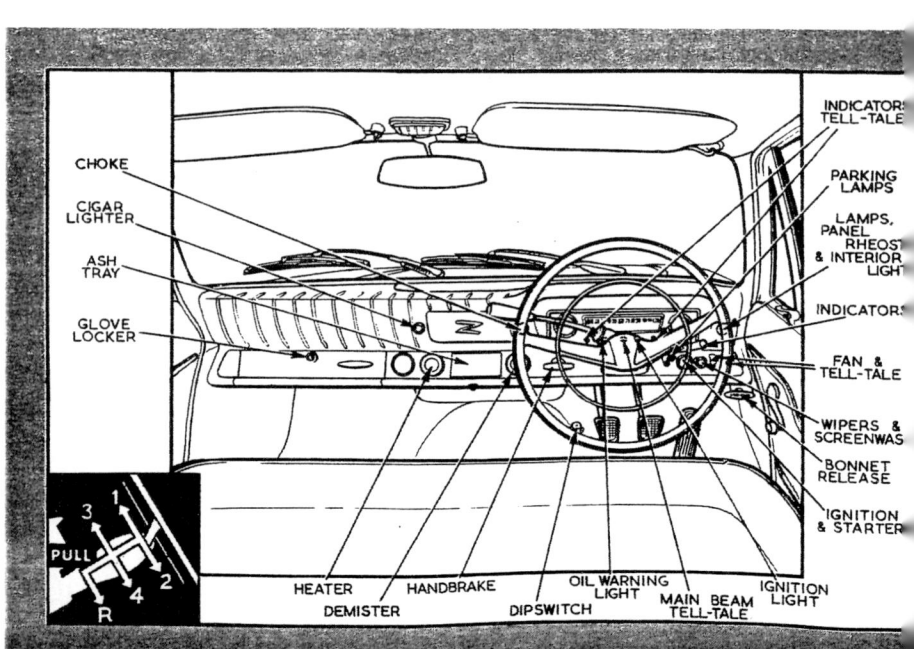

Slender roof pillars like these make for excellent all-round visibility, and the frameless triangular panes behind the rear doors are hinged. Both front and rear signal flashers can be seen from the sides

Ford Zodiac Mark III . . .

Although the Zodiac III is considerably higher geared than its predecessor—for instance, at 80 m.p.h. the engine now turns at about 3,900 r.p.m. as compared with 4,320 r.p.m.—its through-the-gears accelerative powers are improved throughout, more particularly at the "top end." Here are some comparative figures, those for a manual transmission Zephyr tested in September 1960 being given in brackets: 0-30 m.p.h., 4·2sec (4·6); 0-50 m.p.h., 10·0sec (11·2); 0-70 m.p.h., 18·0sec (26·8). Indeed, the Zodiac III reaches 80 m.p.h. 0·8sec quicker than the earlier Zephyr reached 70 m.p.h., and is also fractionally quicker to 90 m.p.h. than the Zephyr was to 80 m.p.h. Because of its lower gearing, however, the Zephyr would pick up speed faster in top up to around 55 m.p.h., after which the Zodiac could leave it easily. In the indirect gears no comparisons could be made because the Zephyr only had three to the new car's four. There is also a 10 m.p.h. gain in all-out speed and a parallel step-up in high speed cruising ability.

As expected, the fuel consumption rates at constant speeds are slightly better where it matters most, the new figure at 80 m.p.h. being 18·1 m.p.g. (Zephyr 17·3 m.p.g.). This seems to be the economical limit, however, for 90

The metal facia panels have a simulated wood grain finish. Above the passenger's knees is a really capacious drop-down locker. Reflections in the screen, seen here, are troublesome in daytime

m.p.h. brings it down to 14·2 m.p.g. Unfortunately our test had to be crowded into a very few days, during which the staff had little opportunity for leisurely driving. Hence an overall consumption of 19·1 m.p.g. may disappoint the manufacturers, but seems perfectly reasonable to us who alone know how hard we drove the car. While the 12-gallon fuel tank is a welcome increase from 10·5, a further two gallons would have been worth while to allow more than a safe 220 miles between refills during really fast runs.

Full Marks for Gearbox

Of the new gearbox one can praise the efficiency of the synchromesh, the quiet running and intelligent ratio spacing. The ability to use third up to a true 80 m.p.h. gives the car real versatility for main road hill-storming and overtaking. First is high enough to be used freely in traffic, low enough for a restart on a 1-in-3—with which the parking brake could not quite cope.

The clutch proved able to absorb repeated full-energy take-offs without developing any roughness or unwanted slip. This pedal had more than usual free travel and a quick take-up, which combined with a rather "sudden" throttle linkage to make smoothly progressive starts from rest rather tricky in normal use. The final drive was practically inaudible at any speed.

While the Zodiac III has basically similar ride characteristics to those of its predecessor, including that familiar slightly rolling gait over steeply cambered or wavy surfaces, lower spring rates have softened it appreciably and back seat comfort is especially improved. The damping is excellent and there is virtually no recurrent pitch nor excessive roll. Little road noise reaches the passengers, and the body is structurally rigid and free from tiresome resonances. There was, however, some very pronounced wind whistle around the seals of one quarter-light on this car, because the locking cam would not pull it tightly shut.

Over special surfaces at the M.I.R.A. proving grounds, the Ford performed in a manner which augurs well for those owners living in countries where the going is much rougher than one finds in the U.K. It steers capably and the mechanism is agreeably light, even at parking speeds, but this has to be paid for by somewhat low gearing at four turns of the steering wheel for a mediocre lock with a mean of 40ft between walls. The car is directionally stable at speed, and quite powerful self-centring action gives an inherent fail-safe characteristic. Fast cornering reveals that the Ford understeers to a degree sufficient to make its behaviour fully predictable and easy to control.

Firestone Sport tyres with nylon casings give sure grip without being noisy at speed or squealing round corners. Only in the wet with the back seat unoccupied would the tail-end sometimes slide outwards earlier than expected, especially when the road surface was none too good.

The braking arrangements are developed from those of the superseded Zodiac, a point being that the rear drums are wider and have properties of endurance more in keeping with the front discs. They give superb stopping power from high speed, repeatedly if necessary, and are smooth and progressive. For the quickest possible stop from 30 m.p.h. 100lb pressure was needed on the brake pedal, which should be within the power of any woman driver.

At night the Zodiac's four sealed beams spread their light over a truly remarkable area, and on the test car at least were set to give more illumination than we can remember on any other car. In fact, this setting was a shade too high because an occasional oncoming driver would flash his lamps in protest against the Ford's dipped beams. On such a potentially fast car the headlamp flasher button is almost essential, not only for signalling but also for those rare occasions when one is travelling with dipped beams and the momentary need arises to extend one's range of vision. A pity that one must then sharply criticize this luxurious car for having no reversing lamps, nor any provision for them.

An unusual item is a parking lamp switch, to leave one front and one rear lamp lit, and at the same time to isolate the self-starter. The interior is lit when any door is opened, with separate lamps for the front and rear compartments. The driving mirror, safely framed in plastic, has tinted glass to reduce dazzle. Operated by a variable speed electric motor, the wipers swept an area of the screen which also varied, according to the prevailing wetness and the speed selected; at times the driver would be faced with a con-

An unusual refinement is the plastic cover, incorporating a pocket for tools, for the spare wheel. The boot is deep and neatly carpeted, and its lid is spring-loaded upwards. The capacity is about 22 cu. ft. Note the outlets for two independent exhaust systems

siderable blind area next to the right-hand screen pillar. Louder horns would be appreciated and, for the driver who smokes, a more accessible ashtray. Apart from a jack, wheelbrace and wheel trim lever, no tools are provided in the car.

There is every indication that the new Zodiac will attract an even wider public than its predecessor, that it will please them more and serve them even better.

Specification

ENGINE
- Cylinders ... 6 in line
- Bore ... 82.6mm (3.25in.)
- Stroke ... 79.5mm (3.13in.)
- Displacement ... 2,553 c.c. (155.8 cu. in.)
- Valve gear ... Overhead, pushrods and rockers
- Compression ratio ... 8.5 to 1
- Carburettors ... Single Zenith downdraught 42WIA-2
- Fuel pump ... A.C. mechanical
- Oil filter ... Full-flow external, replaceable element
- Max. power (net) 109 b.h.p. at 4,800 r.p.m.
- Max. torque (net) 137 lb. ft. at 2,400 r.p.m.

TRANSMISSION
- Clutch ... 8.5in. single dry plate
- Gearbox ... Four-speed, all-synchromesh
- Overall ratios ... Top 3.55, 3rd 5.01, 2nd 7.86, 1st 11.23, reverse 11.88
- Final drive ... Hypoid bevel, 3.55 to 1

CHASSIS
- Construction ... Integral with steel body

SUSPENSION
- Front ... Telescopic struts and dampers, wishbones, coil springs and anti-roll bar
- Rear ... Live axle, half-elliptic leaf springs, lever arm dampers
- Steering ... Recirculating ball. 17in. dia. steering wheel

BRAKES
- Type ... Girling hydraulic; discs front, drums rear, with servo assistance
- Dimensions ... Discs 9.75in. dia., drums 9.0in. dia. with 2.25in. wide shoes
- Swept areas ... F, 203 sq. in.; R, 127 sq. in. (235 sq. in. per ton laden)

WHEELS
- Type ... Pressed steel disc, 5 studs, 4.5in. wide rim
- Tyres ... Firestone Nylon Sports, tubeless. 6.40-13in.

EQUIPMENT
- Battery ... 12-volt 57-amp. hr.
- Headlamps ... Four-lamp system, 50-37 (outer lamps); 37 watt (inner lamps)
- Reversing lamp ... None
- Electric fuses ... 1 (plus 1 for radio)
- Screen wipers ... Two blades, variable speed electric motor, self-parking
- Screen washer ... Standard
- Interior heater ... Standard. Fresh-air type with single-speed booster fan
- Safety belts ... Anchorages provided
- Interior trim ... Leather seat trim, plastic roof lining
- Floor covering ... Carpet
- Starting handle ... None
- Jack ... Screw-pillar type
- Jacking points ... 2 each side under body sills
- Other bodies ... None

MAINTENANCE
- Fuel tank ... 12 Imp. gallons (no reserve)
- Cooling system ... 21 pints (including heater)
- Engine sump ... 8 pints SAE 20. Change oil every 5,000 miles; change filter element every 5,000 miles
- Gearbox and overdrive ... 4 pints SAE 80. Change oil after first 5,000 miles, thereafter top up every 5,000 miles
- Final drive ... 2.5 pints SAE 90. Top up every 5,000 miles. (No recommended change intervals)
- Grease ... 12 points every 5,000 miles
- Tyre pressures ... F and R, 24 p.s.i. (normal driving) F and R, 30 p.s.i. (fast driving)

Scale: 0.3in to 1ft.

Cushions uncompressed.

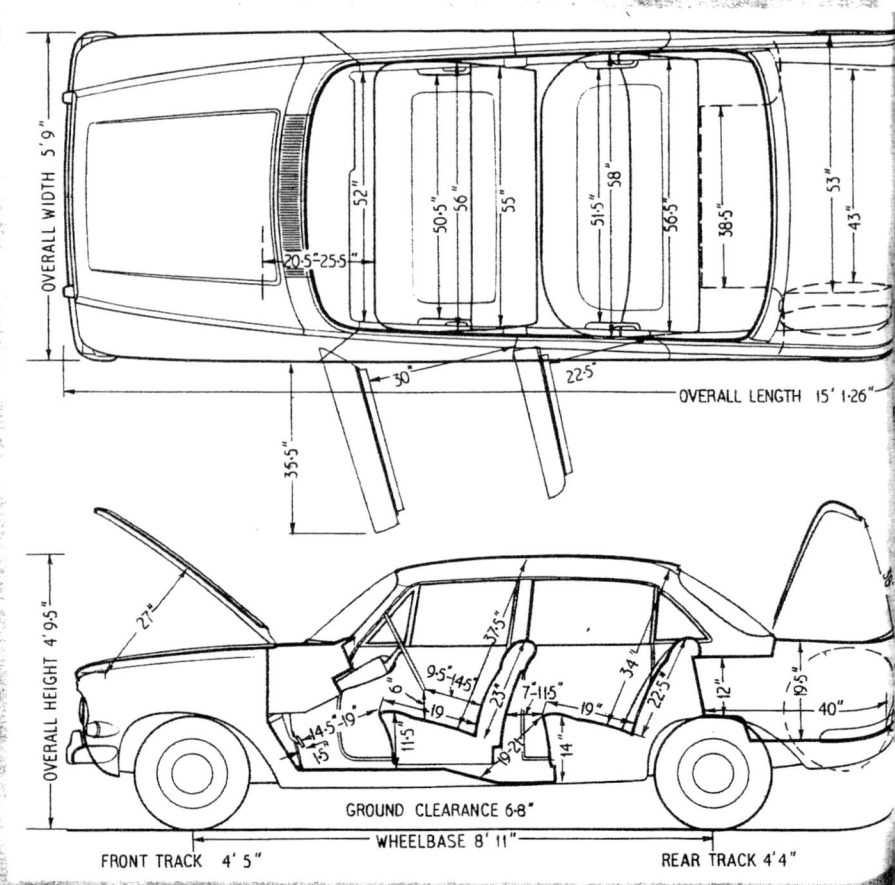

FORD ZEPHYR 4 AND 6 AND ZODIAC MARK III

INDEX TO REPAIR OPERATIONS

BODYWORK
BRAKES
CLUTCH
COOLING SYSTEM
ELECTRICAL SYSTEM
ENGINE
FRONT SUSPENSION AND FRONT END
FUEL SYSTEM

GEARBOX
IGNITION
PROPELLER SHAFT AND UNIVERSAL JOINTS
REAR AXLE AND REAR SUSPENSION
STEERING
WHEELS AND TYRES

GENERAL.—These Mark III versions of the Zephyr and Zodiac models were introduced in April 1962.

BODYWORK

GENERAL.—All-welded pressed-steel integral construction with box section longitudinal members. Front wings are bolted on.

Front suspension upper mounting point is located in engine compartment side valance. When checking accident damage or carrying out repairs, body must be located on jig, picking up on these points to check and ensure correct alignment.

From October 1962, the rear wheel track was increased by 1½ in. and complete bodies to the early dimension are not serviced.

All panels are serviced.

Window regulator handles are retained by hairpin clip (as on Mk. II) fitted in line with handle. Ensure closed end of clip is towards handle when fitting or it becomes impossible to remove afterwards.

Boot lid mounted on adjustable torsion bars which can be located in one of three positions.

When carrying out body repairs, ensure that suitable sealer is applied to all locations.

LOCKS.—Zero-torque locks fitted to all doors with key lock to both front doors. To remove a lock, remove interior handles and trim pad; remove rear glass run, retained by screw at lower end, spring clip at top. On front doors, remove screws securing remote control to door; on rear doors, also disconnect horizontal rod from lock pushrod control. Lock and remote-control assembly can be removed through door after removing lock-retaining screws.

FRONT DOOR WINDOWS.—To remove these, lower windows and remove handles and trim pad. Note plastic sheet fitted behind trim pad must be renewed if damaged and stuck to door panel as this acts as a seal. Remove belt weatherstrip, retained by three clips and glass stop. Detach regulator arm from channel and lay window in bottom of door. Remove self-tapping screw from upper run at top front corner and pull channel to one side. Remove lower vent frame and dividing-channel screw and two screws through face of frame into vent-window frame. Remove regulator and lift out vent window; turn glass through 90° and lift out assembly.

REAR DOOR WINDOWS, ZEPHYR 4 AND 6.—To remove, take off handles, trim pad and lower stop. Wind window down and detach regulator arm. Remove lower screw from vent-window dividing channel and remove belt weatherstrip. Pull down upper glass run adjacent to top of vent window channel and drill out the pop rivet securing the channel to the door. Pull out channel and remove window.

REAR DOOR WINDOWS, ZODIAC.—On the Zodiac, the window is removed upwards after first removing the upper-frame section of the door by drilling out the pop rivets, one either side of the door. The Zodiac opening rear vents can be removed by disconnecting the toggle and removing the three nuts and washers exposed after removing the cover plate from the door-lock pillar.

WINDSCREEN.—To remove windscreen, detach wiper arms and disconnect battery. Remove windscreen pillar and belt-rail panel mouldings, rear-view mirror and radio-speaker grille. Remove lighting-switch knob and bezel and, on Zodiac, detach choke cable from carburetter; remove inner cable and bezel and disconnect cigarette lighter wiring; remove belt rail panel cover. Lever the upper edge of the windscreen weatherstrip under the windscreen opening flange, when approximately two-thirds of this has been done, the assembly can be pushed out. Finally remove the chrome moulding and weatherstrip.

On reassembly, mark the centre of the glass and the centre of the lower chrome moulding and ensure these line up when fitting the lower moulding to the weatherstrip. Assemble the remaining moulding to the weatherstrip. Fit a length of cord to the groove in the weatherstrip so that the ends cross over approximately 6 in. at the bottom. Offer up the assembly so that the upper groove engages the upper flange. Pull on one end of the cord, always towards the centre of the screen until the cord reaches the top centre of the screen, then pull on the other end of the cord to complete installation.
REAR WINDOW.—Rear window is removed and replaced similarly after removing chrome mouldings and the rear quarter trim panels inside the car.

BRAKES
BRAKE DATA

Disc diameter	$9\frac{3}{4}$ in.
Disc run-out	0·004 in.
Front-pad material	Ferodo DS5S
Rear-drum diameter	9 in.
Rear-lining width:	
Zephyr 4	$1\frac{3}{4}$ in.
Zephyr 6/Zodiac	$2\frac{1}{4}$ in.
Rear-lining material	Chekko XL3Z
Rear wheel-cylinder diameter	0·75 in.
Front caliper cylinder diameter	2·25 in.
Master-cylinder diameter (pre-Oct. 1962)	0·875 in.
Master-cylinder diameter (post-Oct. 1962)	0·8125 in.
Tightening torque:	
Disc-caliper bolts	25–30 lb-ft
Disc to hub bolts	27–30 lb-ft
Mounting bracket to spindle body	30–35 lb-ft

Girling hydraulic, disc brakes $9\frac{1}{4}$ in. diameter on front wheels, leading and trailing shoe drum brakes on rear wheels. Zephyr 4 rear drums $9 \times 1\frac{3}{4}$ in.; Zephyr 6 and Zodiac $9 \times 2\frac{1}{4}$ in. Up to October 1962, a vacuum-hydraulic servo was fitted; from that date a vacuum-operated mechanical servo.

BRAKE ADJUSTMENT.—Front disc brakes self-adjusting. On rear brakes, screw in square headed conical adjuster, back off two clicks to free drum.

Handbrake adjustment: If further adjustment is required after adjusting rear shoes, lock drums with adjusters, adjust equaliser on handbrake cable to take up free play, then release drums.

CLUTCH

Single dry-plate with hydraulic operation.

CLUTCH DATA

Clutch-disc diameter:	
Zephyr 4	8·0 in.
Zephyr 6 and Zodiac	8·5 in.
Pressure-plate bolt torque	12–15 lb-ft
Release-arm clearance	0·10 in.
Master-cylinder diameter (pre-1964)	0·75 in.
Master-cylinder diameter (1964 onwards)	0·70 in.
Slave-cylinder diameter	1·0 in.

Zephyr 4, 8 in. diameter; Zephyr 6 and Zodiac, $8\frac{1}{2}$ in. diameter.

ADJUSTMENT.—Release-arm free-travel, 0·10 in., measured at end of release arm. Slave-cylinder pushrod adjustable to give correct setting. The slave cylinder is retained in the clutch housing by an external circlip fitted around the cylinder, remove the circlip and the cylinder can be withdrawn forwards out of the housing.

CLUTCH REMOVAL AND REPLACEMENT.—Clutch disc and pressure plate can be removed from the flywheel after removal of the gearbox. On reassembly, fit disc with damper springs away from flywheel and tighten pressure-plate bolts to 12 to 15 lb-ft torque.

Clutch pilot bearing is a self-aligning ball bearing; this should be packed with lithium-based grease and fitted with the sealed side towards the clutch.

Release bearing is a pre-lubricated ball-thrust type pressed onto the hub. To remove bearing, pull the release arm to detach it from the clips on the hub and retaining clip near the fulcrum pin. The bearing and hub assembly can then be slid off the main drive gear bearing retainer, and the release fork and gaiter removed. On reassembly, lubricate all friction surfaces, e.g. pivot pin, thrust fingers on fork, and lightly grease the main drive gear bearing sleeve.

ASSIST SPRING.—Up to January 1964 an assist spring was incorporated in the clutch linkage. The link is roughly D shaped and should be fitted with the larger portion facing downwards. The spring anchor bolt nut should be adjusted to tension the spring until 0·88 in. on Zephyr 4 (or 1·20 in. on Zephyr 6/Zodiac) of the bolt protrudes from the rear face of the bracket.

If the pedal returns sluggishly, adjust the eccentric bolt securing the master-cylinder pushrod to the pedal to bring the pedal rearwards to give a smooth pedal return. If the pedal is still hesitant, release the spring tension slightly to give a smooth pedal-return action.

MODIFICATIONS.—In January 1964, modifications were made to the clutch and the spring link was eliminated. Changes were made to the clutch pressure plate, clutch disc, pedal, release bearing and hub and the master cylinder was reduced in size from 0·75 in. diameter to 0·70 in. diameter. No change was made to the clutch slave cylinder. It is impractical in service to incorporate the modifications on early vehicles; similarly care must be taken not to mix components on early and current vehicles.

COOLING SYSTEM
COOLING SYSTEM DATA

Filler-cap pressure	13 lb/sq. in.
Thermostat starts to open	80–82°C.
Thermostat fully open	94°C.
Fan:	
Zephyr 4	2 blade 11 in.
Zephyr 6/Zodiac	2 blade 14 in.
Fan belt:	
Length	32 in. approx.
Width	⅜ in.
Tension	½ in. free-movement
Clearance, pump vanes to housing	0·030 in.

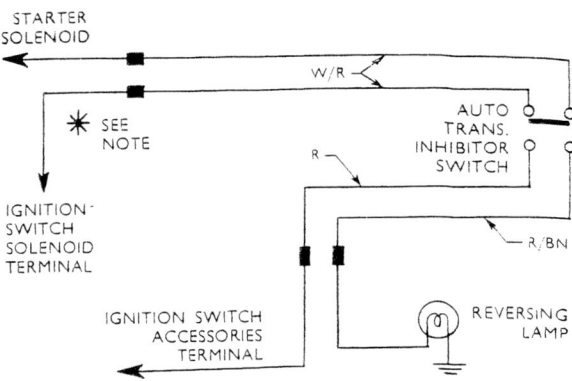

FIG. 2—WIRING DIAGRAM FOR AUTOMATIC TRANSMISSION

Pressurised thermo-syphon, thermostatically controlled, with pump assistance. By-pass tube between water pump and cylinder head. Wax thermostat fitted in cylinder-head outlet.

WATER - PUMP REMOVAL AND REFITTING.—Water pump can be removed with radiator in situ. Drain system and disconnect inlet and heater hose from pump; remove fan belt and unscrew bolts securing fan and pulley to pump flange. Note spacer fitted between the fan blade and pulley on Zephyr 4. Unscrew the four bolts securing pump to block face and detach pump, taking care not to damage by-pass pipe. By-pass pipe was initially of brass with an O-ring fitted at each end to act as a seal. This has now been replaced by a steel pipe rubber-coated; the latest-type pipe should be used if leaks are experienced in this area. When refitting the pump, apply sealer to the pump-to-block bolt threads.

WATER PUMP OVERHAUL.—Pull off pulley hub, withdraw hairpin clip from groove around outside of bearing, press bearing and shaft assembly out of housing and pull off impeller, seal and slinger. Slinger can be split with chisel to remove it.

On reassembly, press bearing and shaft in housing, short end first, until wire clip can be located in groove in bearing and housing. Press on pulley flange, refit slinger so that the flange is 1·41 in. from the end of the shaft, fit the seal with the carbon face away from the slinger and finally press on the impeller. Clearance between impeller vanes and pump body should be 0·030 in.

ELECTRICAL SYSTEM

Twelve-volt positive-earth system. Combined cut-out, current regulator and voltage regulator fitted. Alternator fitted to police cars. C40, 22 amp generator with 37344 regulator, Zephyr 4 and 6; C406, 25 amp generator with 37342 regulator, Zodiac. C42, 30 amp generator with 37331 regulator available as optional equipment. 45 Ah battery standard on Zephyr 4 with 57Ah optional. 57Ah battery standard on Zephyr 6 and Zodiac with 67Ah optional.

ENGINE

GENERAL.—Four or six cylinder, bore 3·25 in., stroke 3·13 in. High or low compression cylinder heads optional, identified by "H" or "L" stamped on machined pad near inlet-manifold flange. Camshaft driven by double-row endless chain;

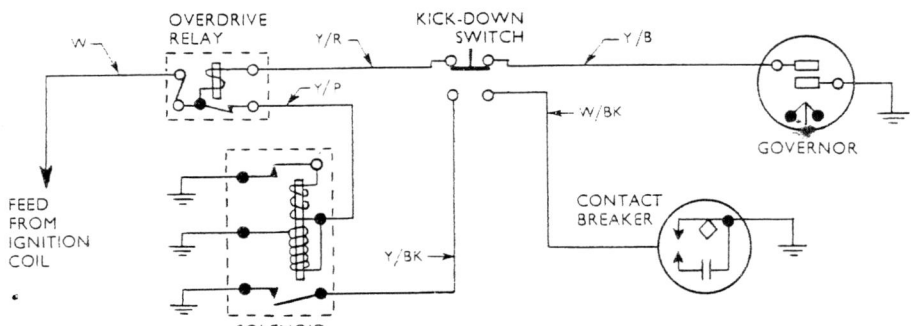

FIG. 3—WIRING DIAGRAM FOR TRANSMISSION OVERDRIVE

ENGINE DATA

General

Bore (all models)	82·55 mm. (3·25 in.)
Stroke (all models)	79·5 mm. (3·13 in.)

Capacity:
- Zephyr 4 . . . . 1,703 c.c. (103·9 cu. in.)
- Zephyr 6 and Zodiac . 2,553 c.c. (155·8 cu. in.)

Compression ratio (all models):
- High-compression . . . 8·3 : 1
- Low-compression . . . 7·0 : 1

Brake horsepower (nett):
- Zephyr 4, h.c. . . 68 at 4,800 r.p.m.
- Zephyr 6, h.c. . . 98 at 4,750 r.p.m.
- Zodiac, h.c. . . 109 at 4,800 r.p.m.
- Zephyr 4, l.c. . . 63 at 4,800 r.p.m.
- Zephyr 6, l.c. . . 91 at 4,750 r.p.m.
- Zodiac, l.c. . . 101·5 at 4,800 r.p.m.

Firing order: 4-cylinder . . 1-2-4-3
6-cylinder . . 1-5-3-6-2-4

Oil-pump relief-valve pressure . 50–60 lb/sq. in.
Lubricant . . . SAE 20 or 20 W

Sump capacity:
- Zephyr 4 . . . 6 pints (+ 1½ for filter)
- Zephyr 6 and Zodiac . 6½ pints (+ 1½ for filter)

Bearings

Big-end end-float	0·006–0·012 in.
Big-end to crankpin clearance	0·005–0·0022 in.
Undersizes available	0·002, 0·010, 0·020, 0·030, 0·040 in.
Crankpin-journal diameter	2·1255–2·1260 in.
Main-bearing clearance	0·000–0·0017 in.
Crankshaft end-float	0·004–0·012 in.
Crankshaft thrust-washer thickness	0·091–0·093 in.
Crankshaft thrust-washer oversizes	0·0025, 0·005, 0·0075, 0·010 in.
Main-bearing undersizes	0·010, 0·020, 0·030, 0·040 in
Main-bearing journal diameter	2·3760–2·3765 in.

Pistons

Piston fit	0·0002–0·0008 in.
Piston oversizes	0·0025, 0·005, 0·015, 0·030 in.
Upper compression-ring gap	0·013–0·018 in.
Upper compression-ring clearance in groove	0·003–0·006 in.
Lower compression-ring gap	0·009–0·014 in.
Lower compression-ring clearance in groove	0·002–0·004 in.
Oil-control ring gap	0·010–0·020 in.
Oil-control ring clearance in groove	0·001–0·0025 in.

Valves

Inlet-valve head diameter	1·555–1·565 in.
Exhaust valve head diameter	1·350–1·360 in.
Valve clearance (cold)	0·014 in.

Valve springs:
- Free length . . . 1·825 in.
- Test length . . . 1·584 in.
- Test load . . . 70–76 lb

Valve-seat angle:
- Inlet . . . 30°
- Exhaust . . . 45°

Tightening Torques (lb-ft)

Main bearings	55–60
Cylinder head	65–70
Big-ends	20–25
Rocker shaft	30–35
Flywheel to crankshaft	70–75

hydraulically-operated tensioner fitted on 4-cylinder engine.

The following operations can be done with the engine in position: Remove cylinder head, remove sump and oil pump, remove pistons and connecting rods, replace main-bearing liners and crankshaft thrust-washers, remove front cover and camshaft, remove water pump, remove flywheel.

ENGINE REMOVAL.—Remove bonnet, disconnect battery and on six-cylinder engines remove battery and carrier. From underneath car, remove splash shield, detach clutch slave cylinder, remove flywheel cover, starter-motor lower mounting bolt, and two block-to-clutch housing bolts on right-hand side of engine. Disconnect gear-change levers from gearbox. Drain and remove radiator and hoses, remove air cleaner, disconnect exhaust pipe from manifold, remove vacuum pipe from inlet manifold and vacuum tank. Disconnect controls from carburetter and throttle cross-shaft at engine bulkhead, remove the cross-shaft. Remove inlet and exhaust manifolds, coil and mounting bracket with heater hoses, if fitted. Disconnect fuel pipe from pump, temperature gauge, oil-pressure switch and generator leads. Remove water pump and generator.

Position lifting tackle to take weight of engine and remove both mounting brackets, lower engine slightly to get access to remaining clutch-housing bolts. Support the gearbox and lift the engine, pulling it forward off the main drive gear splines. Keep the front of the engine raised and turn the engine so that it is diagonally across the engine compartment with the flywheel towards the steering box.

CAMSHAFT.—The camshaft is driven by an endless double-row chain. A hydraulic tensioner, screwed into front cover, is fitted on 4-cylinder engines only. Camshaft sprocket is located on a dowel and retained by two bolts. End-float of camshaft is controlled by thrust plate located between camshaft boss and front bearing. Timing marks on crankshaft and camshaft sprockets. Oil seal fitted in front timing cover.

Camshaft Removal.—Camshaft can be removed with engine in place after removing radiator grille, radiator, sump, and oil pump and releasing push-rods. Remove side cover and suitably retain tappets Remove front cover, timing chain and sprocket. Support engine, remove mounting bolts, lift front of engine and withdraw the camshaft.

Camshaft Bearings.—Replaceable white-metal

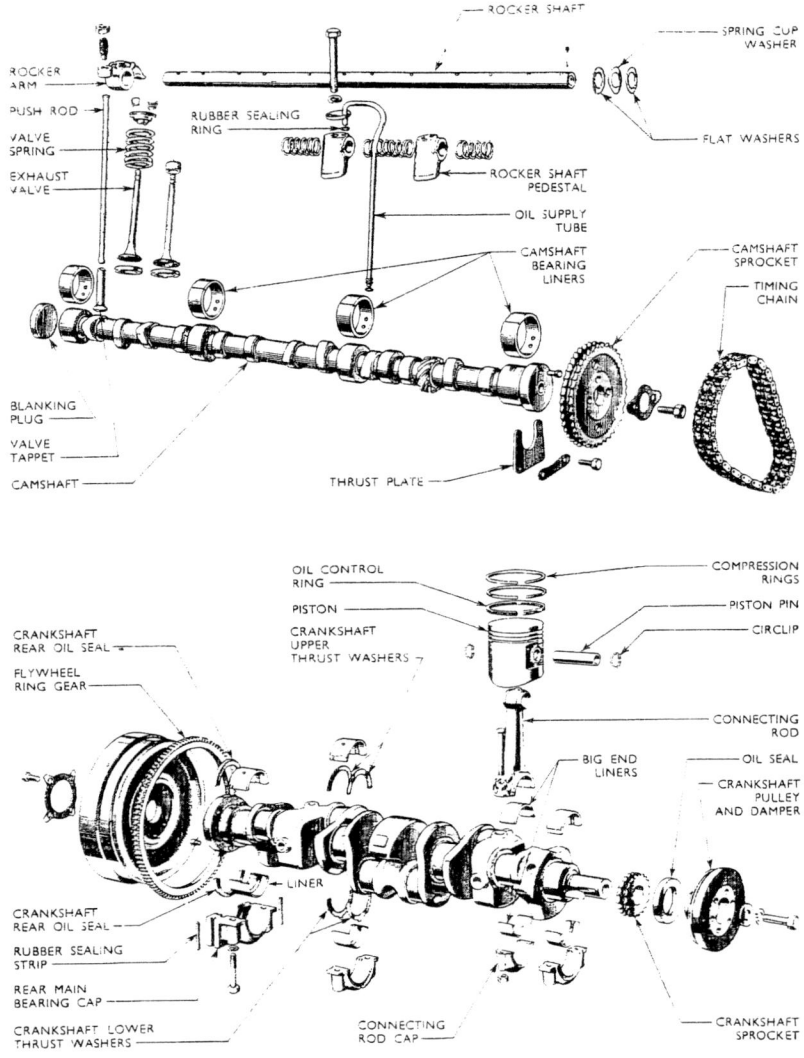

Fig. 5—EXPLODED VIEW OF ENGINE SHOWING VALVE GEAR, CAMSHAFT, TIMING GEAR PISTONS AND CRANKSHAFT ASSEMBLIES

pre-sized bushes are serviced if it is necessary to renew the camshaft bearings. The engine must be removed to do this. Remove sump and crankshaft, push pistons up bores and the bearings can be removed and replaced with special tool. When refitting bushes, ensure that all oil holes line up.

CRANKSHAFT AND MAIN BEARINGS.—Cast-steel crankshaft with three main bearings (4-cylinder), four main bearings (6-cylinder). Copper-lead or lead-bronze liners fitted on 6-cylinder intermediate bearings. Crankshaft end-float, 0·004 to 0·012 in., controlled by split white-metal-faced thrust washer either side of centre (4-cylinder) or number three (6-cylinder) main-bearing cap. Oversize washers + 0·0025, + 0·005, + 0·0075 and + 0·010 in. available. Main-bearing liners available − 0·010, − 0·020, − 0·030 and − 0·040 in. undersize for crankshaft regrinding.

Removing and Replacing Main Bearings.—Main-bearing liners can be replaced *in situ* after removing the cap and pushing the upper half around the crankshaft; thrust washers fitted with oil grooves towards crankshaft thrust face.

Rear main-bearing oil seal in cap and block is a woven graphite-impregnated seal. Press seal fully home in its groove and trim off ends so that protrusion is not more than 0·020 in.

When fitting the rear main bearing cap, apply a film of sealer to the undercut in the block, check that the sealing strips on each side of the cap are in good condition and are not pressed below the cap and block surface. Tighten main-bearing bolts to 55 to 60 lb-ft torque.

CYLINDER HEAD.—To remove the head, drain

cooling system, remove air cleaner, disconnect top hose, fuel pipe, throttle and choke controls, and distributor vacuum pipe from carburetter. Remove inlet and exhaust manifolds, spark plugs, ignition coil and rocker cover. Unscrew rocker-shaft bolts, lift off shaft, remove pushrods and cylinder-head bolts. Note that pushrods on the high-compression head are shorter than those used with the low-compression head and are identified by fins just below the cup.

The rockers can be slid off the shaft, after removing the split-pin and two flat washers with spring washer between them from one end of the shaft.

On reassembly of the head ensure that the oil-supply hole is in the front half of the rocker shaft on 6-cylinder engines, rear half on 4-cylinder engines. Similarly, on 4-cylinder engines the spring between Nos. 4 and 5 rockers is longer than the other two. On 6-cylinder engines a longer spring is fitted between Nos. 4 and 5 and 8 and 9 rockers.

Use studs to ensure gasket alignment when re-fitting cylinder head and take care not to damage the water-pump by-pass pipe. Tighten cylinder head bolts to 65 to 70 lb-ft torque, rocker-shaft bolts to 30 to 35 lb-ft. Valve clearances are set to 0·014 in. and cylinder-head bolt torques should be rechecked after 500 miles.

LUBRICATION.—Spur-gear or eccentric-vane type pump housed in crankcase and driven from helical gear on camshaft. All bearings fed at full pump pressure via full-flow oil filter. Valve gear fed by intermittent feed from camshaft centre bearing (4-cylinder) or No. 2 bearing on 6-cylinder engines via stack pipe to hollow rocker shaft. Rockers are drilled to feed tappets and valves. Groove on front camshaft journal supplies oil to timing gears through small drilling in cylinder block. A drilling in each connecting-rod big-end gives a jet of oil to the cylinder walls.

Sump Removal.—To remove the sump, drain the oil, remove clutch slave cylinder and flywheel cover, and remove the engine splash-shield to obtain access to sump bolts. Gasket is in four pieces dovetailed together; apply sealer to these locations on reassembly and tighten bolts to 5 to 7 lb-ft torque.

Oil-pump Removal and Refitting.—The oil pump is secured to the cylinder block by two bolts and can be withdrawn after removal of the bolts. The oil-pump drive-gear also drives the distributor by integral offset dogs machined on it. On replacement, line up the mark on the crankshaft pulley with the mark on the timing cover and fit oil pump so that when viewed through distributor hole the large D of the gear is towards the fuel pump and the dogs at 45° to a line through the distributor bolt holes. Recheck ignition timing.

Oil-pump Overhaul.—Two types of oil pump, spur-gear or rotating-vane are fitted.

To overhaul the gear-type pump, detach the filter screen and remove the cover and pick-up pipe. O-ring fitted as seal around pick-up pipe. Mark flange and cover, unscrew remaining two bolts and remove cover. The relief valve plunger, spring and spring seat are located in the cover. Pull the idler gear off its stud, the driving gear and shaft are serviced as an assembly; if this has to be renewed, drive out the pin securing the skew gear at the top of the shaft and pull off the gear.

The vane-type pump can be identified by the cast-aluminium body and shroud screwed to the relief-valve housing. When dismantling this pump, remove the pick-up screen and cover and before removing the end cover, invert the pump and slide off the cover to prevent displacing the vanes and spacer ring. Place a straight-edge across the end of the pump and check the clearance between the face of the vanes and rotor assembly; if this exceeds 0·005 in. the end-face of the pump can be carefully lapped to reduce the clearance to this figure. The rotor and shaft are serviced as an assembly and can be withdrawn after removal of the skew gear. A vane spacer ring is fitted on the underside of the rotor.

Oil-feed to Valve Gear.—Modifications have been made to improve the oil supply to the valve gear. Initially, the lower end of the feed pipe was pushed direct into a drilling in the cylinder block possibly damaging the O-ring on the end of the pipe. A guide tube is now pressed into the block, the feed pipe locates in this. The later feed pipe is shorter than the early one and the latest parts can be fitted to earlier engines. At the same time, the position of the drillings in the rocker shaft were modified to improve lubrication to the valves and rockers.

PISTONS AND CONNECTING RODS.—Aluminium-alloy autothermic pistons fitted with two compression and one oil-control ring. Piston pin is retained by end circlips and is offset $\frac{1}{16}$ in. towards thrust side of engine. Cast arrow on piston crown denotes front on assembly. Pistons selected by measurement to give 0·0002 in. to 0·0008 in. cylinder-bore clearance. Cylinder bores to be measured at right angles to piston pin 1·31 in. below centre of pin, this point being level with the top of the cut-outs in the piston.

Compression rings marked "Top", upper ring tapered and chrome-plated, this being treated with a reddish brown bedding-in compound which must not be washed off. If necessary to degrease this ring, use only petrol. Lower compression ring also marked "Top" and is stepped.

Connecting Rods and Big-ends.—Forged-steel connecting rods fitted with steel-backed copper-lead bearing liners. Small-end bush of phosphor bronze is not serviced separately. Big-end of rod drilled for oil feed to cylinder walls. Rod and cap numbered on camshaft side, rod marked "Front".

Undersize bearing liners available — 0·002, — 0·010, — 0·020, — 0·030, — 0·040 for reground crankshafts. New self-locking nuts should be fitted to big-end bolts and tightened to 20 to 25 lb-ft torque.

VALVES.—Larger valves fitted than on Mark II engines. Inlet-valve head diameter, 1·432 to 1·442 in. on Mark II, 1·555 to 1·565 in. on Mark III. Exhaust valve head diameter, 1·182 to 1·192 in. on Mark II, 1·350 to 1·360 in. on Mark III.

The valve-seat angles are inlet 30°, exhaust 45°.

Valves operate in guides cast in cylinder head. Valves with oversize stems, + 0·003, + 0·015 and + 0·030 in., are serviced to cater for worn guides. Valve guide must be reamed to fit the + 0·015 in. and + 0·030 in. oversize valves. Oversize marked on valve stems.

Umbrella type seals fitted to valve stems. Springs fitted with close coils to cylinder head.

Valve clearance, inlet and exhaust, 0·014 in. cold.

Push-rods for high-compression engines are ribbed at the upper end for identification.

FRONT SUSPENSION AND FRONT END

Macpherson-type independent suspension with coil spring located between seat on vertical double-acting shock absorber body and piston rod. Upper end of piston rod located in rubber-mounted ball-thrust bearing; mounting bolted to front-wing valance. Lateral wheel alignment controlled by track-control arms located on ball-joints to steering arms and to front cross-member by rubber bushes. Longitudinal alignment controlled by stabiliser bar, rubber-bushed in track-control arm and clamped to mounting feet located in rubber bushes in side-member; steering arms bolted to suspension-unit foot; wheel spindle forged integral with suspension-unit foot.

Before attempting to remove the suspension unit, the coil spring must be clamped; similarly, if removing track-control arms on stabiliser bar, the spring must be clamped before jacking up the car.

TO REMOVE SUSPENSION UNIT.—Clamp spring, remove road wheel and brake caliper (do not break hydraulic unions), unscrew bolts securing steering arm to suspension unit and nuts securing suspension top mounting to wing valance. Depress track-control arm to separate steering arm from suspension unit and remove unit.

TO DISMANTLE SUSPENSION UNIT.—Unscrew nut from piston rod and pull off upper mounting, spring seat and spring.

Note from May 1964 the right-hand spring is ¾ in. longer than the left-hand one.

Relieve the staking of the cylinder to the upper gland nut and unscrew the nut; remove the rubber seal and withdraw the assembly from the outer cylinder. Pull the compression and foot-valve assembly from the bottom of the cylinder; this is pre-set and the adjustment sealed and should not be altered. Pull the gland, gland seat, wave spring and upper guide off the piston rod; note that the lower face of the gland is marked "This way down". Push the piston rod down out of the cylinder. The piston valve is retained in the piston by a nut; unscrew the nut which forms the valve seat and remove the piston valve and spring. The piston-valve adjustment is sealed and should not be altered. The piston and rod are machined as an assembly and no attempt should be made to separate them. If necessary, the rebound-stop tube can be removed from the top of the cylinder.

FRONT-END DATA

Castor	— 0°19' to + 0°41'
Camber	1°37' to 2°37'
Kingpin inclination	5°40' to 6°40'
Toe-in	1/16 – 3/16 in.
Toe-out on 20° turn (inner wheel)	1°–2°

FRONT SPRING DATA

Free length and colour (to May 1964):
Standard	16·79 in. blue
Heavy-duty	15·40 in. red

Free length and colour (from May 1964)*:
Standard, right-hand	17·54 in. blue/yellow
Standard, left-hand	16·79 in. blue
Heavy-duty, right-hand	16·15 in. red/yellow
Heavy-duty, left-hand	15·40 in. red

* From May 1964, longer spring fitted to right-hand side of right-hand drive cars.

TIGHTENING TORQUES (lb-ft)

Piston-rod gland cap	35–40
Piston-rod nut	55–60
Upper mounting to wing valance	30–35
Stabiliser-bar nuts	50–60
Stabiliser-bar V bolts	25–30
Stabiliser-bar mounting foot	20–25*
Track control-arm ball-joint	30–35
Track control-arm bushing	30–35*

* Tighten with car standing on ground unladen.

TRACK-CONTROL ARMS.—The track-control arms can be removed after clamping spring. Disconnect steering arm and track-control arm from ball-joint on steering arm, remove the nut securing it to the crossmember pivot, unscrew the nut on the end of the stabiliser bar and pull off the track-control arm. Track-control arms are handed—lubricator (pre-June 1964) to front. From that date, plastic-seated ball-joints have been used; these arms have "Front" forged on them.

To replace track-control arm ball-joints (early type), remove plug from housing and compress spring with clamp. Remove circlip, spring plate,

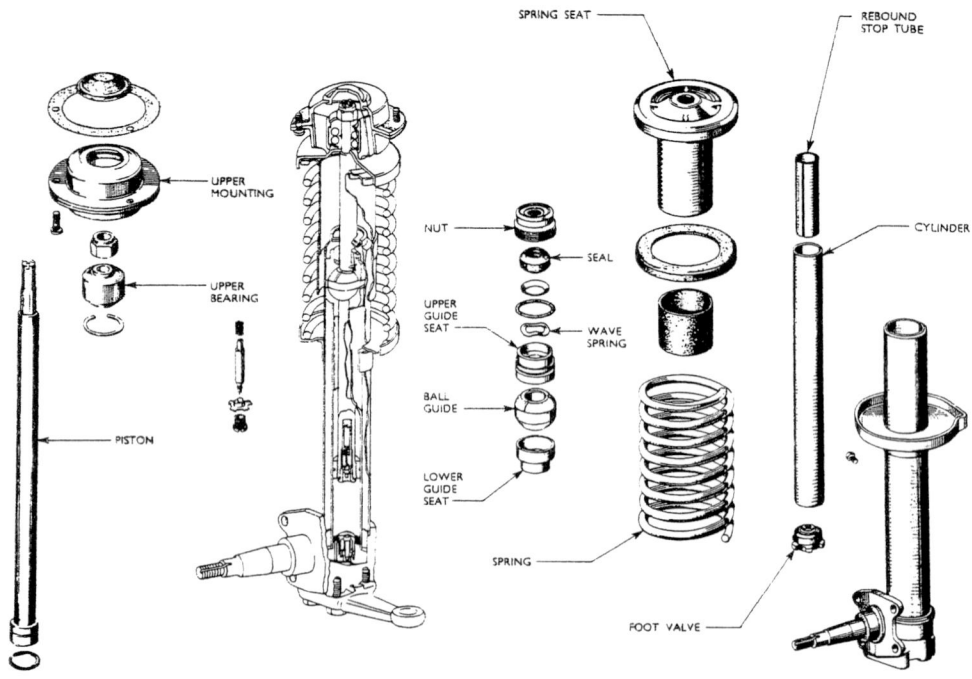

Fig. 6—COMPONENT PARTS OF FRONT SUSPENSION

spring lower seat, ball-stud and upper seat.

On reassembly, grease all parts with molybdenum-disulphide grease, fit parts removed in reverse order and again compress spring and install circlip. Check clearance between retainer and circlip (still clamped); this should be 0·003 to 0·010 in.; if not, select a circlip to give this clearance. Eleven circlip thicknesses available from 0·1050–0·1084 to 0·1400–0·1434 in. in 0·0035 in. steps. Refit plug after establishing correct clearance and stake housing.

Fit a dust seal over the stud and fit spring clip with gap away from brake disc.

On the plastic joints, the ball operates in a split plastic seating, dismantle as greased type joints. On reassembly, grease all parts with molybdenum-disulphide grease, install upper ball seat, ball, lower seat, pack recess with grease and fit spring seat, spring and retainer; compress spring to fit circlip (one thickness only). Fit plug and stake housing to retain plug. The dust cover should be packed with grease before fitting to the ball stud.

STABILISER BAR.—Secured to mounting feet pivoted on rubber bushes in mounting bracket, ends of bar located in rubber bushes in track control arm.

To Remove.—Fit spring clips and jack up car. Remove U-bolts from mounting feet; unscrew nuts at each end of stabiliser bar in track-control arms. Remove locking plate, flat washer and conical rubber bush from each end and pull bar out of track-control arms. Note sweep of bar is upwards and it must be fitted this way. Pull the other conical bushes off the bar and unscrew the sleeve nuts. The mounting foot bushes can be renewed after removing the mounting foot.

To Reassemble.—On reassembly, screw sleeve nut onto bar so that with the slots in line, $\frac{11}{16}$ to $\frac{3}{4}$ in. of thread protrude beyond the end of the sleeve. Fit conical bush to each sleeve and locate bar in track-control arms; fit bush, flat washer and lockwasher, taking care that keys enter slot in bar and fit nut but do not fully tighten. Refit U-bolts, making sure they locate on the flats on the bar; fit locking plates and nuts, tighten nuts to 25 to 30 lb-ft.

Lower car to ground and check castor angle ($-0°19'$ to $+0°41'$). If correct, tighten stabiliser bar nuts to 50 to 60 lb-ft. If incorrect, check fitment of bar, U-bolts and sleeve nuts. If mounting feet bushes have been replaced, tighten nut to 20 to 25 lb-ft. These must only be tightened with the car on its wheels.

FRONT HUBS.—Mounted on taper-roller bearings. Check adjustment every 5,000 miles, clean and replace with fresh grease. Two types of adjusting nut have been used. Initially a castellated nut was used; this has been replaced by a plain nut onto which a pressed metal retainer is fitted.

To adjust the hub bearings, if castellated nut fitted, tighten nut to 30 lb-ft torque and back off between $1\frac{3}{4}$ and $2\frac{1}{4}$ castellations. If plain nut is fitted, tighten nut to 30 lb-ft, fit retainer with a slot in line with pin hole in spindle and back off two castellations. Dust cap in hub must be fitted dry.

FUEL-SYSTEM

Rear-mounted fuel tank, 12½ gallons capacity, non-vented filler cap. A.C. mechanical pump operated from engine camshaft. Pump pressure 2–3½ lb/sq. in. Zenith 36VN carburetter on Zephyr 4, 36 WIA-2 on Zephyr 6 and 42 WIA-2 on Zodiac.

AIR CLEANER.—Air cleaner on Zephyr 4 and 6, oil-wetted-gauze type, cleaned every 5,000 miles. Zephyr 4 element cannot be removed from body, remove cleaner from carburetter and pour petrol into body to clean, pour small quantity of oil through the spout to reoil gauze. On fitting to carburetter align one edge of cut out on sealing-ring flange with centre of choke spindle to prevent accelerator-pump link fouling on full throttle.

On Zephyr 6, top cover of air cleaner is removable for access to gauze.

Paper-element cleaner on Zodiac. Remove and clean every 5,000 miles; element and sealing rings renewed every 15,000 miles.

CARBURETTER JET SIZES

Zephyr 4
Carburetter type	Zenith 36VN
Main jet	100
Compensating jet	130
Accelerator-pump jet	50
Idling jet	50
Choke-tube diameter	32 mm.

Zephyr 6
Carburetter type	Zenith 36WIA-2
Main jet	142
Compensating jet	120
Accelerator-pump jet	70
Idling jet	55
Choke-tube diameter	31 mm.

Zodiac
Carburetter type	Zenith 42WIA-2
Main jet	170
Compensating jet	190
Accelerator-pump jet	70
Idling jet	50
Choke-tube diameter	36 mm.

GEARBOX

Four-speed all-synchromesh box, floor or column change.

Borg-Warner Type 35 automatic transmission optional; Zephyr 4 converter 9½ in. diameter, Zephyr 6, and Zodiac 11 in. diameter.

Borg-Warner overdrive can be fitted with column change only.

TO REMOVE GEARBOX.—Disconnect exhaust pipe from manifold and throttle operating link from carburetter. Remove engine splash shield, starter motor, clutch slave cylinder (do not disconnect pipe) and flywheel cover. Disconnect drive shaft from pinion flange and remove shaft. Unscrew speedo-cable retaining bolt, disconnect cable, remove exhaust stay (if fitted) from box and disconnect gear-change levers from gearbox. (On floor-change cars, remove gear-lever assembly, see later). Support gearbox and remove cross-member, lower jack to allow gearbox to drop, remove clutch housing bolts and withdraw the gearbox.

TO DISMANTLE GEARBOX.—Remove clutch fork, bearing, clutch housing and selector housing. Unscrew bolts securing extension housing to gearbox and remove extension housing and mainshaft; on 4-cylinder engines, the countershaft must be removed to let the cluster gear lay in the bottom of the box before removing the mainshaft. Remove main drive-gear bearing retainer and tap out main drive gear. Remove cluster gear and reverse-idler gear. Reverse idler gear shaft tapped 5/16-24UNF2 for extraction.

GEARBOX DATA

Lubricant	SAE 80 E.P.
Capacity	4 pints

Ratios

Zephyr 4:
First	4.412 : 1
Second	2.353 : 1
Third	1.564 : 1
Top	1 : 1
Reverse	4.667 : 1

Zephyr 6 and Zodiac:
First	3.163 : 1
Second	2.216 : 1
Third	1.412 : 1
Top	1 : 1
Reverse	3.366 : 1

End-float
First and Second gear	0.005–0.009 in.
Third gear	0.005–0.016 in.

Speedometer drive gear, no. of teeth
3.900 : 1 axle (standard Zephyr 4)	7
4.111 : 1 axle (alt. Zephyr 4)	6
3.545 : 1 and 3.900 axle (Zephyr 6, Zodiac) standard and alternative	7

Speedometer driven gear, no. of teeth and colour
3.900 : 1 axle	22 red
4.111 : 1 and 3.545 axle	20 blue
3.900 : 1 axle (Zephyr 6, Zodiac)	22 red

Overdrive transmission
Speedometer drive gear: Zephyr 4	6
Zephyr 6 and Zodiac	7
Speedometer driven gear	20 blue

Bolt-tightening torques (lb-ft)
Extension housing	40–45
Clutch housing	40–45
Speedometer drive gear	20–25

Interlock sleeve lengths
EOA 7233 A	1.2865–1.2885 in.
B	1.2895–1.2915 in.
C	1.2925–1.2945 in.
D	1.2955–1.2975 in.
E	1.2985–1.3005 in.
F	1.3015–1.3035 in.

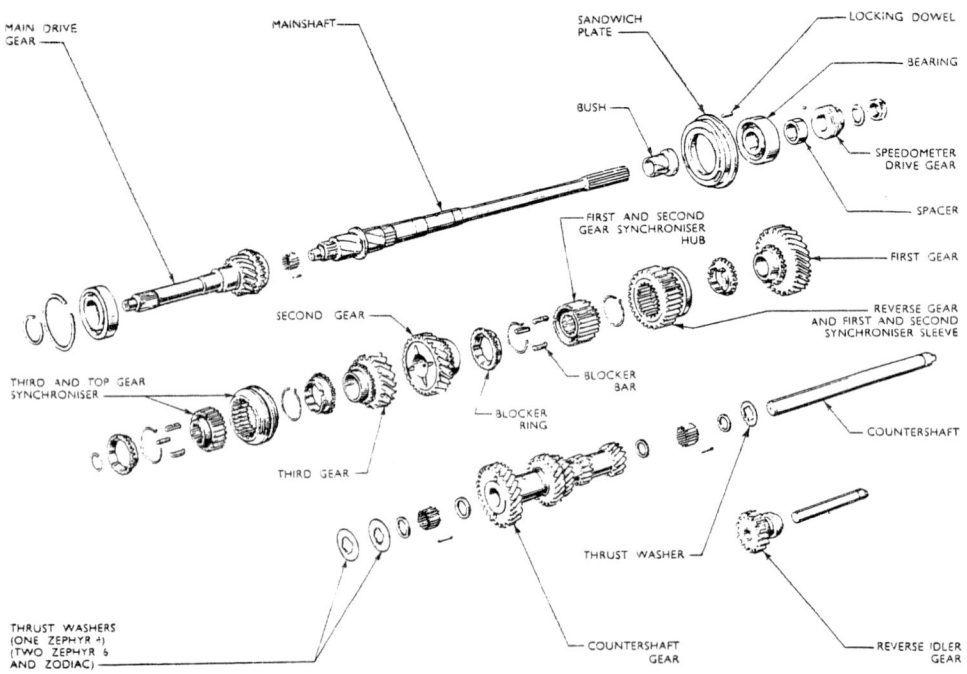

Fig. 7—EXPLODED VIEW OF FOUR-SPEED ALL-SYNCHROMESH GEARBOX

To dismantle the mainshaft, remove the 3rd and top synchroniser snap-ring and press off the 3rd gear and synchronizer. Unscrew the speedometer drive-gear retaining nut and remove the speedometer drive gear, locking ball located in the mainshaft and the spacer. Press off the mainshaft bearing, sandwich plate and 1st gear. Note the 1st-gear sleeve is locked to the mainshaft by a ball and this must be removed before 2nd gear and 1st and 2nd gear synchroniser can be pressed off the shaft.

TO REASSEMBLE GEARBOX.—Reassembly is the reverse of the above procedure but the following points should be noted.

1. Synchroniser hubs and sleeves are mated together, etch marks in line; also the assemblies to mainshaft, etch marks on shaft and hub.

2. Speedometer drive-gear nut tightened to 20 to 25 lb-ft.

3. Cluster-gear needle rollers (22 in each set) assembled with thrust washer at each end of bearing with white petroleum jelly. On Zephyr 6, two thrust washers fitted at front; assembly can be installed before fitting mainshaft. On Zephyr 4, lay cluster gear in bottom of box and lift into mesh after fitting mainshaft.

4. Caged needle-roller bearing in main drive gear should be well oiled before installation.

5. Assemble sandwich plate in gearbox with dowel hole central between upper bolt holes to line up with dowel in extension housing.

6. Flats on countershaft and reverse-idler shaft to be horizontal to locate in locking recess on extension housing.

7. Cover main drive-gear splines with masking tape before fitting retainer to prevent scoring oil seal.

8. Only forged blocker rings to be used on floor-change boxes.

SELECTOR MECHANISM OVERHAUL.—Remove operating levers from shafts, remove 3rd and top selector cam-interlock sleeve, spring and two bolts and remove 1st and 2nd selector and reverse selector. Lift out reverse interlock plungers. Slide reverse-selector shaft rearwards, cover hole in rear support when extracting shaft to trap locking ball and spring. Forward selector shaft can be removed after driving out tension pin in front boss.

On reassembly, after fitting forward selectors and shaft, install reverse-shaft locking ball and spring (note the spring is shorter than the one in the forward gear-interlock sleeve) and slide in reverse shaft until ball locates in the first notch. Install reverse interlock plungers and fit selector levers Fit 1st and 2nd selector cam with reverse plunger located in cut out at bottom of selector and fit operating lever to relay lever. Fit interlock plunger but not balls and spring and fit the 3rd and top selector cam. Set the 1st and 2nd selector cam in neutral (central cut out in line with interlock) and 3rd and top cam with high point between cut outs in line with interlock plunger and check clearance at this point. This should be 0·005 to 0·0075 in., if not select sleeve to give this clearance. When clearance is correct remove 3rd and top cam and fit spring and balls to interlock plunger and refit cam in neutral position. Fit reverse-relay lever

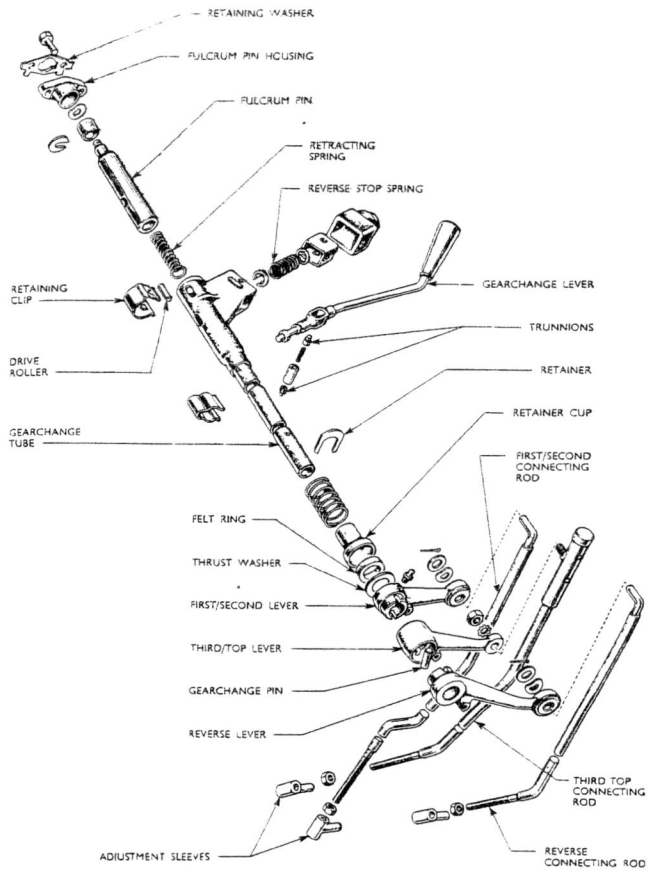

FIG. 8—STEERING-COLUMN GEAR-CHANGE COMPONENTS—EARLY TYPE

On later models, no ball joint and sleeve is fitted to the upper end of the top/3rd connecting rod—rod has a right-angle bend as other two connecting rods.

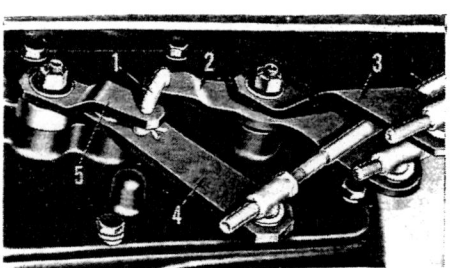

FIG. 9—GEAR-OPERATING LEVERS ON COLUMN-CHANGE GEARBOX

1, Link; 2, reverse relay lever; 3, third and top gear operating lever; 4, first and second gear operating lever; 5, reverse gear operating lever.

FIG. 10—COLUMN GEAR-CHANGE LINKAGE ADJUSTMENT

1. Setting pin ($\frac{11}{64}$ in. diameter) inserted through small hole in each lever.

over camshaft and fit 3rd and top operating lever. Connect reverse operating lever to relay lever.

COLUMN GEAR-CHANGE.—The gear-change lever operating mechanism has been modified after production of the Mark III models commenced and the setting instructions vary according to the particular linkage fitted. The top/3rd connecting-rod upper end with the ball joint and sleeve shown in Fig. 8 is of the earlier type. The current linkage has no ball joint and sleeve, the connecting-rod having a right-angle bend as in the case of the other two rods. These gear change connecting rods have also been increased in diameter, from $\frac{5}{16}$ to $\frac{7}{16}$ in. on Zephyr 4 and from $\frac{3}{8}$ to $\frac{7}{16}$ in. on Zephyr 6 and Zodiac models.

The gear-change lever is now slightly shorter and the lower gear-change levers longer to reduce the overall movement when changing gear. Further, the gear-change column-retainer thickness has been reduced from 0·057 in. to 0·040 in. and by using some three in combination, the column-change end-float has been reduced to approximately 0·030 in. maximum.

To adjust linkage, first engage reverse gear and then pull gear lever upwards, relieving spring pressure so that end-float between lower face of reverse lever and steering box can be checked. If it exceeds 0·030 in., fit additional retainers, not more than three in all, to obtain this end-float. Fit these retainers after straightening each lug on the adjacent bracket, so that additional retainers can be added or removed to suit. With the correct end-float, and lugs bent back proceed as follows.

Select neutral and then disconnect the operating levers (Fig. 9). Remove rubber button from floor-board cover plate. Insert a setting pin through this hole in the steering-column bracket, through small hole in each lever and then enter it fully in its location in steering box. (Use $\frac{11}{64}$ in. silver steel, tapered at one end and a right-angled bend at the other, approximately 7 in. in straight length.)

Now adjust each sleeve to just fit in its operating

lever. All three current type rods can now be reconnected, but on the earlier type reconnect only the reverse-lever connecting rod at this stage. Then unscrew sleeve on the other two connecting rods four full turns before reconnecting them.

Remove setting pin and check for easy and correct gear engagement. If necessary, unscrew these sleeves to a maximum of ten turns if this setting does not give easy gear selection. The gear-lever ball stud must be tight, a screwdriver slot enabling it to be held with a cranked screwdriver whilst the nut is tightened. An internal-toothed lockwasher must be used with this nut.

FLOOR GEAR-CHANGE.—Mounted on extension housing, the floor gear-change lever operates through rods to selector cover on left-hand side of box.

To remove, detach boot and retainer from car floor, remove two screws securing gear lever to bracket and lift out lever. Unscrew self-locking nuts retaining operating rods to levers and detach rods. Unscrew three bolts securing assembly to extension housing and remove assembly.

To dismantle, remove plastic gaiter, circlip, washer and spring, unscrew retainer-bracket bolts and remove bracket. Pull off the cone washer and levers. The gear-lever support is pinned to the operating shaft; drive out the pin if this is to be dismantled, polyurethene bushes are fitted in each side of the support. The gear-lever and reverse-latch assembly cannot be dismantled. Reassembly is the reverse of the above procedure.

To adjust the linkage, slacken the self-locking nuts securing the operating rods to the levers, line up the levers so that a ¼ in. rod can be passed through the hole in the bracket and in each lever into the hole in the opposite side of the bracket. Check that the levers on the gearbox are in neutral and tighten the self-locking nuts to 15 to 20 lb-ft torque.

IGNITION

TUNE-UP DATA

Firing order:
   Zephyr 4 1-2-4-3
   Zephyr 6 and Zodiac . . . 1-5-3-6-2-4
Initial ignition timing:
   High-compression . . . 8° b.t.d.c.
   Low-compression . . . 4° b.t.d.c.
Contact-breaker point gap . . 0·014–0·016 in.
Contact-breaker spring tension . 18–22 oz.
Sparking plugs:
   Type . . Champion N5 or Autolite AG3
   Gap . . . . 0·023–0·028 in.

Distributors fitted on high-compression and low-compression engines differ in the automatic advance springs and cam assemblies. Low-compression distributor identified by green l.t. washer or marking; high-compression distributor, red l.t. washer or marking.

DISTRIBUTOR DATA

Distributor identification:
   Zephyr 4 . . . 40852 (h.c.), 40851 (l.c.)
   Zephyr 6 and Zodiac . 40841 (h.c.), 40840 (l.c.)
Automatic advance starts (crankshaft r.p.m.):
   Zephyr 4 . . . . 1,000 (h.c.), 950 (l.c.)
   Zephyr 6 and Zodiac . . 900 (h.c.), 925 (l.c.)
Automatic advance ends (crankshaft r.p.m.):
   Zephyr 4 . . . . 5,000 (h.c.), 4,200 (l.c.)
   Zephyr 6 and Zodiac . . 5,000 (h.c. and l.c.)
Maximum centrifugal advance (distributor degrees):
   High-compression . . . . 9°–11°
   Low-compression . . . . 11½°–13½°
Vacuum-advance begins (in. mercury):
   4-cyl., h.c. and l.c., 6-cyl., h.c. . . 6 (approx.)
   6-cyl. l.c. . . . . . . 3½ (approx.)
Max. vacuum advance (distributor degrees):
   4-cyl., h.c. and l.c., 6-cyl. h.c.
                8°–10° (18 in. mercury)
   6-cyl. l.c. . . . 8½°–10½° (12 in. mercury)

IGNITION TIMING.—Timing set with notch in pulley in line with timing pointer on front cover; with fourth line on vacuum-unit scale in line with body gives 8° b.t.d.c. and is correct for high-compression engines. On low-compression engines set to this, then retard one division on vacuum-unit scale to give 4° b.t.d.c.

PROPELLER SHAFT AND UNIVERSAL JOINTS

Fixed-length open drive-shaft with needle-roller universal joints front and rear. Rear flange spigot-mounted on pinion-drive flange. Front yoke slides on mainshaft splines and is supported by white-metal bush in gearbox extension housing. Oil seal fitted in extension housing.

REAR AXLE AND REAR SUSPENSION

REAR AXLE DATA

Ratios:	Zephyr 4	Zephyr 6, Zodiac
Standard . . .	3·90 : 1	3·545 : 1
Automatic transmission	3·545 : 1	3·545 : 1
Overdrive . . .	4·111 : 1	3·545 : 1

Lubricant . . . . . SAE 90 Hypoid
Capacity . . . . . . 2½ pints
Pinion-bearing preload (excluding oil-seal drag)
                               12 to 15 lb-in.
Crown-wheel and pinion backlash . 0·005–0·007 in.
Differential-bearing cap spread . 0·005–0·007 in.
Tightening torques (lb-ft):
   Crown-wheel bolts 30–35
   Differential-bearing cap bolts . . . 70–80
   Differential-bearing locking-plate bolts . 15–20
   Rear-hub nut . . . . 100 (minimum)

REAR AXLE.—Three-quarter-floating hypoid axle. Crown-wheel and pinion, mounted on carrier fitted in front face of axle casing, can be removed as a unit after disconnecting drive shaft and removing axle shafts. Oil seal in end of axle casing. Differential assembly must be removed to replace oil seal as seal is fitted from inside axle tube.

Special tools are required for crown-wheel and pinion overhaul or adjustment. Pinion depth of mesh controlled by shim behind teeth. Ten thicknesses available ranging in 0·001 in. steps from 0·1506 to 0·1596 in. thick. Pinion-bearing preload controlled by collapsible spacer between bearings.

On reassembly, tighten drive-flange retaining nut to just remove end-float but without causing preload. Check rotating torque on flange to determine oil-seal drag x lb-in.). Tighten flange nut to preload pinion bearings, rotating torque to be (12 to 15) + x lb-in. and stake nut securely. If over-torqued, dismantle, fit new collapsible spacer and repeat. If necessary to fit new oil seal in service, differential assembly must be removed and pinion dismantled.

Crown-wheel and pinion backlash is adjustable by bearing ring-nuts. Adjust to give 0·005 to 0·007 in. backlash and, at the same time, spread the differential caps 0·005 to 0·007 in. to preload differential bearings. To do this, adjust nuts to give 0·001 to 0·002 in. backlash, then rotating crown-wheel all the time screw in the differential-side adjusting nut to spread the caps 0·005 to 0·007 in. Check crown-wheel and pinion backlash, which should be 0·005 to 0·007 in. Tighten differential-bearing cap bolts to 70 to 80 lb-ft and fit adjusting-nut locking plates. The running-in oil supplied with each crown-wheel and pinion must be used for the initial fill.

REAR HUBS.—Mounted on deep-groove ball bearing on axle casing. Grease seal fitted in hub, lip towards bearing; spacer pressed into hub on outside of bearing. Hub-bearing nut to be tightened to at least 100 lb-ft. Exceed this torque if necessary to align locking tab on washer with slot in bearing nut.

REAR SUSPENSION.—Semi-elliptic assymetrical springs. Split rubber bushes in front eye and rear shackles. Length 52·0 in., five leaves standard, six leaves heavy-duty suspension. Armstrong double-acting piston-type shock-absorbers fitted.

STEERING

STEERING BOX.—Burman recirculating-ball type worm and nut. Adjustment provided for worm shaft and rocker-shaft. Rocker-shaft can be adjusted in car but it is recommended to remove the box for worm-shaft adjustment.

Rocker-shaft Adjustment.—To check rocker-shaft adjustment, disconnect steerage linkage from drop arm, set steering wheel in the centre of its travel. Attach spring balance to wheel at spoke junction; wheel should turn through straight-ahead position with 1 to 1¼ lb pull on balance. Adjust shims under cover to give correct reading. Shim thicknesses available, 0·002–0·003 in., 0·004 in. and 0·010 in.

To Remove Steering Box.—Disconnect battery, remove horn button or embellishment, horn ring

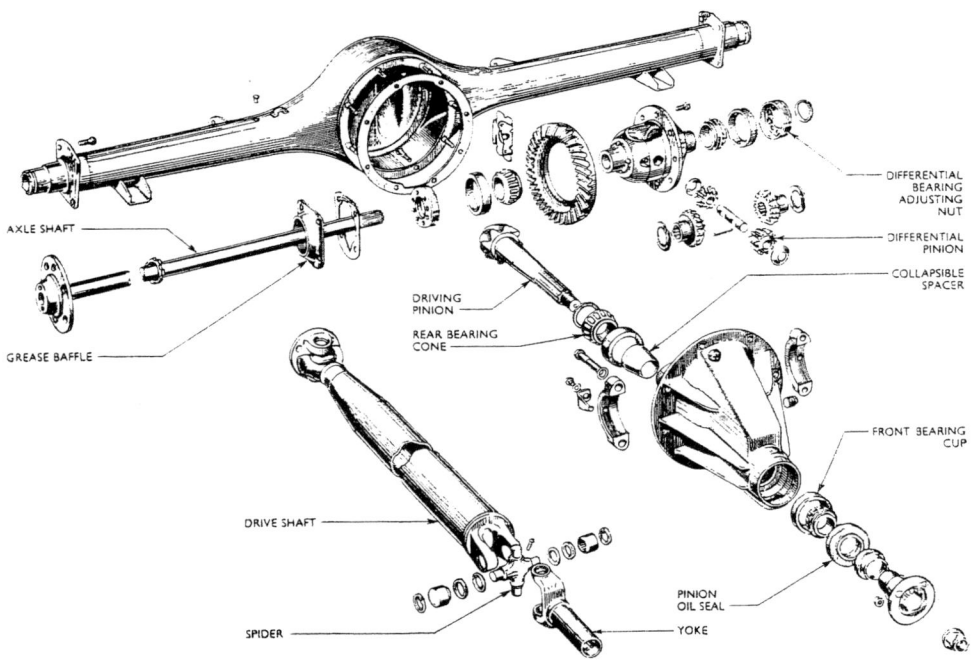

Fig. 11—REAR-AXLE DIFFERENTIAL AND DRIVE SHAFT

STEERING DATA

Worm-shaft adjustment	Shims (0·004 and 0·010 paper), 0·010 steel
Worm-shaft bearing preload	0·003 in.
Rocker-shaft adjustment	Shims 0·002–0·003, 0·004–0·005, 0·010 in.
Worm-shaft rotating torque	$8\frac{1}{2}$–$10\frac{1}{2}$ lb-in. (box assembled)

Tightening torques (lb-ft):

Drop-arm nut	70–80
Steering-wheel nut	25–30
Steering ball-joints	20–25
Steering-box top cover	17–22
Idler-arm grease caps (pre-June 1964)	70–80
Idler-arm bushes (post-June 1964)	30–35
Track-rod clamps	15–18
Steering arm	30–35

on contact plate, steering wheel, washer and spring. Remove column lower shroud and surround. Disconnect indicator and flasher wiring and remove indicator switch. Depress spring-loaded plungers under plastic shroud and remove gear lever. Remove lower half of mounting bracket and rubber insulator. Disconnect throttle pedal, remove toeboard cover-plate, disconnect gear linkage and horn wire, disconnect drop-arm to idler arm rod, pull off drop-arm and remove steering box.

Worm-shaft Bearing Adjustment.—Worm-shaft bearing adjustment by shims 0·004 in. thick and 0·010 in. paper gaskets under end-plate. Shim pack to be sandwiched between two gaskets. Adjust number of shims to give 0·003 in. preload on bearings. Install rocker shaft, springs and thrust button and refit cover-plate and shims. Adjust number of shims under cover plate so that the rotating torque of the worm shaft is $8\frac{1}{2}$ to $10\frac{1}{2}$ lb-in. This can be checked by refitting steering wheel and pulling with a spring balance at the spoke to rim junction; pull to turn steering wheel should be 1 to $1\frac{1}{4}$ lb.

STEERING-IDLER ARM.—Mounted in bracket on left-hand side-member. Screwed bushes locate arm to bracket and to idler-arm rod.

If arm has been dismantled fit seals to studs and push them past their location on to the idler arm. Screw on the bushes so that the clearance between the inner face of the bush and idler-arm boss is 0·22 in., relocate seals between bush and idler arm boss. Refit the arm with steering straight ahead, locate internal tongue on lockwasher in slot in bush and the two tabs in the bracket or idler-arm rod, it may be necessary to turn the bush slightly to fit the plate. Refit grease caps and tighten to 70 to 80 lb-ft and lock with two tabs on lockwasher.

Some cars have a steering damper fitted in place of the idler-arm assembly; a screwed bush is fitted on the damper-arm stud to connect it to the drop-arm rod. The bush and seal should be assembled as above.

From June 1964, the screwed bushes have been replaced by steel-sleeved rubber bushes in the idler-arm bracket and drop-arm rod. Press the bush into the idler-arm bracket from the top, pressing on the outer flange only, until the outer sleeve is just flush with the lower face of the bracket. Fit the bush in the drop-arm rod similarly so that the non-flanged end is flush with the face of the rod and towards the idler arm. This bush is shorter than the other one; fit a flat washer and nut to each end of the idler arm, tighten nuts to 30 to 35 lb-ft. The latest assembly supercedes the steering damper.

TRACK RODS.—Separate track rods fitted between each steering arm and drop-arm to idler-arm rod. Plastic-seated ball-joints fitted from June 1964 onwards.

Adjust both track rods equally when adjusting toe-in.

Renewing Track-rod Ends.—If renewing track rod ends fit the shorter one towards the steering arm (grease nipple if fitted to rear) longer one to drop-arm to idler-arm rod. Locate clamps between pips on tube, with slot in clamp in line with slot in tube, clamps to be pendant with bolt heads facing forward. Clamp nuts tightened to 15 to 18 lb-ft with ball-joint in the middle of its travel. Pack plastic gaiter with grease before fitting to track-rod ball-stud.

On pre-June 1964 cars, the drop-arm to idler-arm rod was connected to the drop-arm by a detachable ball-stud located in the end of the rod, and located in a spring-loaded split seat. To adjust this screw the end plug right home and back off $\frac{3}{4}$ turn.

Post-June 1964 drop-arm to idler-arm rods have a plastic-seated ball-stud integral with the rod. Ball-stud is not serviced separately. Plastic gaiter should be packed with grease before fitting to stud.

STEERING STOPS.—Fitted on crossmember to contact abutments on drop-arm to idler-arm rod. To adjust, screw stops in, turn left-hand wheel through 38° on left-hand lock and adjust stop-to-contact abutment. Repeat for right-hand wheel on right lock.

WHEELS AND TYRES

Pressed-steel $13 \times 4\frac{1}{2}$J wheels; heavy-duty wheels, identified by aluminium paint, fitted to Zodiac and police cars.

Tyres, 6·40—13 4-ply. rayon cord on Zephyr 4 and 6, nylon sports on Zodiac.

Tyre pressures (front and rear): Zephyr 4 and 6, 22 to 28 lb/sq. in. Zodiac, 24 to 30 lb/sq. in.

FORD ZODIAC Mk III

A BARE ten years ago, 100 m.p.h. was still rather exclusive. Large, expensive saloons or sports cars which were either costly or stark (or both) mastered it easily. But middle-class saloons were often trying very hard at eighty-five, and completely out of breath at ninety. Now, well-established after twenty-one months' production, the Mark III Ford Zodiac holds five comfortably and six when the need arises, *just* manages the magic hundred—and costs under a thousand pounds.

Large by British standards, the interior space of the Zodiac is curiously allocated, making legroom limited at the back and the boot big, but awkwardly shaped. The test car's excellent floor gearshift made a third occupant in the front bench seat problematical; otherwise the accommodation is good and the decor pleasing. With a 2½-litre, six-cylinder engine the car is smooth and quiet; the good performance is not bought at the expense of refinement. Apart from steering which is rather lifeless, the handling is safe and the ride level. It would obviously benefit from back suspension which did not bump and judder on rough corners, but for most practical purposes the non-independent rear is adequate. The new gearchange works satisfactorily, unflattered by a slow clutch, and the brakes are light and free from fade. If the performance of the Zodiac is exploited and its capacity for fast cruising used as fully as it was during our test, fuel consumption looks rather unimpressive at 18.1 m.p.g. overall, but the Touring figure of 22.56 m.p.g. indicates that despite its size and weight, the Zodiac need not be greedy.

Without offering anything for nothing, the latest development of Ford's luxury car represents outstanding value for money, both to buy and run. It has an effortless gait, an easy way of covering big mileages very quickly indeed, without fatigue to its driver. A day filled with 600 miles of motorway and fast main-road cruising left one fresh and relaxed with only the over-75 m.p.h. wind noise ringing in the ears. Yet reasonable dimensions, lively acceleration, and a striking appearance make the Mark III Zodiac attractive in traffic and town.

Performance

ALTHOUGH an instant starter from cold, the six-cylinder, 2,553 c.c. engine is slow to warm up. After about half a mile on a wintry morning however, it runs smoothly enough, picks up easily, and the heater becomes effective. Once warm, it delivers its 109 b.h.p. smoothly and quietly but not very evenly. A light flywheel makes it responsive, but jerky at low r.p.m. and the engine is rather easy to stall. There is also a flat spot which makes acceleration around 40 m.p.h. in top gear leisurely and although 90 m.p.h. is reached fairly quickly, acceleration tails off thereafter. This is not to say that there is a pause, or a reluctance to pick up on opening the throttle but merely that at some speeds there isn't much punch in top.

Premium fuel suffices for the 8.3:1 compression ratio and it is interesting that the engine does not have the complication of a twin-carburetter layout with its attendant tuning problems. After 1,500 hard miles, there was no apparent deterioration in performance; the Zodiac seems quite untemperamental. A restart was possible on the 1 in 3 test hill on the second attempt, the first failing on account of furious clutch slip in first gear. Although the last few m.p.h. of the 100.2 m.p.h. maximum speed are gained with some difficulty, there is little indication of the engine working hard. In the nineties, it makes little more than a low humming noise and if taken near its maximum in the gears there is a deep buzz from the valve-gear but this is rarely heard in ordinary driving, and is almost inaudible when idling.

Transmission

THE new floor gear change for the four-speed, all-synchromesh gearbox is smooth and light. It is bent through a right angle, bringing the substantial knob close to the driver's left knee, and moves through an unusual plane at a shallow angle to the horizontal. Movements are short against powerful (but not heavy) synchromesh and they can be made quickly, but working the clutch quickly as well results in slip. To guard against inadvertent engagement of reverse, there is a neat sliding ring round the lever, below the knob, which is pulled back naturally when selecting reverse. It is difficult to gauge clutch grip by the feeling through the pedal, making starts and gearchanges sometimes jerky or perhaps unnecessarily slow. The movement is moderately light with a peak pressure of 40 lb. Third is only of much value up to about 68 m.p.h. when the effective rev. limit is being reached and the engine becomes noisy; one tends to forget this because of the normal smoothness of the engine and

In Brief

Price £813 plus purchase tax £169 18s. 9d. equals £982 18s. 9d.	
Capacity	2,553 c.c.
Unladen kerb weight	24¾ cwt.
Acceleration:	
20-40 m.p.h. in top gear	8.8 sec.
0-50 m.p.h. through gears	9.6 sec.
Maximum top gear gradient	1 in 9
Maximum speed	100.2 m.p.h.
Overall fuel consumption	18.1 m.p.g.
Touring fuel consumption	22.56 m.p.g.
Gearing: 19.9 m.p.h. in top gear at 1,000 r.p.m.	

The pronounced curve of the side windows gives plenty of shoulder room in front and rear. Note the cranked gear lever on the small gearbox hump in the front. The door handles are neat, being small levers under the armrests.

FORD ZODIAC Mk. III

change down at too high a road speed. The synchromesh on first is welcome for traffic driving and all the gears are quiet.

Running costs

THE Zodiac's consumption of premium petrol (mixture caused pinking) is not light when high speeds are habitually used, as they were during the greater part of our test. It works out at 3.2d. per mile, and with the Touring Fuel Consumption (a more realistic figure for everyday user/drivers) at 2.7d. per mile.

Fuel consumptions under special conditions were as follows:

**Cold start (choke in operation for about ¼ mile),
5.3 miles, average 24.4 m.p.h.: 19.2 m.p.g.
Motorway, fast cruising, 27.9 miles, average 88 m.p.h.: 13.8 m.p.g.
Gentle driving on main roads, mostly in top gear: 22.1 m.p.g.**

Service intervals extend to 5,000 miles (or six months) when use of a molybdenum disulphide lithium base grease is obligatory, otherwise greasing should be every 1,000 miles. The Ford book of service vouchers has a table of maximum charges which are exclusive of the cost of oil and materials. They are £4 10s. every 5,000, with an additional £1 every 15,000 miles for additional attention to brakes, steering geometry, suspension, and running gear. Access under the self-supporting bonnet is fair; the screen wash bottle, dipstick, oil filler, etc. are easy to get at, and the battery, hydraulic reservoirs and radiator are easily inspected and topped up. The fuel pump and the distributor are rather low however.

Handling

THE rather lifeless steering conceals the Zodiac's good handling until one becomes accustomed to it. It is by no means heavy but there is little feeling of the road transmitted to the driver's hands; it seems imprecise and woolly at first, although familiarity leads one to accept, but never like it. On corners there is moderate understeer which the driver combines with the generous power available to make the car very stable and safe. Roll is quickly checked and only sudden changes in direction cause any lurching. In the wet the understeer asserts itself more strongly and corners are best taken under power (a desirable, but not always possible practice in any car) to maintain a steady line. Adhesion in both wet and dry is good and there is ample warning of breakaway when it does eventually take place, either at the front (with the throttle shut) or the back (with it open). Wheelspin can occur with the inside back wheel tending to lift on sharp corners but this is less pronounced than on earlier six-cylinder Fords which could be distinctly skittish. The chief shortcoming of the live back axle is the uncomfortable, noisy tramp over bumps, making steering corrections necessary on uneven corners. Tyre squeal is absent except under extreme provocation.

Brakes

UNDER about 70 m.p.h., stopping the Zodiac is no problem. The brakes are light, free from fade, and pull up in a straight line. Care has sometimes to be exercised when making hard applications at very high speeds, however, for there is a tendency to wander, particularly in the wet. Efficiency remained unimpaired in our test down a long hill, and after the watersplash and prolonged fade tests. The handbrake failed to hold the car on a 1 in 3 hill, only just managing to do so on a 1 in 4.

Comfort and control

OVER most main roads, the ride is good. Long bumps are taken with a gentle rise and fall whatever the speed, but short bumps result in sharp, vertical movements and a certain amount of body shake if they are severe. Although set rather low, the seats are comfortable and give the driver plenty of firm support for thighs and shoulders, making them comfortable over many hours' occupation. Curiously, a bench front seat is retained even when the central gear lever is fitted but sideways location is good nonetheless—even without using the central armrest. The back compartment suffers from a shortage of legroom despite the efforts Ford have made to improve matters since the introduction of the model. When the front seat is at its middle fore-and-aft adjustment, which is nearer the wheel than most drivers prefer it, a tall passenger in the back has less than a hand's width between his knees and the seat in front of him. The driver sits upright; the position is a good compromise for a big saloon, and most sizes fit it quite well.

Quietness is one of the Zodiac's greatest virtues. The engine and transmission are subdued and road noise is hardly ever noticeable. Above about 75 m.p.h. there is a certain amount of wind roar which, in gusty conditions makes it necessary to turn up the radio. In the 90-100 m.p.h. range which is the natural motorway speed, this is the most obtrusive noise in the car, highlighting the quietness of everything else. On the overrun there is a rasp from the dual exhaust system only noticeable from outside the car, or audible with a window open.

The heater and demister is powerful and effective. The demister serves the double duty of keeping the windscreen clear and warming (or cooling) the upper part of the car. By manipulation of the controls, you can have warm feet and a cool head. The adjustments have to be made with some care however—the installation is rather of "all or nothing" character. The heating became of major importance in the test car because of some annoying draughts round the doors which seemed to fit well (and closed quietly with a gentle push) but somehow let in unwelcome cold.

The windscreen pillars are quite thick, the driving mirror huge, and there is a bad reflection both in daylight and after dark from the demister grilles in the top of the facia, making the Zodiac's visibility poorer than it might have been. Glass area is generous and the view aft is good, the fins making reversing easy. After dark the automatically operated reversing lights make the task simpler still. But judgement of the width at the front of the car is more difficult because of the falling-away front wings, the left-hand one being invisible from the low driving seat for all but the very tall. Quadruple headlights give a splendid spread for fast night driving and the headlight flasher stalk beside the steering column is most useful for daytime signalling.

Fittings and furniture

THE facia has two levels. The upper, in front of the driver contains most of the instruments and some of the switches. The lower is recessed with the heater controls, handbrake, clock, and some more switches—an unsatisfactory arrangement because the upper switches are difficult to get at past the steering wheel and the lower ones are too far away. The lights switch to the upper right, for example, is close to the door and the driver's sleeve is caught between the window winder and the steering wheel. The heater controls cannot be operated by a driver wearing a seat belt; they are shallow wheels which have to be turned with the tips of the fingers and on the test car they were very stiff anyway. The ashtray in the middle has a useful capacity. A weak, plunger-operated screenwasher delivers a meagre quantity of water which tends merely to smear, and the wipers flutter at speed.

Behind a flat glass, the instruments in the middle of the facia (speedometer and mileage recorders) are more easily read after dark, when annoying reflections disappear, and the same is true of the vaguely calibrated fuel gauge and temperature gauge behind curved glasses. The upper part of the facia is plastic crash padding and the lower part and the instrument console have panels of simulated wood. Upholstery is plastic and the floor is covered with a neatly fitting carpet. There are map pockets beside the front occupants' feet and a glove box in the facia with a curious downward opening which seemed to hold little advantage over the conventional sort. The boot is big but has lots of projections taking up space. Apart from the spare wheel, there is the fuel filler in the middle of the extreme rear, the counterbalance torsion bars, and the hinges in the lid. It is, however, usefully lit after dark.

Reversing lights are recessed into the back bumpers where casual bumps are unlikely to cause them damage. (*Right*)

Fluid levels in the radiator, battery and hydraulic reservoirs can easily be inspected. (*Lower, right*) **The bonnet is held open by counterbalance springs.**

The boot lid stays up by means of torsion bar springs. Its capacity (*below*) is good, but the shape is irregular. It held a total of 11.9 cu. ft. of dummy luggage comprising two 28×21×9 in., two 21×15×7 in., two 17½×13×6 in. and three 14×11×5 in. boxes. There was still space unoccupied near the extreme rear because of encroachment by the fuel filler behind the number plate.

Extended Road Test No. 1/64

MAKE Ford ● TYPE Zodiac Mk. III
● MAKERS Ford Motor Company Ltd., Dagenham, Essex.

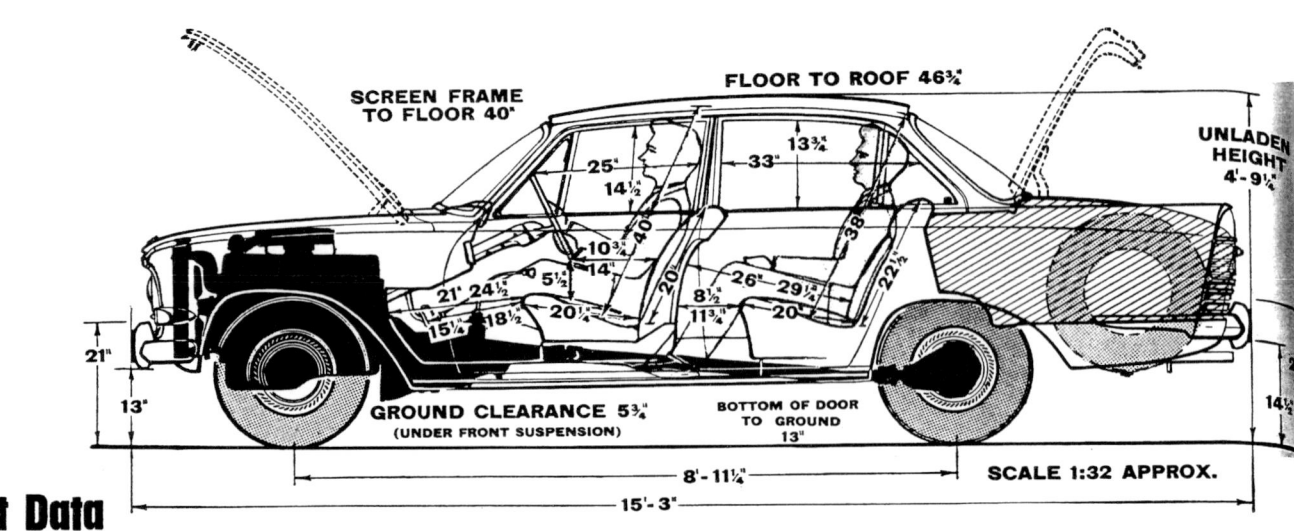

Test Data

World copyright reserved; no unauthorized reproduction in whole or in part.

Conditions: Weather: Dry, cool, light wind. (10-20 m.p.h.) (Temperature 39°-43°F., Barometer 29·5-29·6 inHg.) Surface: Dry concrete and tarmacadam. Fuel: Premium grade pump petrol (98 Octane by Research Method)

MAXIMUM SPEEDS
Flying mile
Mean of four opposite runs .. 100·2 m.p.h.
Best one-way time equals .. 100·3 m.p.h.

"Maximile" Speed: (Timed quarter mile after one mile accelerating from rest)
Mean of four opposite runs .. 95·9 m.p.h.
Best one-way time equals .. 96·8 m.p.h.

Speed in gears
Max. speed in 3rd .. .. 80 m.p.h.
Max. speed in 2nd .. .. 48 m.p.h.
Max. speed in 1st .. .. 36 m.p.h.

ACCELERATION TIMES
from standstill
0-30 m.p.h. .. .. 3·9 sec.
0-40 m.p.h. .. .. 6·3 sec.
0-50 m.p.h. .. .. 9·6 sec.
0-60 m.p.h. .. .. 13·4 sec.
0-70 m.p.h. .. .. 17·9 sec.
0-80 m.p.h. .. .. 26·2 sec.
0-90 m.p.h. .. .. 37·6 sec.
Standing quarter mile .. .. 19·0 sec.

on upper ratios

	Top gear	Third gear
10-30 m.p.h.	9·1 sec.	6·1 sec.
20-40 m.p.h.	8·8 sec.	5·8 sec.
30-50 m.p.h.	9·3 sec.	6·2 sec.
40-60 m.p.h.	10·4 sec.	6·9 sec.
50-70 m.p.h.	11·8 sec.	8·3 sec.
60-80 m.p.h.	13·4 sec.	13·1 sec.
70-90 m.p.h.	18·8 sec.	

Overtaking
Starting at 40 m.p.h. in direct top gear, distance required to gain 100 ft. on another car travelling at a steady 40 m.p.h. = 620 ft.

HILL CLIMBING
Max. gradient climbable at steady speed
Top gear .. 1 in 9 (Tapley 245 lb./ton)
3rd. gear .. 1 in 6·6 (Tapley 335 lb./ton)
2nd. gear .. 1 in 4·1 (Tapley 540 lb./ton)

FUEL CONSUMPTION
Overall Fuel Consumption for 1,531 miles, 84·5 gallons, equals 18·1 m.p.g. (15·6 litres/100 km.)

Touring Fuel Consumption (m.p.g. at steady speed midway between 30 m.p.h. and maximum, less 5% allowance for acceleration.) .. .. 22·6 m.p.g.
Fuel tank capacity (makers' figure) 12 gallons

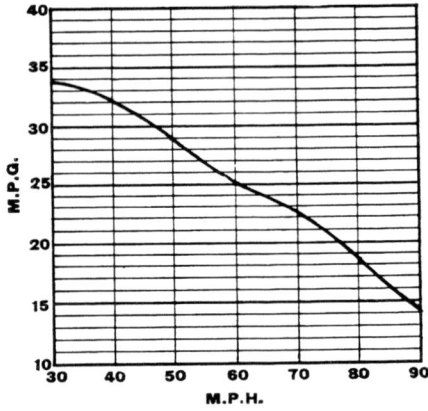

BRAKES
Deceleration and equivalent stopping distance from 30 m.p.h.
0·25 g with 25 lb. pedal pressure .. (=120 ft.)
0·59 g with 50 lb. pedal pressure .. (=51 ft.)
0·74 g with 75 lb. pedal pressure .. (=40½ ft.)
0·97 g with 85 lb. pedal pressure .. (=31 ft.)

Handbrake
0·35 g deceleration from 30 m.p.h. (=86 ft.)

Brake Fade
TEST 1. 20 stops at ½ g deceleration at 1 min. intervals from a speed midway between 30 m.p.h. and maximum speed (=65 m.p.h.)
Pedal force at beginning = 45 lb.
Pedal force for 10th stop = 50 lb.
Pedal force for 20th stop = 50 lb.

TEST 2. After top gear descent of steep hill falling approximately 600 ft. in half a mile, increase in brake pedal force for ½ g stop from 30 m.p.h. = 0 lb.

PARKABILITY
Gap needed to clear 6 ft. obstruction

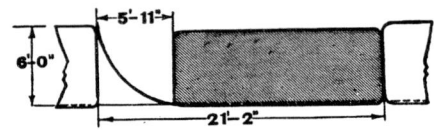

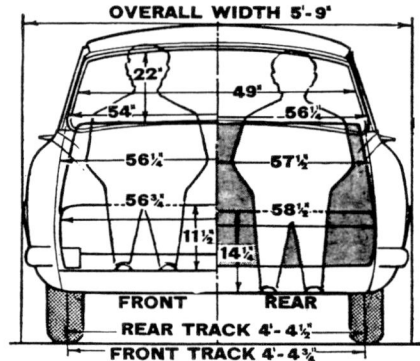

Waterproofing
Increase in brake pedal force for ½ g stop from 30 m.p.h. after two runs through shallow watersplash at 30 m.p.h. = 0 lb.

CLUTCH
Free pedal movement.. .. .. = 1 in.
Additional movement to disengage clutch completely .. .. .. = 3 in.
Maximum pedal load .. .. = 40 lb.

STEERING
Turning circle between kerbs.
Left .. .. 34¾ ft.
Right .. .. 34¾ ft.
Turns of steering wheel from lock to lock 4½

INSTRUMENTS
Speedometer at 30 m.p.h. .. 6% fast
Speedometer at 60 m.p.h. .. 2½% fast
Speedometer at 90 m.p.h. .. 2% fast
Distance recorder .. .. 2½% fast

WEIGHT
Kerb weight (unladen, but with oil, coolant and fuel for approximately 50 miles) .. .. 24¾ cwt.
Front/rear distribution of kerb weight 54/46
Weight laden as tested.. .. 28½ cwt.

FORD ZODIAC Mk. III

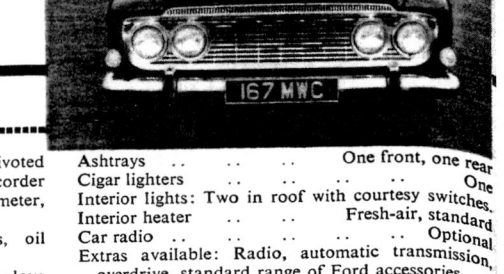

Coachwork and Equipment

Starting handle	None
Battery mounting	Under bonnet
Jack	Triangular screw type
Jacking points:	Two each side under door sills.
Standard tool kit	Jack and wheelbrace
Exterior lights:	Four headlights, two side/flashers, two stop/tail, two rear flashers, number-plate light.
Number of electrical fuses:	One (plus one for radio).
Direction indicators	Self-cancelling flashers
Windscreen wipers	Two-speed, self-parking
Windscreen washers	Manual plunger
Sun visors	Two, universally pivoted
Instruments:	Speedometer with total mileage recorder and decimal trip, fuel gauge, water thermometer, clock.
Warning lights:	Ignition, direction signals, oil pressure, main beam, heater fan.
Locks:	with ignition key: Both front doors, glove locker, and boot; no other keys.
Glove lockers	One
Map pockets	Two in front compartment
Parcel shelves	One behind rear seat
Ashtrays	One front, one rear
Cigar lighters	One
Interior lights:	Two in roof with courtesy switches.
Interior heater	Fresh-air, standard
Car radio	Optional
Extras available:	Radio, automatic transmission, overdrive, standard range of Ford accessories.
Upholstery material	Cirrus 500 P.V.C.
Floor covering	Carpet on felt
Exterior colours standardized	Ten
Alternative body styles	None

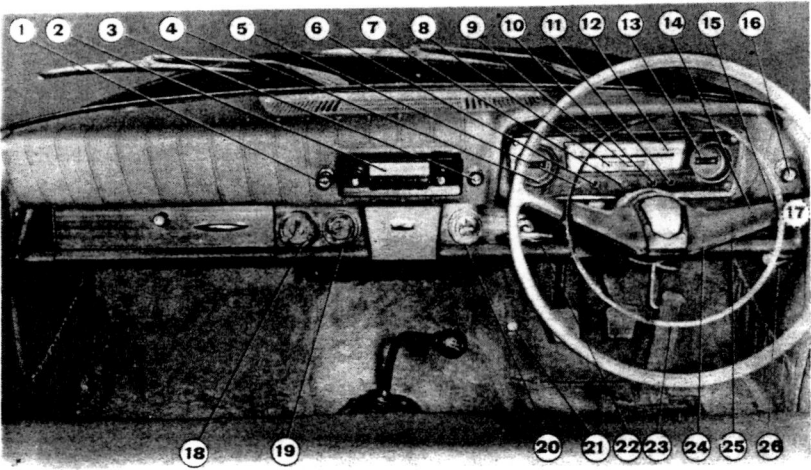

Key to facia

1, Cigar lighter. 2, Radio. 3, Choke. 4, Fuel gauge. 5, L.H. direction indicator warning light. 6, Oil pressure warning light. 7, Main beam warning light. 8, Trip mileage recorder. 9, Total mileage recorder. 10, Ignition warning light. 11, R.H. direction indicator warning light. 12, Speedometer. 13, Water temperature gauge. 14, Windscreen wiper switch/washer plunger. 15, Heater fan switch and warning light. 16, Lights switch. 17, Stalk for direction indicator and headlight flasher. 18, Clock. 19, Heater temperature control. 20, Demister/de-icer control. 21, Dip switch. 22, Handbrake. 23, Horn ring. 24, Parking lights switch. 25, Ignition/starter switch. 26, Bonnet release.

Specification

ENGINE
- Cylinders: 6
- Bore: 82.55 mm.
- Stroke: 79.5 mm.
- Cubic capacity: 2,553 c.c.
- Piston area: 49.74 sq. in.
- Valves: Pushrod o.h.v.
- Compression ratio: 8.3/1 (7.0/1 optional)
- Carburetter: Zenith 42 W.I.A.-2 downdraught
- Fuel pump: A.C. mechanical
- Ignition timing control: Centrifugal and vacuum
- Oil filter: Full flow
- Maximum power (net): 109 b.h.p. at 4,800 r.p.m.
- Maximum torque (net): 140.5 lb./ft at 2,400 r.p.m.
- Piston speed at maximum b.h.p.: 2,500 ft./min.

TRANSMISSION
- Clutch: Ford/Borg & Beck 8¼ in. s.d.p.
- Top gear (s/m): 3.545
- 3rd gear (s/m): 5.005
- 2nd gear (s/m): 7.849
- 1st gear (s/m): 11.213
- Reverse: 11.861
- Propeller shaft: Open Hardy Spicer needle roller
- Final drive: Hypoid bevel
- Top gear m.p.h. at 1,000 r.p.m.: 19.9
- Top gear m.p.h. at 1,000 ft./min. piston speed: 38.1

CHASSIS
- Brakes: Girling hydraulic with vacuum servo.
- Brake dimensions: Front, 9¾ in. diameter discs, Rear, 9 in. diameter drums 2¼ in. wide.
- Friction areas: 99.2 sq. in. of friction lining operating on 345 sq. in. swept disc and drum surface.
- Suspension: Front: Independent by Macpherson coil-spring-damper strut and bottom wishbone incorporating anti-roll bar. Rear: Live axle and semi-elliptic leaf springs.
- Shock absorbers: Front: Armstrong telescopic. Rear: Armstrong lever arm.
- Steering gear: Ford/Burman recirculating ball.
- Tyres: 6.40/13 4-ply Nylon sports, tubed or tubeless.

Maintenance

- Sump: 6½ pints, S.A.E. 20W (plus 1½ pints in filter).
- Gearbox: 4 pints, S.A.E. 80
- Rear axle: 2½ pints, S.A.E. 90
- Steering gear lubricant: S.A.E. 90, E.P. oil
- Cooling system capacity: 19 pints (two drain taps)
- Chassis lubrication: By grease gun every 5,000 miles to 12 points.
- Ignition timing: 8° b.t.d.c.
- Contact breaker gap: .015 in.
- Sparking plug type: Champion N.5 or Autolite AG4-A
- Sparking plug gap: .023/.028 in.
- Valve timing: Inlet opens 17° b.t.d.c. and closes 51° a.b.d.c.; exhaust opens 49° b.b.d.c. and closes 19° a.t.d.c.
- Tappet clearances (cold): Inlet .014 in.; exhaust .014 in.
- Front wheel toe-in: 1/16 to 3/16 in.
- Camber angle: 1° 37′ to 2° 37′
- Castor angle: 0° 19′ to 0° 41′
- Steering swivel pin inclination: 5° 40′ to 6° 40′
- Tyre pressures: Front 24-30 lb.; Rear 24-30 lb.
- Brake fluid: Castor oil Polyglycolether mixture
- Battery type and capacity: 12-volt, 57 amp./hr.

Visibility
180° from the driving seat. Shaded areas show one-eye visibility.

90°   75°   60°   45°   30°   15°   0°   15°   30°   45°   60°   75°

For Performance Comparisons, see page 148

TWO PEDAL version of the Zephyr 4 cockpit is shown here. The lighting switch is convenient on the right of the facia, the wiper switch on the left is usually reached through the wheel.

LARGEST four-cylinder Ford, this four-door saloon with conventional headlamps is neatly designed.

FORD ZEPHYR 4 (Automatic)

Six into Four

AMONGST all the many four-cylinder cars built by British manufacturers, the new Ford Zephyr stands out as almost the only true six-seater. Bigger than any other car which can be bought for its "starting price" of £846 12s. 9d., and very well sprung, it is an attractive proposition in its simplest form. For those who can afford to spend about £110 more than this but do not wish to spend upwards of £1,070 on a Ford Zodiac, two interesting propositions at comparable prices are a Zephyr 6-cylinder with synchromesh gears, or the Zephyr 4-cylinder with fully automatic two-pedal transmission which is the subject of this report.

Whereas in a Road Test Report published two weeks ago we described the new Ford Zodiac as "a car which will appeal particularly to the long-distance business motorist by virtue of the outstanding performance and impressive appearance . . ." this Zephyr 4, with the optional automatic transmission, offers as much or more room to the man or woman who puts emphasis on economy and ease of driving rather than on exceptional standards of speed and acceleration—the hydraulic torque converter of our test model made four cylinders operate quite as smoothly as would the "six" with mechanical transmission.

In Brief

Price (including automatic transmission as tested) £695 plus purchase tax £261 12s. 9d. equals £956 12s. 9d.

Price with synchromesh gearbox (including purchase tax), £846 12s. 9d.

Capacity .. .. 1,703 c.c.
Unladen kerb weight .. 22½ cwt.
Acceleration :
  20-40 m.p.h. in kick-down gear 5.9 sec.
  0-50 m.p.h. through gears 14.7 sec.
Maximum top gear gradient approx. 1 in 8.9
Maximum speed .. 78.9 m.p.h.
"Maximile" speed .. 76.0 m.p.h.
Touring fuel consumption 27.2 m.p.g.
Gearing: 19.9 m.p.h. in top gear at 1,000 r.p.m.

Go-anywhere Suspension

IT is no coincidence that some of the first Fords of this series were sent to East Africa, where they won their class in the Safari Rally. Long-travel suspension with very little friction in it lets this Zephyr 4 stride over really rough roads with exceptional ease, not "bottoming" audibly even when carrying its full complement of six passengers although, conversely, one example could reach the rebound limit of its rear suspension rather noisily if hustled over potholed going when unladen. Careful thought has been given to the elimination of vulnerable projections beneath the body, and whilst (as usual!) our measurements showed less than the claimed amount of ground clearance, this is a car which should not suffer damage in negotiating rutted tracks.

On ordinary British roads which do not require a long range of spring movement the Zephyr 4 provides good average standards of riding comfort, with a fair amount of rise and fall on the suspension but no pitching. Road noise is extremely inconspicuous, despite the fact that this model carries a much smaller weight of sound-absorbing material than does the Zodiac, and the back seat ride is not noticeably inferior to that enjoyed by the driver.

Steer and Stop

WITH its 4-cylinder engine in a car designed to cope with a 6-cylinder unit, this Zephyr 4 has an advantage in respect of steering which remains conveniently light even during parking manœuvres. Whilst it has not quite the dart-like stability of the faster and heavier Zodiac, needing slightly more conscious "driving" on roads with varying camber, the Zephyr 4 responds to the helm promptly and with average touring car precision: it comes as a surprise to find that more than four turns of the wheel are needed from lock to lock.

BROAD enough to give six people comfortable elbow room, the Zephyr 4 is shown here with woven upholstery. A glove locker and parcel tray face the front passenger.

Exploration of the narrow lanes through Cornish fishing villages showed the steering lock available to be good for what is, by British standards, a bulky car. Some sorts of rough going could induce shake of the steering column, but there was no " kick " of the wheel to make the wearing of gloves desirable.

Vacuum-assisted braking, with discs at the front and drums at the rear, is another feature which the Zephyr 4 inherits from more powerful Fords. We tried to produce brake fade by making a long series of stops from speeds in the 60-70 m.p.h. range at the shortest possible intervals, and failed utterly to produce any appreciable loss of braking performance. Wet roads caused no loss of power, and even a watersplash about 12 in. deep had very little effect. There are cars which produce more instant " bite " in an emergency stop from 20 m.p.h., usually at the cost of locking the wheels too easily in bad weather or being subject to " fade " after hard usage, but for all-round merit the Zephyr 4's brakes would be hard to beat. Emerging through the facia panel at a convenient angle, the twist-to-release handbrake could just hold the car on a 1-in-4 test hill if applied really forcefully, but worked easily in more normal circumstances.

Creature Comforts

FURNISHING inside the Zephyr 4 is simple compared with the Zodiac, but neat and practical when judged in its own right. Quadrant speedometers seldom please us much, but at least this one faces the driver squarely, has clear figures and has good variable-brightness lighting. Other instruments are merely a contents gauge for the 12-gallon petrol tank (big enough to give quite a long cruising range), a radiator thermometer and a total distance recorder indicating in 1/10th mile units. A capacious shelf below the passenger's half of the facia panel is supplemented by a small but welcome lockable glove box.

Seating is on a simple bench at the front, low enough for the not-very-tall to find the steering wheel rim near to their sight line, and with just enough adjustment range to let a 6-ft. man be reasonably well at ease. One car which we drove had leathercloth upholstery, the other was furnished in a woven plastics fabric which we found more pleasing, and although the seat is not shaped to give lateral support one does not slide about on this fabric. A further option (but at extra cost) is hide upholstery. Quite long drives showed the backrest shaping to give comfortable support for the spine. Whilst rear seat kneeroom is not really adequate unless the driving seat is one notch short of its full-back setting (even then, a rather sharp lower rear corner to the front seat invokes a little criticism) the less-bulky seat cushions make this model a useful fraction roomier internally than is the Zodiac. In either model, three-abreast seating is truly comfortable save for restricted footroom in the centre-front seat due to a big transmission hump; a high-set mirror in conjunction with the tall rear window lets the driver retain a rearward view over the heads of passengers during six-up motoring. All-round vision is reasonably good, but slimmer pillars at the flanks of the broad windscreen would make it much better still.

Windscreen wipers with two wiping edges per blade do a good job of removing dirty water from curved glass, audible clonking from the drive mechanism of relatively new cars hinting at the considerable effort needed to move them. After dark, two sealed-beam headlamps gave plenty of light though without such a broad spread as would give four lamps: a headlamp mounting about 20% lower than on Consuls increases very slightly the tendency for pools of darkness to be left beyond humps in an undulating road. Less-brilliant lighting of the automatic transmission quadrant, and non-reflective trim on top of the padded facia, would diminish windscreen reflections.

The optional extra interior heater was fitted to each of our test cars. Powerful as a heater-up of incoming fresh air, it can pass a not-very-large volume of either cold or hot air onto the windscreen interior, regardless of whether cold or hot air is being blown down onto the front floor: temperature control by the excellent system of admitting variable

MECHANICAL elements visible under the bonnet include battery and brake servo on the left of the picture, the vacuum reservoir and heater blower on the other side of the overhead-valve engine.

33

proportions of cold and hot air would be much more satisfactory if the two air-streams were mixed instead of emerging separately from below two sides of the facia panel. The hinged ventilation panels on the front doors, being pivoted almost at their front edges, can be opened some way to let air out of the body without letting rain into the car on wet days, but both they and the four wind-down windows of curved glass were sometimes very stiff to move.

What'll She Do?

WHEN a higher-powered version of the same car is offered, this inevitable question is not asked in expectation of a sensational answer, but for reassurance that the lower-powered of two cars is not in any sense under-engined. We drove two different examples of the Zephyr 4 whilst preparing this test report, and were able to time the synchromesh-geared version at a mean speed of just over 85 m.p.h., a pace some 5 m.p.h. above anything we were ever able to record with Ford Consuls. For cars fitted with the optional automatic transmission, a rear-axle ratio too high to let the engine reach the peak of its power curve has been chosen (presumably in the interests of fuel economy and of quiet running) but even so our two-pedal car was timed at a mean speed of almost exactly 79 m.p.h. Whilst this somehow felt a leisurely car, its gentle surge away from rest is not broken by pauses to change gear and it astonished us by recording a better average time for the standing start ¼-mile than did Consuls with their 3-speed synchromesh gearbox.

Selection of a high axle ratio for use with the automatic transmission means that the indirect gears also are high. Accelerated at full throttle, our test car would remain in bottom gear until about 40 m.p.h. and only changed from middle to top gear at just over 60 m.p.h. Top-gear acceleration in the upper ranges of speed is leisurely, so that whereas on M1 a cruising gait in the seventies is natural

TALL and wide, the curved glass rear window provides all-round vision even when the car is fully laden. A counterbalanced lift-up lid gives easy access to the capacious boot.

and reasonably quiet, on ordinary roads one seldom seems to exceed 65 m.p.h. Kick-down pressure on the accelerator will produce a downward change from top to middle gear at any speed below 55 m.p.h., so that on most occasions the car has reasonably good overtaking performance. If the moderate but quite perceptible "second pressure" on the accelerator pedal is not used, this two-pedal car will pull away from as low a speed as 20 m.p.h. in top gear, the hydraulic torque converter letting the engine get up into the middle of its speed range where it is smooth but not unduly fussy. At small throttle openings, upward changes of gear occurred at low speeds, and so smoothly that they could hardly be detected. Our testing included some of the steepest hills of Somerset, Devon and Cornwall, an ability to restart a moderate passenger load on a 1-in-4 hill sufficing for all normal purposes although for caravan-towing it might prove inadequate. Reverse gear is higher than first, and we found hills on which a stop-and-reverse (such as might be necessary on meeting other traffic when descending a narrow lane) was impracticable.

Automatic transmission control was by the usual lever moving over a very simple and entirely positive quadrant. A driver who wanted to help the automatic "brain" could hold or select middle gear instantly—this ratio could be engaged at any speed up to about 60 m.p.h. for braking purposes, the fact that first gear braking was only available at very low speeds being no bother with this car's powerful and well-cooled servo disc brakes.

Our tests were run on premium-grade petrol of around 97 R.M. Octane rating, but both the cars which we drove proved willing to tolerate "mixture grade" fuel (90 octane approx.) without much pinking. Oil consumption lay in the 500-1,000 miles per pint region, according to driving speed. Cold starting and warm-up performance did not come up to the best modern standards, but once warm the two-pedal car's engine was smooth enough to pass as a "six" at any but idling r.p.m.

With Synchromesh

AS has been indicated already, sampling a car with the synchromesh gearbox and the slightly lower rear axle ratio, we recorded a substantially higher maximum speed. Overall petrol consumption checks also favoured the non-automatic car by about 3½%, but running conditions were not by any means identical and we would hesitate to make very precise comparisons on this account.

With synchromesh gearing we found the Zephyr 4-cylinder engine markedly less smooth than the Zodiac six—neither engine was especially fond of being asked to pull at low r.p.m., but below 30 m.p.h. the "four" boomed considerably during top gear acceleration. Torque converter transmission let the engine run faster and more smoothly whenever it was under load, without making it unduly fussy.

For a keen driver, four gears (all with synchromesh) are much preferable to the three of the superseded Consul, although the gear-shy would notice that 7% higher effective gearing makes this less of a top gear model than was its predecessor. Reasonably quiet but by no means as silent as the epicyclic gearing of two-pedal cars, this new gearbox has well-chosen ratios, but its steering column lever moves rather a long way to the first and third gear positions, and an over-centre helper spring which reduces clutch disengagement effort tends to result in the pedal coming back with a thud after changes of gear.

Coachwork and Equipment

Starting handle	None
Battery mounting	Alongside engine on right
Jack	Bipod pillar type
Jacking points	2 external sockets under each side of body
Standard tool kit	Jack and wheelbrace, in bag
Exterior lights:	2 headlamps, 2 sidelamps/flashers, 2 stop/tail lamps, rear number plate lamp
Number of electrical fuses	1 (in turn indicators circuit)
Direction indicators:	self cancelling flashers, white front and amber rear
Windscreen wipers:	Twin-blade electrical, variable-speed and self-parking
Windscreen washers	Extra
Sun vizors	Two, universally pivoted
Instruments:	Speedometer with decimal total distance recorder, fuel contents gauge, coolant thermometer
Warning lights:	Dynamo charge, oil pressure, headlamp main beam, turn indicators (also for heater fan if fitted)
Locks: with ignition key:	Ignition/starter switch, both front doors, luggage locker, glove box
With other keys	None
Glove lockers	One on facia, lockable
Map pockets	None
Parcel shelves	One on nearside of facia, one behind rear seat
Ashtrays	One on facia, one behind front seat
Cigar lighters	extra
Interior lights	One above windscreen, controlled from facia and by courtesy switches on front doors
Interior heater	Optional extra, fresh air type with screen demisters
Car radio	Optional extra (manual or push-button tuning)
Extras available:	Automatic transmission (as tested) or overdrive, heater, radio, hide upholstery, whitewall tyres, and range of Fomoco accessories
Upholstery material	PVC or woven plastics fabric (at extra cost, hide)
Floor covering	Laminated rubber mats
Exterior colours standardized	12 single colours
Alternative body styles	None (Zephyr 6 and Zodiac are more-powerful versions of same basic car)

Maintenance

Sump capacity	6 pints plus 1½ pints in filter, S.A.E. 20W for temperate summer and winter
Gearbox	2¼ pints, S.A.E. 80
Rear axle	2½ pints, S.A.E. 90 hypoid oil
Steering gear lubricant	EP gear oil
Cooling system capacity	15.3 pints plus 1.7 pints in optional heater (2 drain taps)
Chassis lubrication	By grease gun every 5,000 miles to 12 points
Ignition timing	8° before t.d.c. static (low-compression engines 4° before t.d.c.)
Contact breaker gap	0.015 in.
Sparking plug type	Champion N5, 14 mm.
Sparking plug gap	0.030 in.
Valve timing:	
Inlet opens 17° before t.d.c. and closes 51° a.b.d.c.	
Exhaust opens 49° before b.d.c. and closes 19° a.t.d.c.	
Tappet clearances (cold):	
Inlet and Exhaust	0.014 in.
Front wheel toe-in	1/16 to 3/16 in.
Camber angle	1° to 2°
Castor angle	0° to 1°
Steering swivel pin inclination	6° 17′ to 7° 17′
Tyre pressures: According to load, 22 lb. minimum at front and rear	
Brake fluid	Fomoco (castor oil-polyglycolether mixture)
Battery type and capacity	12 volt, 57 amp. hr. (with synchromesh gearbox, 45 amp. hr.)

The Motor

MAKE: Ford. TYPE: Zephyr 4 (with automatic transmission).
MAKERS: Ford Motor Co., Ltd., Dagenham, Essex.

ROAD TEST • No. 17/62

DATA

World copyright reserved; no unauthorized reproduction in whole or in part.

CONDITIONS: *Weather: Cool and damp, with low barometer and light breeze. (Temperature 40°-45° F., Barometer 29.3 in. Hg.) Surface: Damp concrete and tarred macadam. Fuel: Premium grade pump petrol (approx. 97 Octane Rating by Research Method).*

INSTRUMENTS

Speedometer at 30 m.p.h.	5% fast
Speedometer at 60 m.p.h.	4% fast
Speedometer at 80 m.p.h.	3% fast
Distance Recorder	3½% fast

WEIGHT

Kerb weight (unladen, but with oil, coolant and fuel for approximately 50 miles)	22½ cwt.
Front/rear distribution of kerb weight	54/46
Weight laden as tested	26¼ cwt.

MAXIMUM SPEEDS

Mean lap speed around banked circuit	78.9 m.p.h.
Best one-way ¼-mile time equals	81.1 m.p.h.

"Maximile" Speed (Timed quarter mile after one mile accelerating from rest.)

Mean of opposite runs	76.0 m.p.h.
Best one-way time equals	77.9 m.p.h.

Speed in gears (Automatic upward changes at full throttle.)

Max. speed in 2nd gear	61 m.p.h.
Max. speed in 1st gear	40 m.p.h.

FUEL CONSUMPTION

37.5 m.p.g.	at constant 30 m.p.h. on level
34.0 m.p.g.	at constant 40 m.p.h. on level
30.5 m.p.g.	at constant 50 m.p.h. on level
26.5 m.p.g.	at constant 60 m.p.h. on level
22.5 m.p.g.	at constant 70 m.p.h. on level
18.5 m.p.g.	at constant 80 m.p.h. on level

Overall Fuel Consumption for 1,230.5 miles, 53.5 gallons, equals 23.0 m.p.g. (12.3 litres/100 km.

Touring Fuel Consumption (m.p.g. at steady speed midway between 30 m.p.h. and maximum, less 5% allowance for acceleration) 27.2 m.p.g.
Fuel tank capacity (maker's figure) 12 gallons.

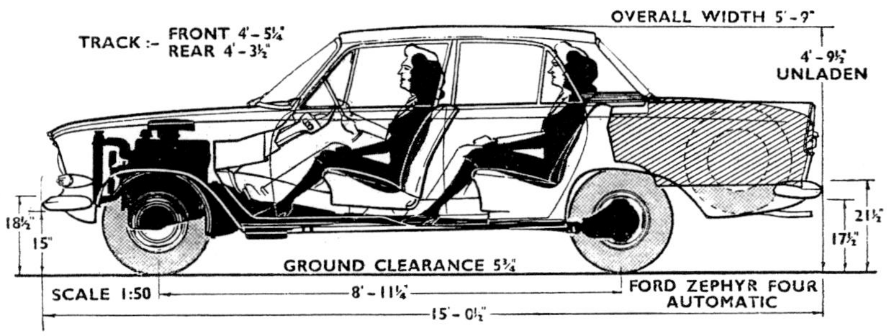

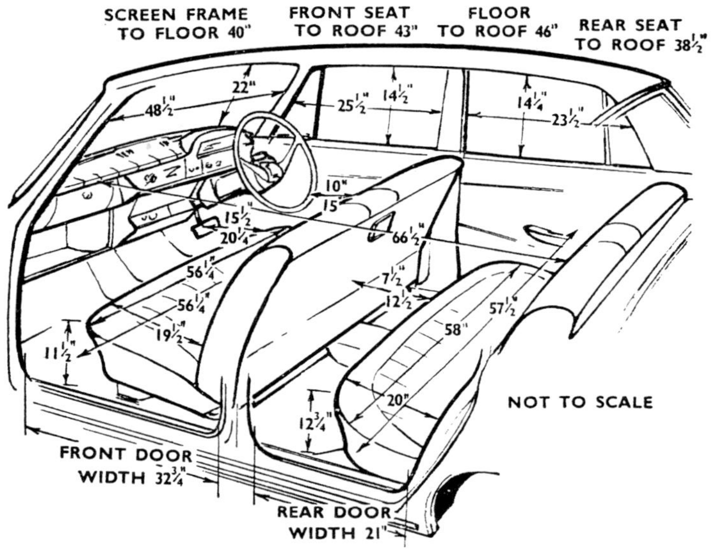

BRAKES from 30 m.p.h.
0.95 g retardation (equivalent to 31¾ ft. stopping distance) with 70 lb. pedal pressure.
0.73 g retardation (equivalent to 41¼ ft. stopping distance) with 50 lb. pedal pressure.
0.35 g retardation (equivalent to 86 ft. stopping distance) with 25 lb. pedal pressure.

HILL CLIMBING at steady sustained speeds

Max. gradient on top gear approx. .. 1 in 8.9 (Tapley 250 lb./ton)

ACCELERATION TIMES from standstill

0-30 m.p.h.	6.7 sec.
0-40 m.p.h.	9.8 sec.
0-50 m.p.h.	14.7 sec.
0-60 m.p.h.	22.8 sec.
0-70 m.p.h.	42.9 sec.
Standing quarter mile	22.8 sec.

ACCELERATION TIMES from rolling start

	Kick-down range	Top gear
10-30 m.p.h.	4.8 sec.	—
20-40 m.p.h.	5.9 sec.	10.0 sec.
30-50 m.p.h.	8.0 sec.	14.0 sec.
40-60 m.p.h.	13.0 sec.	20.7 sec.
50-70 m.p.h.	28.2 sec.	32.4 sec.

STEERING

Turning circle between kerbs:	
Left	35½ ft.
Right	33¼ ft.
Turns of steering wheel from lock to lock	4⅓

SYNCHROMESH-GEARED CAR

A second car was also driven, with the lower-ratio axle and 4-speed all-synchromesh gearbox, giving ratios of 3.9, 5.87, 9.17, and 17.21.

Distance Recorder on this car was 2% fast.

Maximum Speed was 85.1 m.p.h. mean, with a best one-way speed of 88.9 m.p.h.

Overall Fuel Consumption for 457 miles (corrected distance) was 23.8 m.p.g.

Specification

Engine

Cylinders	4
Bore	82.55 *mm.*
Stroke	79.5 *mm.*
Cubic capacity	1,703 *c.c.*
Piston area	33.16 *sq. in.*
Valves	*o.h.v. (pushrods)*
Compression Ratio	8.3/1 (*optional* 7.0/1)
Carburetter	*Zenith 36 VN downdraught*
Fuel pump	*AC mechanical*
Ignition timing control	*centrifugal and vacuum*
Oil filter	*Full Flow*
Maximum power (net)	68 *b.h.p.* (73.5 *b.h.p. gross*)
at	4,800 *r.p.m.*
Piston speed at maximum b.h.p.	2,500 *ft./min.*

Transmission (automatic)

Clutch	*Borg Warner torque converter with 2/1 maximum multiplication*
Top gear	3.55
2nd gear	5.147
1st gear	8.48
Reverse	7.419

Propeller shaft	*Hardy Spicer series* 1140 *single-piece open*
Final drive	*hypoid bevel*
Top gear m.p.h. at 1,000 *r.p.m.*	19.9
Top gear m.p.h. at 1,000 *ft./min. piston speed*	38.1

Chassis

Brakes	*Girling hydraulic with vacuum servo, disc front and drum rear*
Brake dimensions	*Front discs* 9¾ *in. dia. rear drums* 9 *in. dia.* × 1¾ *in. wide*
Friction areas	81 *sq. in. of lining working on* 301.6 *sq. in. rubbed area of discs and drums*
Suspension:	
Front	*Macpherson telescopic coil spring and damper struts, with lower wish-bone incorporating anti-roll bar*
Rear	½*-elliptic leaf springs*
Shock absorbers:	
Front	*Armstrong, incorporated in suspension struts*
Rear	*Armstrong lever-arm*
Steering gear	*Ford-Burman recirculating ball-bearing*
Tyres	6.40-13 4*-ply, tubed or tubeless*

NEW FORDS

The Zephyr Six is recognizable from the exterior by its divided radiator grille while . . .

. . . the Zephyr Four, replacing the old Consul, has a simpler style

Enter the Zodiac Zephyr 6 Zephyr 4

The Zephyrs have a different roofline to the Zodiac, noticeable in the squarer rearward part of the roof and lack of separate quarter light

TWO weeks ago Ford introduced the first of their new big car range, the Zodiac. Now they have announced two more Zephyr models, the Zephyr Six and the Zephyr Four, the latter being a replacement for the old Consul model. All three models are basically the same car in terms of body-chassis unit, suspension and mechanical components except, of course, in the case of the Zephyr Four which has the four-cylinder engine of 1703 cc similar to the old Consul model.

Outwardly the lines of all three cars are alike although each has a different grille, only the Zodiac sporting four headlamps, and the new Zephyrs also have an altered roof line which conveys a rather elegant squared-off effect to the back of the roof by incorporating a quarter light in the rear door and bringing a wider roof panel down behind it. As would be expected, the interiors of the cars change with the price bracket, the Zephyr Four being simple but tasteful, the Zephyr Six rather more elaborate and the Zodiac with the full treatment, including simulated walnut. Unlike the previous Zodiac and Zephyr, the new cars have differences in the engine compartment where the Zodiac produces 109 bhp net at 4,800 rpm as against the Zephyr's 98 at 4,750 rpm. The Zodiac also boasts a dual exhaust system using a common silencer.

A feature of the range is the option of automatic transmission on any of the models, this being the latest Borg-Warner unit which is impressing so favourably on the range of BMC 1½-litre cars.

Having covered a fair number of miles in each of the new models in both manual and automatic form, the most significant thing one can say about them is that they do not give the impression of being new models at all. This is meant in no derogatory sense but absolutely the opposite. These cars feel like vehicles which have been in production for a number of years and in which the bugs have been ironed out. They are big cars with plenty of room for four people and adequate capacity for six, while at the rear there is a luggage boot of truly cavernous proportions. The driving position is good and all-round visibility excellent on all the cars. Controls are well thought

Sporting Motorist

out, seats comfortable although, of course, being of bench type in the front not perfect for fast cornering, and the performance very lively indeed even on the four-cylinder model. Steering has a progressive ratio which varies between 18.6 to 1 and 21 to 1 towards maximum lock. This is a useful feature for parking a fairly large car. Brakes, which are disc on the front and drum at the rear, are powerful and progressive with very light pedal pressures required for maximum stopping power. New sound-deadening techniques have been used to give a notably quiet passenger compartment, the four-cylinder again being particularly noteworthy in this respect. One of our few criticisms centres around the wind noise experienced at high speed, although in fairness this is probably more obvious because of the lack of noise from any other source. There are a number of thoughtful touches, such as the concealed catches in the door handles which make it difficult for children to open the doors from inside, the excellent plastic seat covering material called Cirrus Fabric which feels for all the world like good quality hide, the reduced-service suspension and steering components which now require lubrication only every 5,000 miles, the one-side parking lights with isolator to prevent the driver from moving off without lighting all four lights, and so on.

A full analysis of the new Fords' detail engineering and road performance we will leave for the time when a road test is undertaken. Suffice it to say that this is a really notable addition to the country's large medium-priced cars, and that it adds, in the Zodiac, one more model to the very many now on sale in this country that can exceed the magic 100 miles per hour.

The difference in interior trim is readily apparent in these views of the Zephyr 4 (above) and 6 (below)

A vestige of the old Zodiac remains in the grille treatment of the latest version, which boasts four headlamps

The Zodiac (below) takes luxury even further, the model shown being equipped with automatic gearbox

Sporting Motorist

Ford Executive Zodiac 2,555 c.c.

AT A GLANCE: Performance and comfort below expectations; Powerful and stable braking; Suspension satisfactory in the U.K., less so on continental roads; Smooth and quiet engine; Good detail finish and full equipment.

MANUFACTURER:
Ford Motor Co. Ltd., Warley, Brentwood, Essex

PRICES
Basic	£1,099
Purchase Tax	£216
Total (in G.B.)	£1,315

PERFORMANCE SUMMARY
Mean maximum speed	94 m.p.h.
Standing start ¼-mile	20·1 sec
0-60 m.p.h.	15·2 sec
30-70 m.p.h. in intermediate	18·0 sec

FUEL CONSUMPTION
Overall fuel consumption	17·7 m.p.g.
Miles per tankful	212

CERTAINLY not demonstrative by nature, the British sometimes display surprising quirks of exhibitionism and individuality when it comes to personal possessions. Whether the Ford market research department were relying on this to account for the success of their latest "new" model, the Executive Zodiac with its extra fittings, or simply the status-conscious young businessman eager to make his mark, is not known. Whatever the reasons, the car has caught on, and already examples can be seen quite often on the streets. With no noticeable styling changes since the range was introduced over three years ago, the Zodiac now covers a broader potential market.

Among the items Ford consider essential to the executive are radio, seat belts, fog and spot lamps, separate reclining front seats and automatic

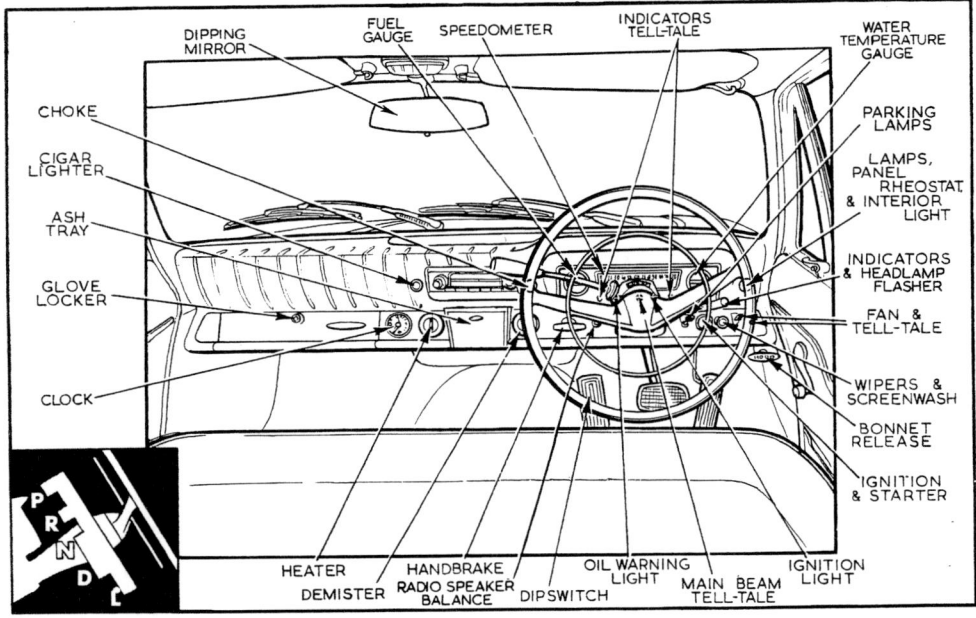

transmission. To convey an impression of aristocratic sobriety, the inside is trimmed in a mixture of black leather, p.v.c. and carpet (even in the boot), and special paints are available like the acrylic gold of our test car. Even after two Alpine crossings through snow and slush, and parking for several nights under trees inhabited by birds, a quick wash was sufficient to restore the gleaming gloss.

Mechanically the car is a Zodiac with the 2½-litre six developing a claimed 109 b.h.p. net at 4,800 r.p.m. (11 more than the Zephyr 6). A recent change to all Zodiacs has been to replace the dual-outlet exhaust system with a single, large-bore one, which leaves a vacant niche under the tail of the car, as on the Zephyr 4 and 6. We say "claimed" advisedly, because by comparison with the automatic Zephyr 6 tested 1½ years ago not all this power seems to be realized.

Performance

Despite the encouragement of a speedometer that is a full 10 m.p.h. fast at the top end, the mean maximum of our test car was only 94 m.p.h.—just 0.7 better than the Zephyr. Acceleration times, too, show little difference, the step-off being a bit smarter and saving just over a second from rest to 60 m.p.h. (Executive Zodiac 15.2; Zephyr 6 16.5sec). From 30 to 70 m.p.h. in top gear took 24.2sec on our Zodiac, compared with 24.6sec on the Zephyr.

The automatic changepoint from low to intermediate takes place at 36 m.p.h. and we found that, although the engine would run happily up another 10 m.p.h. when held in low, these extra revs made no difference to the acceleration times. Holding intermediate gave a corresponding lift to its speed range, from the automatic limit of 60 to about 70 m.p.h., and here it cut the times by about a second if one delayed the change into top.

On the open road one tends to use this over-ride quite a lot, partly to avoid the surge of a kick-down change at full throttle, but chiefly to engage intermediate above the maximum kick-down speed of 49 m.p.h. From 50 to 70 takes 3sec less in intermediate, so overtaking is appreciably quicker and one has the added security of full engine braking when tucking back into a line of traffic.

Transmission

In towns, of course, it is best to leave the selector in its "D" slot and let the transmission do the work instead. Normally there is only very slight creep (one could just hold the car static on the flat without the brake lamps lighting), but the idling speed of our engine was set rather slow; a little too slow, perhaps, because after a cold start the choke knob had to be left about half an inch out for two or three miles to avoid the embarrassment of the engine dying in the middle of a junction just as one moved off; restarts take a little longer with an automatic because one must first move the selector to neutral (or Park), operate the starter, then move the lever back to D.

Upward gear changes of this Borg-Warner type 35 box were not as smooth as other examples we have tried. At full throttle from intermediate to top the car seemed to take a great gulp which set passengers' heads nodding, although with a bit of practice one could do better lower down the speed range by letting up the accelerator for an almost imperceptible engagement. Engaging intermediate to supplement the braking was somewhat delayed. Downward changes from top to intermediate on the over-run—for instance, at the approach to a roundabout—had to be anticipated by about 3sec, as there was this delay between the message and the action. This lag represents about 100yds at 60 m.p.h.

For such a large car without power steering the effort is light, and even when parking one does not have to heave at the wheel. The low gearing is not a handicap either, and with its compact turning circle of 37ft between kerbs, the Zodiac is an easy car to manoeuvre through city streets. The sides bulge slightly, but one sits high enough to see the near side edge of the bonnet, and the standard wing mirrors act as "sights." Reversing presents no problems either, with the high rear wings giving a good guide to the tail overhang. Twin reversing lamps are built into the bumper.

Steering and Cornering

At speed the steering loses some of its directional precision and the car sometimes surprises the driver by darting slightly one way or the other. Joints and ridges in the road surface deflect the tyres off course quite noticeably.

Cornering is aided by the stabilizing influence of slight understeer, although in the wet this becomes more neutral as the tail swings slightly. With a fluid torque converter in the transmission, power cannot be applied so abruptly as with a manual gear train, so tail slides from this source are far less frequent. The biggest discouragement to fast cornering is the way the car lurches over on to its front suspension as a bend is entered, causing loose articles to roll about and passengers to clutch for something firm. This non-executive treatment is out of character with the car, and it feels happiest trickling round much more sedately in top.

However, when really pushed to the limit there is far more adhesion than one might expect, and the car always remains stable. Braking from high speeds gives every feeling of confidence as the large front discs pull the car up with commendably light pedal loads. Maximum braking efficiency required only 75lb on the pedal, anything more causing wheel-lock. The handbrake, too, was powerful—unusually so for its type—holding the car securely and easily on a 1-in-3 test hill. Getting away again

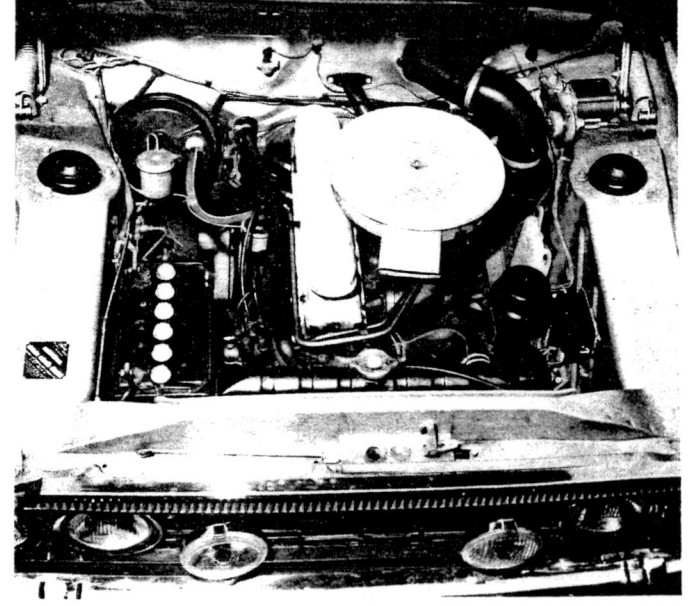

MAKE: **Ford**
TYPE: **Executive Zodiac 2,555 c.c.**

Speed range, gear ratios and time in seconds

m.p.h.	Top (3·55-7·10)	Inter (5·16-10·32)	Low (8·48-16·96)
10—30	—	6·5	4·2
20—40	8·5	6·6	4·7
30—50	10·3	7·1	—
40—60	12·1	8·3	—
50—70	13·9	10·9	—
60—80	18·2	—	—

TEST CONDITIONS
Weather ... ... Showery with 10-15 m.p.h. wind
Temperature ... ...7 deg C. (45 deg. F.)
Barometer, 22·00in. Hg. Mainly dry concrete and tarmac surfaces

WEIGHT
Kerb weight (with oil, water and half-full fuel tank) 25·2cwt (2,833lb-1,286kg)
Front-rear distribution, per cent ... 52·4F., 47·6R
Laden as tested ... ... 28·2cwt (3,159lb-1,438kg)

TURNING CIRCLES
Between kerbs ... ... L, 38ft. 0in.; R, 36ft. 10in.
Between walls ... ... L, 40ft. 2in.; R, 39ft. 0in.
Steering wheel turns lock to lock ... ... 4·6

PERFORMANCE DATA
Top gear m.p.h. per 1,000 r.p.m. ... ... 20·3
Mean piston speed at max. power ... 2,500ft/min.
Engine revs at mean max. speed 4,630
B.h.p. per ton laden ... ... 77·2

FUEL CONSUMPTION
At constant Speeds
30 m.p.h. ... ... 33·0 m.p.g.
40 ,, ... 30·0 ,,
50 ,, ... 26·3 ,,
60 ,, ... 21·6 ,,
70 ,, ... 18·2 ,,
80 ,, ... 15·2 ,,
90 ,, ... 12·3 ,,

Overall m.p.g. ... ... 17·7 (15·9 litres/100km)
Normal range m.p.g. 15-20 (18·8-14·1 litres/100km)
Test distance ... ... 1,453 miles
Estimated (DIN) m.p.g. ... 16·6 (17·0 litres/100km)
Grade ... ... Premium (95-97RM)

OIL CONSUMPTION
SAE 20W/20 ... ... 3,700 m.p.g.

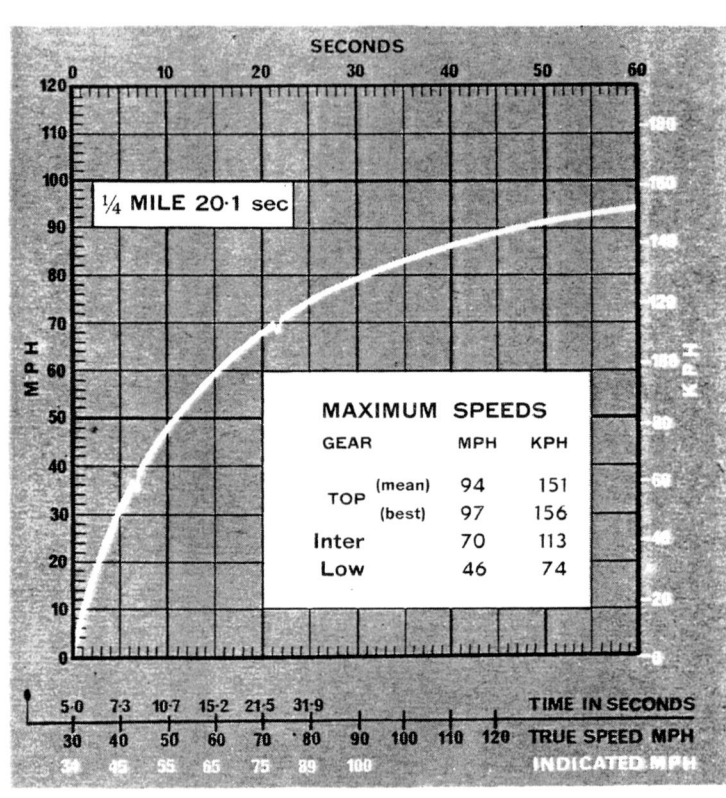

¼ MILE 20·1 sec

MAXIMUM SPEEDS

GEAR		MPH	KPH
TOP	(mean)	94	151
	(best)	97	156
Inter		70	113
Low		46	74

BRAKES (from 30 m.p.h. in neutral)	Pedal load	Retardation	Equiv. distance
	25 lb	0·22g	137ft
	50lb	0·55g	55ft
	75lb	0·97g	31·0ft
	Handbrake	0·35g	86ft

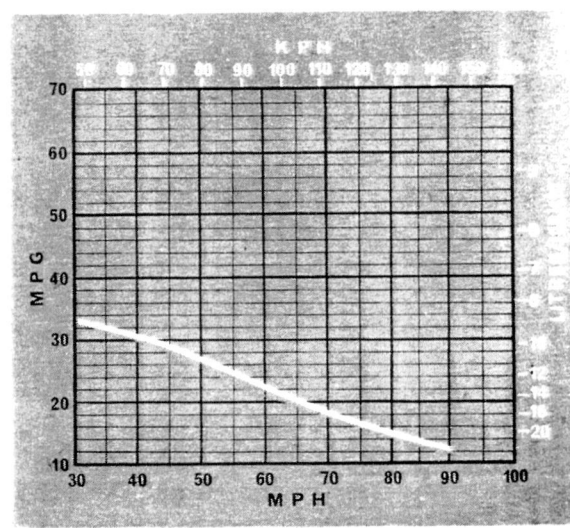

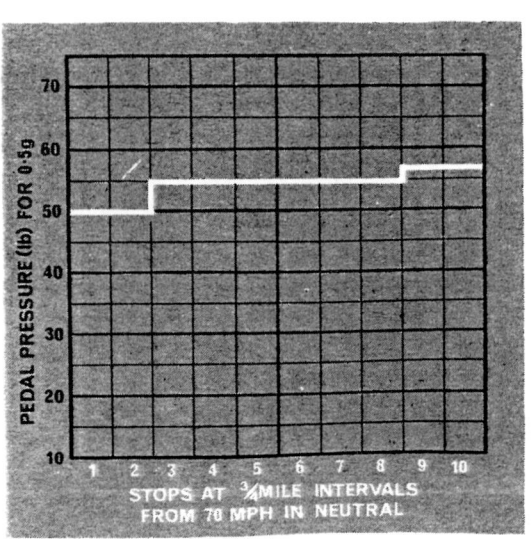

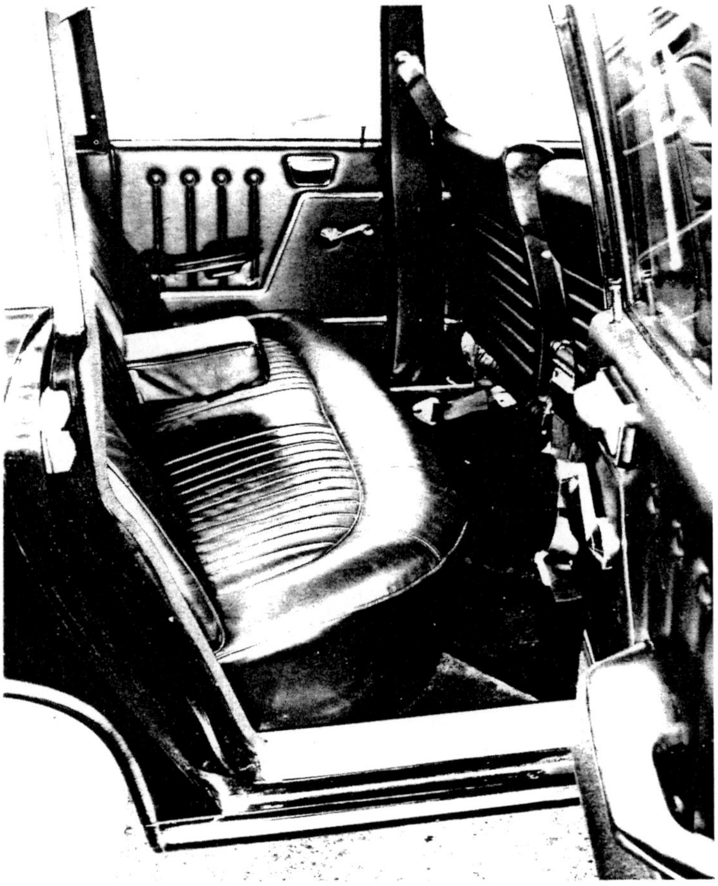

Left: Interior trim is all in black, with dark wood panels below the facia capping. The armrest between the front seats has a lift-up lid, with a useful tray in front. Right: There are three armrests and three ashtrays in the back, but the gap for getting feet in and out is narrow

Ford Executive Zodiac...

on a damp surface caused wheelspin, and the transmission could be felt changing up and down with the variations in grip, but the car pulled away smoothly.

On English roads the suspension of the Zodiac gives a reasonably favourable impression. It has a big car feel with a comfortable ride most of the time, although rough patches of roadworks and bumpy tracks set the suspension thumping around noisily. A lot of these disturbances are accentuated rather than deadened by seats which are too firmly sprung. Taking the car abroad on French roads proved somewhat revealing, all the passengers complaining of the choppy ride. In the front the seat springs could be felt quivering beneath—one driver even finding this numbed his posterior! And with these movements one's shoulders fret against the backrest. In the rear compartment it was a good deal better, although the curvature of the backrest padding does not support the shoulders much unless one slumps down.

The back seat is not really up to executive travel, for legroom is cramped even when those in the front aren't being greedy with the adjustment. Moreover, the gap between front and back seats makes it difficult to climb out without the feet getting jammed, or tied up with the seat-belt loops. In other aspects back-seat passengers are well catered for. There are three ashtrays, a swinging assist-strap each side above the door (white plastic which soon showed grubby finger marks), armrests and an extra radio speaker on the rear shelf.

Driving Position

Most of our drivers found the steering wheel too close to the chest, and with no clutch to press to the floor even a 5ft 8in. tester would have liked to get farther from the pedals. Through the steering wheel the driver sees a ribbon-type speedometer flanked each side by spherical dials for the fuel gauge and engine thermometer. The figures on the speedometer are pale, and there are times when bright sunlight catches the glass and makes them illegible. At night the instrument lighting turns them into a clear white-on-black.

The rest of the dashboard layout is new and individual to the Zodiac. Dark wood veneer panels are set beneath matt black capping with

The boot floor is lined with black carpet, which also covers the spare wheel on the left. Over-riders have rubber pads, and there are twin reversing lamps built into the bumper

Zodiacs have opening rear quarterlights as well as swivelling ones in the front doors. Twin wing mirrors are standard, and the single exhaust system is new

switches well scattered in accessible positions. Most controls are down on the right, with the main lighting switch sensibly remote. This is the excellent universal type which does everything, including dimming the panel lamps and turning on the interior light. The wiper switch is pressed to work the washers, and twisting it varies the wiping speed from 52 to 66 strokes a minute. Unfortunately most of the dirt is left on the edge by the right-hand screen pillar where it can mask the driver's view. Above 80 m.p.h. in a crosswind the wiper blades lift off the glass.

To left and right of the large central ashtray (big enough for executive cigar ash, incidentally) are the circular controls for the latest heater. This has a hot-matrix air-mixing system which can be adjusted instantly for temperature, and the air to the floor and screen can be regulated independently. Although the heater knob was a little stiff and insensitive, it was not difficult to arrange for a good wafting flow of warm air right through to the back footwells, yet at the same time to keep the temperature at face level refreshingly cool. Seldom was the single-speed booster fan needed, so long as the car was moving; it is not noisy, but not really quiet enough to justify the red warning lamp alongside its switch.

Noise Level

With front and rear swivelling quarterlights it is easy to promote a through-flow of air, but even with everything shut tight there is a lot of wind roar above about 75 m.p.h. Most of this seems to come from around the front door edges and it makes conversation difficult during a long day's motoring.

In each of its three gears the transmission worked quietly, and there was never any signs of mechanical noises intruding on the interior. The engine ran up to its maximum revs with the characteristic smoothness of a straight six and we thought the new exhaust system muffled more decibels than the older one Only when cold, and perhaps lightly coated with rust after a damp night, did the brakes issue a subdued groan when being dragged by transmission creep on a fast warm-up idle.

During our continental tour we returned 17·7 m.p.g. while cruising most of the time in the 80s. Back home on normal domestic duties, the same car managed nearly 20 m.p.g. in stop-start conditions of gentle running. Family owners therefore should find no difficulty in getting this figure, but on a quick business trip by motorways to the north would most likely drop some 4 m.p.g. With a 12-gal tank the safe range between fill-ups is well under 200 miles.

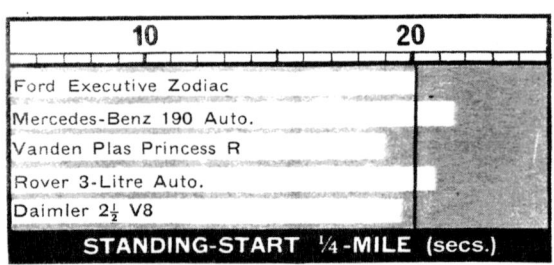

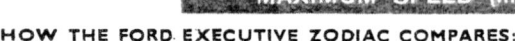

HOW THE FORD EXECUTIVE ZODIAC COMPARES:

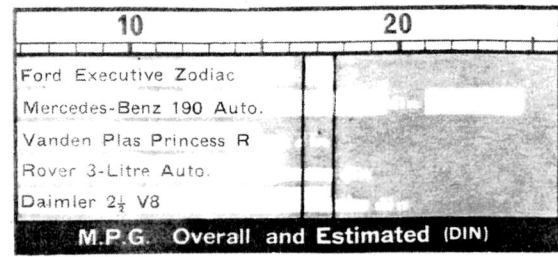

Ford Zephyr 4   MANUAL and AUTOMATIC 1,703 c.c.

So far as the British market is concerned, the familiar Ford model name of Consul now becomes one mainly of the past. It is still used abroad in connection with the 1,340 c.c. Classics but the public at home already omits to use the full title of these cars. With the introduction of the new, big range of Fords, the Consul Mark II or 375 is replaced by the more logically named Zephyr 4, which is the cheaper Zephyr powered by the similar 1,703 c.c., four-cylinder engine. Unlike its predecessor, however, it is not shorter than the six-cylinder Zephyr but is identical in exterior dimensions. Minor differences in appearance have been introduced purposely to permit immediate model identification.

This new Zephyr 4 is a sensible, work-horse design; it is spacious, yet its price falls among those of medium-sized cars. Provided the driver is prepared to sit rather close to the steering wheel, it is to be regarded as an ample six-seater having plenty of luggage accommodation, but it is a pity that some 3in. more rear seat legroom has not been provided.

Owners of Mark II Consuls, on the whole, are a satisfied bunch; if pressed, they might mention the inadequacy of the three-speed gearbox and a certain lack of smoothness in engine and transmission. Ford have tried hard with the new Zephyr range—4 and 6—to meet desires and criticisms. Thus a four-speed, all-synchromesh gearbox has been provided and the engine and transmission have been made appreciably smoother and quieter. A quite good example of its kind, the column gearchange has a rather longer movement than one would wish. Purchasers are offered the option of a Borg-Warner overdrive (operative in all gears), which would seem to be superfluous on the Zephyr 4, or three-speed automatic transmission of the new Borg-Warner type at an extra cost of £110 0s 0d. This report covers both the manual transmission and the automatic cars, and full performance figures are listed for each variant. Both Zephyr 4 and 6 are also described in detail in the article preceding this test report.

Drivers familiar with the earlier Consul and Zephyr models will have no difficulty in detecting similarities in the new four-cylinder Zephyr, but only when the engine is being used to its full capacity does it become obtrusive—this feature being more apparent with the automatic transmission car than with the manual one.

With the manual box, the performance is quite a lot brisker now throughout the range of acceleration, and the standing quarter-mile figure is 21·4sec compared with 22·7 sec for the Consul Mk. II. This is also by virtue of the car's extra 9 b.h.p. net with a weight increase of only 55lb with the two cars laden as tested.

There is an increase in maximum speed, which rises from a mean of 76·3 m.p.h. for the Consul Mk. II to 84·0 m.p.h.,

PRICES		
Basic	£615	
Purchase tax	£231 12s	9d
Total (in G.B.)	£846 12s	9d
	£ s	d
Extras (total)		
Overdrive	58 8	9
Automatic transmission	110 0	0
Heater	20 12	6
Screenwasher	8 13	3
Hide upholstery	20 12	6

The orderly modern facia design has a padded top and a composite instrument presentation. The attractiveness of corrugated bright metal trim is a matter of taste

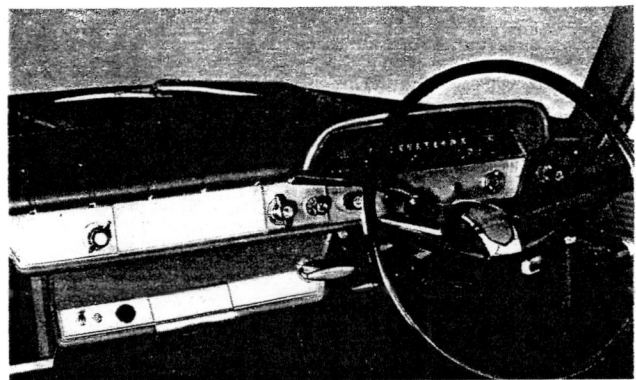

The interior is spacious and the seat cushions are wide. The front seat is shown two notches forward from its backstop, where many drivers would set it

but the Zephyr 4 will cruise without fuss at over 70 m.p.h. and, with its high 3·9-to-1 top gear ratio, it is particularly restful when cruising at about 60 m.p.h. This same high top gear does bring the need for an earlier downchange, both in slow traffic and for overtaking, but this is the natural outcome of the pleasant new four-speed box and sensibly-selected ratios. The Consul II accelerated from 30 to 50 m.p.h. in top gear in 13·4 seconds, while the Zephyr 4 takes 14·8 seconds but, for example, the Zephyr 4 manages 40 to 60 m.p.h. in third gear in 10·8 seconds and the Consul, which had to use second and top, took 17·3 seconds. The minimum comfortable top gear speed is now about 18 m.p.h.

With automatic transmission the picture is rather different and all the performances recorded are somewhat lower than those for the manual model. It takes 22·9 seconds to cover a quarter-mile from a standstill and the maximum speed is only just over 76 m.p.h. Overtaking usually needs careful timing and plenty of space. This version is 60lb heavier.

Since the automatic transmission is of the new Borg-Warner type with the torque convertor operative in all ratios, a brief reminder of its characteristics may be helpful. The selector lever can be moved to Low, Drive, Neutral, Reverse or Park, in that order on the quadrant from left to right, and as usual the engine can be started only when Neutral or Park are selected. Low, intermediate and high ratios are provided. In D automatic gear changes take place at predetermined points according to road speed and throttle opening. If the selector lever is moved from D to L when driving normally, intermediate is obtained at any speed. Intermediate having been engaged, and if the road speed is below about 35 m.p.h., operation of the kick-down switch will then bring in low and hold it.

To return to intermediate and to hold that ratio, the selector lever is moved back to D; as soon as intermediate re-engages in the normal manner at the change-up point, the lever is moved back to L. The maximum speed in intermediate is approximately 68 m.p.h. and the limit is one of power falling off, not of reaching valve bounce; the equivalent figure in low hold is 44 m.p.h. Automatic up-changes on full throttle are made at 38 and 60 m.p.h., using kick-down.

For those drivers who find virtues in automatic transmission but regret the inability to select a gear to suit an occasion, this box offers a compromise technique. As one approaches a corner to be taken fast, L is selected on the quadrant and this gives the equivalent of third gear engine braking with the manual box and ready pick-up. If an even lower gear is needed, this is obtained with a quick kick-down to give full low gear engine braking followed by acceleration. Coming out of a corner with maximum acceleration, whether in low or intermediate, D can be reselected to give automatic up-changes.

For normal driving the automatic changes are very smooth indeed and can scarcely be detected, up or down. An outstanding virtue of this transmission is that, once top has been engaged—or intermediate in the "hold" position—the next lower ratio can be obtained only by operation of the kick-down switch, unless the road speed falls to the pre-determined automatic drop-out point. Thus the annoyance of frequent automatic changes between ratios, or "hunting," is avoided.

The basic design of the suspension of the Zephyr 4 is similar to that of previous models. However, there are important detail changes, as described in the preceding article. The outcome is somewhat less firm springing and a softer ride. Roll is restrained, although when a full load is carried the back of the car will take on appreciable bank when cornering fast; this in turn has some effect on the cornering characteristics. Under heavy braking forces the nose is made to dip but the ride is normally free from pitching and well damped.

Good Road-holding

Adhesion in dry weather is very good indeed and it is difficult, with the power available, to make the back of the car move across unless the road surface is unusually rough. In wet conditions the adhesion is also good and definitely an improvement on that of the previous model.

Road noises and shocks are well insulated; only on one particular kind of road surface, dressed with small stones, is a mild droning heard inside the car.

With all the windows properly closed and fitting, comparatively little wind noise is heard by the occupants. On certain of the early production models we have tried, the relative silence has been upset by a slightly proud seal in the vicinity of the driver's side quarterlight. These have a front edge hinge which helps to prevent rain entering when they are opened and which also avoids wind roar when they are very slightly opened. A side window at front, back or both may be opened by as much as 2in. without causing draughts, buffeting or excessive noise. The car's excellent heating and ventilation system immediately works to greater capacity if a side window is opened to allow the air to flow through the interior.

Our test drivers were of the opinion that the steering wheel is larger than necessary, since the steering is quite light, and that were the ratio to be higher—say, 3½ instead of 4¼ turns from lock to lock—less arm-work would be needed. In other respects the steering is very acceptable, giving precise control of direction. These cars understeer mildly when cornering normally, but if plenty of power is used the characteristics become almost neutral, particularly when a full load is carried. In these conditions the roll already referred to has an initial oversteer influence. The Zephyr is not sensitive to side winds and holds a very straight course on a motorway. Self-centring action is

Make · FORD Type · Zephyr 4

Manufacturers: Ford Motor Co. Ltd., Dagenham, Essex

Test Conditions
Weather............ Dry, with 5-15 m.p.h. wind
Temperature .... 49 deg. F. (9 deg. C.).
Barometer .... 26·6in. Hg.
  Dry concrete and tarmac surfaces.

Weight
Kerb weight (with oil, water and half-full fuel tank)
  22·8cwt (2,547lb-1,155kg)
Front-rear distribution, per cent: F, 52·8; R, 47·2
Laden as tested: ......25·8cwt (2,883lb-1,307kg)
  Automatic: ....26·25cwt (2,940lb-1,333kg)

Turning Circles
Between kerbs .... L, 37ft 1in.; R, 36ft 8in.
Between walls ...... L, 38ft 10in.; R, 38ft 5in.
Turns of steering wheel lock to lock .... 4·25

Performance Data
Top gear m.p.h. per 1,000 r.p.m. .... 18·45
  (Automatic 20·3)
Mean piston speed at max. power ...... 2,510 ft/min.
Engine revs. at mean max. speed .... 4,550 r.p.m.
B.h.p. per ton laden .... 52·8

FUEL AND OIL CONSUMPTION

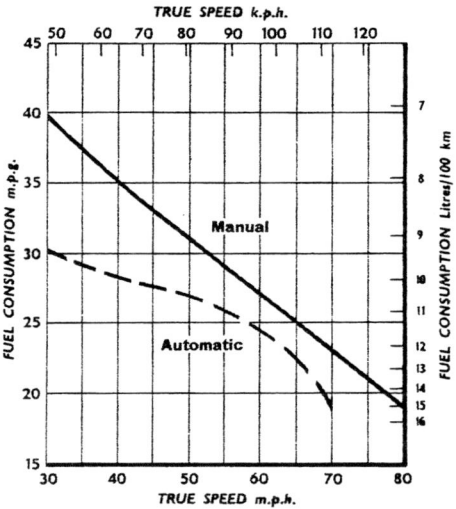

FUEL .... Premium Grade
  (96 octane RM)

Test Distances
  711 miles (Manual), 654 miles (Automatic)
Overall Consumption .... 23·8 m.p.g.
  (11·9 lit/100km)
  Automatic .... 23·1 m.p.g.
  (12·3 lit/100km)
Normal Range (both cars): 20-30 m.p.g.
  (14-9·4lit/100km)
OIL: SAE 20W .... Consumption: None
  measurable on either model

MAXIMUM SPEEDS AND ACCELERATION (mean) TIMES

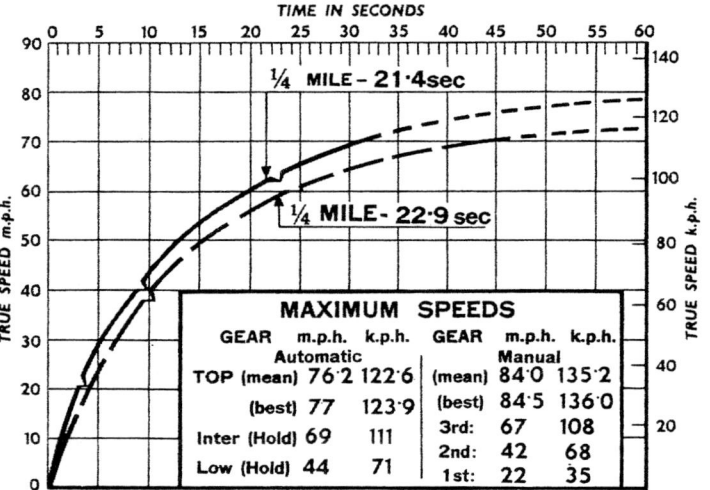

MAXIMUM SPEEDS					
GEAR	m.p.h.	k.p.h.	GEAR	m.p.h.	k.p.h.
Automatic			Manual		
TOP (mean)	76·2	122·6	(mean)	84·0	135·2
(best)	77	123·9	(best)	84·5	136·0
Inter (Hold)	69	111	3rd:	67	108
Low (Hold)	44	71	2nd:	42	68
			1st:	22	35

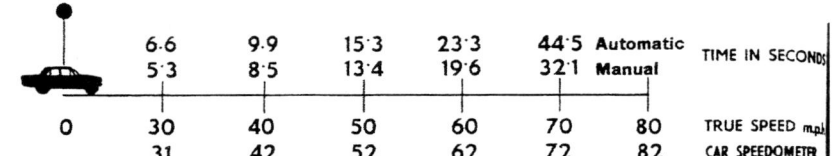

Speed range and time in seconds
Manual
m.p.h.	Top	Third	Second	First
10—30	—	8·3	5·1	—
20—40	13·2	7·7	5·5	—
30—50	14·8	8·4	—	—
40—60	17·2	10·8	—	—
50—70	21·2	—	—	—

Automatic
m.p.h.	Top	Inter	Low
10—30	—	7·0	5·4
20—40	10·3	8·8	6·1
30—50	14·4	11·4	—
40—60	24·4	13·8	—
50—70	34·8	—	—

BRAKES	Pedal load	Retardation	Equiv. distance
(from 30 m.p.h. in neutral)	25lb	0·36g	83ft
	50lb	0·75g	40ft
	70lb	0·96g	31ft
	Hand brake	0·41g	74ft

CLUTCH Pedal load and travel—38lb and 5·5in.

HILL CLIMBING AT STEADY SPEEDS

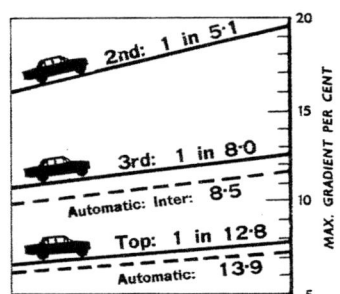

Manual
Gear	Top	3rd	2nd
PULL (lb per ton)	175	277	433
Speed Range (m.p.h.)	34—40	28—32	22—28

Automatic
Gear	Top	Inter
PULL (lb per ton)	160	263
Speed Range (m.p.h.)	30—35	25—28

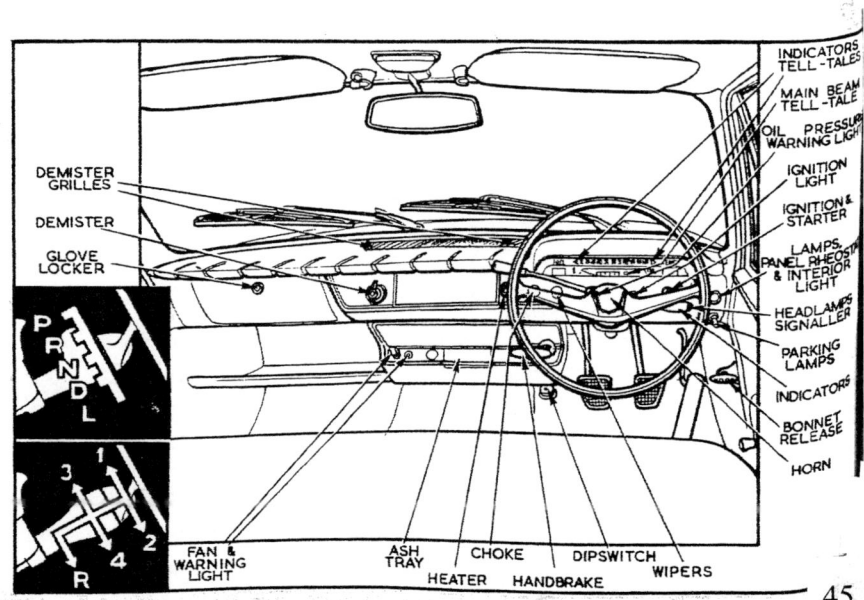

Note the Galaxie-type rear window and associated side panels, which clearly distinguish the Zephyrs from the Zodiac, "Automatic" appears below the Zephyr motif on the appropriate model

Ford Zephyr 4 . . .

only slight for small movements of the wheel from the straight-ahead position.

There is no doubt that the new disc front, drum rear brake system will be greatly appreciated. It has powerful, though not over-sensitive, servo assistance and moderate pressure on the pedal gives smooth and very powerful retardation. The pull-out handbrake is substantial, efficient and conveniently positioned. The rubbing areas of the rear drums have been increased to provide adjustment periods comparable with front disc pad life.

Even in the extreme conditions of standing start acceleration measurement and restarting on a 1-in-3 gradient, the clutch of the manual gearbox was smooth and effective. The travel is not unduly long and pressure is quite light. The automatic transmission car also starts without difficulty on 1-in-3, and on the same incline the handbrakes of both cars held firmly.

A new throttle linkage is provided which is much better than the rather abrupt and springy system on the previous cars; some drivers thought that the initial opening was still rather abrupt.

Although the Zephyr 4 engine now gives more power than that of its predecessor, fuel consumption figures are likely to work out almost exactly the same, and although, as would be expected, the automatic transmission car uses slightly more fuel, the difference is very small. Even "press-on" drivers should obtain in the region of 24 m.p.g. on journeys and those who drive gently should obtain 27 or 28 m.p.g.

Anything which needs topping up is conveniently placed in the engine compartment. The brake servo unit is just behind the battery

Since the total mileages covered during our tests of the two variants were somewhat less than usual, yet the full list of performance figures was obtained with each, the overall test averages give a rather pessimistic impression.

Drivers will approve of the bright and spacious interior, from which a good driving view is obtained, apart from the fact that the passenger side wing cannot be seen by the driver because of the height of the bonnet; the toggle opener for the latter is labelled "Hood" in the American way. Available equipment is thorough for a car of this class and is arranged in the modern manner, and while we prefer a hand lever for headlamp dipping (this does not apply to the automatic model in which the left foot is free to operate the foot switch), the additional flasher switch on the end of the direction indicator lever is appreciated.

An extra switch is provided which cuts out the near side lamps so that those on the off side can be used for parking. When this is operated, the panel lamps are switched off as a warning.

New Heater

A very effective layered system for heating and ventilation is listed as an extra in the case of the Zephyr 4. Two winged controls are twisted to obtain the desired temperature and to cut off or select demisting, defrosting or de-icing flow to the screen. At demist, cold air flows over the windscreen and ventilates the upper part of the car while either hot or cold air to choice is directed rearwards at seat level. The booster fan has an indicator light and delivers a large volume of air. The direction of flow is inclined to miss the driver's feet and ankles. In the padded scuttle top are two large grilles for the screen air. They lie flush and are of matching colour. Pale trims cause some unwelcome reflections in the screen in spite of the matt finish.

Interior detail finish is neat and synthetic trimming materials are used throughout. An open parcel shelf and, above it, a locker with key, are seen on the passenger side. No door pockets are provided on this model. Soft padded sun vizors are fitted, which can be swung across to give shade from the sides.

There is plenty of support area in the front bench seat; it is quite comfortable and there is sufficient rearward adjustment. For other than gentle driving, the absence of shaping to give lateral location leads the passengers to sway sideways on corners. Our test staff are agreed that the mounting of the seat is some 2in. too low. By using a cushion we found that the view over the scuttle and bonnet was at once improved, the angle between feet and pedals, —which meet the soles of the shoes edge-on—is slightly better and the driving attitude is more alert. Headroom and steering wheel clearance is ample to permit this small modification.

Three grown-ups can sit reasonably comfortably on the

back seat. It is not as easy as it might be for elderly people to get in and out, because the spaces between the central door pillar and the front corners of the seat are narrow. Armrests are provided on all four doors.

Single, low-mounted headlamps, on each side of the undivided grille, are a recognition point of the Zephyr 4; they give ample range and spread for the car's performance. The finish to the edges of the metalwork above them leaves much to be desired. The side lamps, applied somewhat vulnerably, are protected in part by substantial wrap-round bumper extremities, which st   proud of the wing edges by ?in. The main lamp sw   is of the double pull-out type and, as found increasingly on modern cars of most nationalities, a twist of the same knob operates a rheostat for the instrument panel lamps; at the extremities of twist, the interior lamps are turned on or the panel lamps turned off. No reversing lamp is provided.

While it is pleasant to have an uninterrupted view of the instruments through the dished, two-spoke steering wheel, the flush horn button is now too difficult to hit in an emergency and the note produced is very humble. On the automatic model the illumination of the selector quadrant is too bright after dark.

A variable-speed electric windscreen wiper is fitted. Its blades clear a large area, leaving only a portion of the curved edges obscured. They did not park as low as they should on the manual model tested, and after prolonged use ceased to be silent, producing a slapping noise. A screen washer is extra on this model. The wide, shallow interior rear-view mirror is very satisfactory.

Both the bonnet and the boot lid are self-supporting—an almost essential feature these days. Some manufacturers have wry fun hiding the release for the second safety catch and giving it an illogical movement; not so Ford, who has placed it just where it should be. The bonnet opens wide and accessibility is quite good. The dipstick and its tube might well be extended and the diameter of the oil filler-breather on the rocker cover increased. When attending to contact breaker points, mechanics will find the distributor rather buried. Other than those for wheel changing, which are contained in a sack wedged between the spare wheel and the side of the car, there are no tools.

A welcome advance has been made in reducing servicing requirements. With the introduction of this new model, greasing of the 12 points is needed only at 5,000-mile intervals and when more experience is gained, it may be possible to increase this figure to 7,000 or even 10,000 miles.

With the introduction of their new Zephyr 4s Ford have again made substantial improvements over the models replaced; they offer greater refinement and several new features which owners will appreciate. Equally important, the price has been held at a very competitive level.

Specification

ENGINE
- Cylinders ... 4 in line
- Bore ... 82·55mm (3·25 in.)
- Stroke ... 79·5mm (3·13in.)
- Displacement ... 1,703 c.c. (103·9 cu. in.)
- Valve gear ... Overhead, pushrods and rockers
- Compression ratio 8·3 to 1
- Carburettor ... Zenith 36VN
- Fuel pump ... AC mechanical
- Oil filter ... Full flow, external
- Max. power ... 68 b.h.p. (net) at 4,800 r.p.m.
- Max. torque ... 93·5 lb. ft. at 3,000 r.p.m.

TRANSMISSION
- Clutch ... Borg and Beck 8in. dia. single dry plate.
- Gearbox ... Four-speed, all synchromesh
- Overall ratios ... Top 3·90, 3rd 5·87, 2nd 9·17, 1st 17·21, reverse 18·20.
- Automatic transmission ... Borg-Warner model 35.
- Overall ratios ... Top 7·10-3·55; Inter 10·30-5·15; Low 16·96-8·49; Reverse 14·84-7·42.
- Final drive ... Hypoid bevel, 3·90 to (Automatic 3·55 to 1).

CHASSIS
- Construction ... Integral with steel body.

SUSPENSION
- Front ... Strut type, coil springs and wishbones, Armstrong telescopic dampers, anti-roll bar.
- Rear ... Live axle and semi-elliptic leaf springs, Armstrong lever arm dampers
- Steering ... Burman recirculating ball; wheel dia. 17in.

BRAKES
- Type ... Girling hydraulic; discs front, drums rear, with servo assistance
- Dimensions ... Discs 9·75in. dia. Drums 9·0in. dia., 1·75in. wide shoes
- Swept area ... F. 203 sq. in.; R. 99 sq. in. Total: 302 sq. in. (234 sq. in. per ton laden)

WHEELS
- Type ... Pressed steel disc, 5 studs, 4·5in. wide rim.
- Tyres ... Goodyear tubeless 6·40-13in.

EQUIPMENT
- Battery ... 12-volt, 45-amp. hr.
- Headlamps ... 50-40 watt bulbs.
- Reversing lamp ... None
- Electric fuses ... 1
- Screen wipers ... 2, variable speed, self-parking
- Screen washer ... Extra
- Interior heater ... Extra
- Safety belts ... No anchorages provided
- Interior trim ... P.v.c., optional cloth, hide extra
- Floor covering ... Rubber
- Starting handle ... None
- Jack ... Triangular screw type
- Jacking points ... 2 each side under body sills
- Other bodies ... None

MAINTENANCE
- Fuel tank ... 12 Imp. gallons (no reserve)
- Cooling system ... 17 pints (including heater)
- Engine sump ... 6 pints. Change oil every 5,000 miles; change filter element every 5,000 miles
- Gearbox ... 2·5 pints SAE80. No oil change specified
- Final drive ... 2·5 pints SAE90 Hypoid. No oil change specified.
- Grease ... 12 points every 5,000 miles
- Tyre pressures ... F and R, 22 p.s.i. (normal driving) F, and R, 26 p.s.i. (fast driving) F, and R, 28 p.s.i. (full load)

Scale: 0·3in. to 1ft.
Cushions uncompressed.

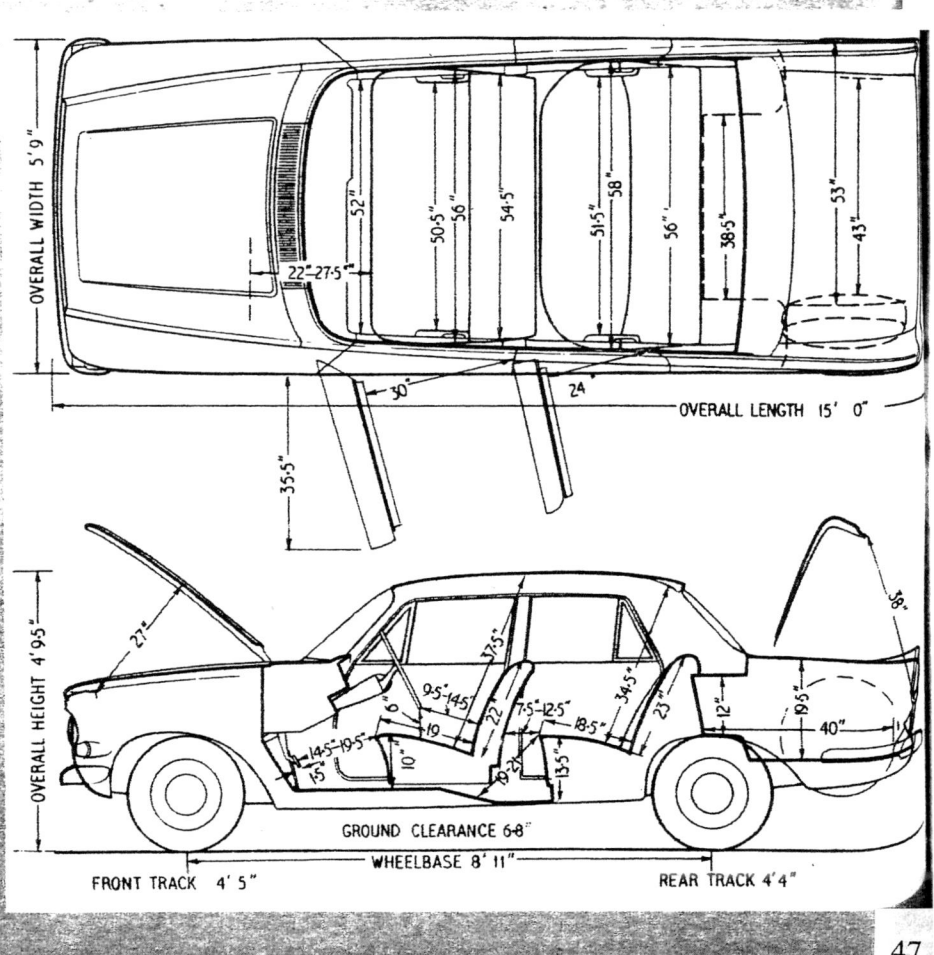

Ford Zephyr 6 (Automatic)

OFFERING hard-to-beat motoring value for money, the Ford Zephyr Six with automatic transmission should appeal greatly to the hard-pressed business man who seeks swift, reliable and easy-to-drive transport for every day of the week. The automatic drive spares him the trouble of depressing the clutch and selecting his own gears, while the effortless top gear performance of the 2.6-litre six-cylinder o.h.v. engine makes this a lazy man's motorcar, requiring little physical or mental effort to progress quickly and safely.

With its big overhang at front and rear, and its high, wide flanks, this Ford seems a larger car than in fact it is; indeed, leg room at the rear is markedly restricted, in favour of the currently fashionable vast luggage boot, but the seats are wide, and with a clear front floor space devoid of a gear lever, three people are comfortably installed in the front, and three less comfortably in the rear.

On performance, the Six Automatic is disappointing when contrasted with its more powerful and luxurious brother, the Zodiac Mk. III. The mean maximum speed recorded during our test was 87.4 m.p.h., admittedly under damp and blustery conditions (the maximum one-way speed was 91.0 m.p.h.), compared with 100.7 m.p.h. by the Zodiac with 11 b.h.p. more under its bonnet and a manual gearbox. As an effortlessly performing big six saloon at a basic price of under £700, however, this car represents excellent value for money, even though some necessities in the way of equipment have to be purchased as extras.

Brawny and oversquare

MECHANICALLY, the Zephyr Six Automatic has ample resources for motoring on roads anywhere in the world, with its brawny oversquare (82.55 × 79.5 mm.) engine of 2,553 c.c. with pushrod overhead valves, giving a net output of 98 b.h.p. at 4,750 r.p.m. The chassis and springing follow current convention, with independent front suspension by Dagenham's familiar Macpherson spring-cum-damper strut units, and live rear axle with time-honoured semi-elliptic leaf springing and Armstrong lever arm shock absorbers.

Entering the car, the driver of average length will find the driving position comfortable, but the longer-legged are less enthralled, since rearward movement of the bench seat is restricted so as not to impair the already limited leg room of the rear seat passengers. The front seat squab is well-shaped to support the small of the back, and the steering wheel is at a comfortable angle. The 17-in. two-spoked steering wheel embodies a horn ring which cuts off the view of the strip type speedometer from about 25 to 85 m.p.h. for the driver of average height.

Instruments are few, comprising the speedometer, reading up to 120 m.p.h., and temperature and fuel gauges, sharing the facia with direction indicator warning and red ignition lights, plus the usual inept green one showing that all is not well with the engine oil, and also, most usefully on the test car amidst the noise of surrounding traffic, that the engine had stalled. The headlight and ignition switches are to the right, and wiper, heater, choke and de-mister controls to the left, with a compact handbrake below the facia, not too well located for instant use.

Before the driver, on the steering column, is the automatic transmission control, a simple lever moveable to five positions

In Brief

Price (including automatic transmission as tested) £772 plus purchase tax £161 7s. 11d. equals £933 7s. 11d.	
Capacity	2,553 c.c.
Unladen kerb weight	24¼ cwt.
Acceleration:	
20-40 m.p.h. in top gear	8.8 sec.
0-50 m.p.h. through gears	12.4 sec.
Maximum speed	87.4 m.p.h.
Overall fuel consumption	16.1 m.p.g.
Touring fuel consumption	19.1 m.p.g.
Gearing: 19.9 m.p.h. in top gear at 1,000 r.p.m.	

Ford Zephyr 6

Top: There's plenty of room, said Alice. Not all of the overall 21¾ cu. ft. of boot capacity can be utilized for luggage, the wheel arches and spare wheel demanding their share, but there is room for the luggage of six people.

Top right: The bold, almost aggressive styling of the Zephyr makes it appear a larger car than it is. Good points are the curved windows, slender screen pillars and wide doors.

Right: Seating for six is provided, those at the front with floor space unimpeded by gear lever or handbrake, those at the rear with less ample legroom.

Bottom right: Two-pedal control makes driving the Zephyr Automatic an easy matter. The pedal on the left operates the dipper switch for the headlights. The handle below the dash on the extreme right operates the bonnet catch.

—Lock-up, Drive, Neutral, Reverse and Park, each denoted by their first letters in a small panel which is illuminated at night by use of the rheostat headlight control. There are three forward speeds, but for all the driver need worry about them, there might well be none. With the Borg-Warner torque converter, gear-changing and declutching are forgotten by the driver, who merely engaged D, presses the accelerator pedal, and drives.

Starting, effected only when Neutral or Park are engaged, was immediate regardless of damp or cold. Engaging Reverse or Drive with the engine running faster than on normal tickover on initial choke caused a jerky start, and sometimes a stalled engine, but warming up is swift and the choke can soon be dispensed with. Driving the Zephyr Six thereafter is a restful business, progress being quiet and smooth.

There is, of course, no clutch or clutch pedal, and the driver's left foot is thus unemployed, but a left-foot-braking, right-foot on accelerator technique is practical and useful in traffic, and is quite normal driving practice in the United States, where automatic drive is the rule rather than the exception. On the test car, which was irritatingly prone to stall on tickover when warm, such left-foot braking proved necessary in traffic to hold the car while light throttle pressure kept the engine just above stalling speed. Obviously accurate throttle setting for clean idling is all-important on cars with automatic transmission, but apart from this, the system is remarkably efficient and proof against abuse, while its advantages for those who habitually drive long distances or for long periods in town in reducing fatigue are immeasurable.

While it is possible, of course, to remain in Drive throughout a journey, use of the throttle "kick down" switch produces notably brisker acceleration. Using full-throttle but not kick-down, the car took a mean of 5.9 sec. from 10 to 30 m.p.h., whereas with use of kick-down it required 4.1 sec. only; the value of this where traffic conditions permit is obvious. Use of Lock-up (generally misinterpreted as meaning Low) below 60 m.p.h. provides full engine braking by changing down to second gear, or, on continued slowing, into first, besides imparting notable agility in traffic or on hilly ground. Thus the characteristics of normal drive are retained to a degree, without the burden of having to operate a clutch pedal or gear lever.

Engine pick-up is swift for a 24-cwt. car, and the changes from first to second when accelerating in Drive on small throttle openings are so smooth as to be almost imperceptible. The change-up from second to top, however, proved notably jerky on hard acceleration, but in contrast progress from full throttle downward was very smooth. The engine works with commendable quietness except at high revs., and on kick-down acceleration, when the gearbox also gives voice.

The car withstood a considerable amount of full-throttle driving without protest, and will cruise happily all day at 80 m.p.h. in motorway conditions. Apart from marked front wheel patter at around 70 m.p.h., attributable to ill-balanced wheels, stability at high speed is commendable in spite of occasional 40 m.p.h. side gusts of wind encountered during the test.

Steering and handling

STEERING is pleasantly light, being low geared at 4½ turns lock to lock. The Zephyr Six is not the kind of car to fling exuberantly into roundabouts and corners; its reaction is simply to scrub its tyres sideways, wallow through the turn, and make the occupants uncomfortable, although at no time does it feel unsafe or uncontrollable. Cornered at speeds more compatible with a substantial six-seater saloon—but faster than could be attempted in some—handling is smooth and confidence-inspiring, there is only slight roll and very little tyre squeal. Under all conditions the car retains a comforting modicum of understeer, any rear end breakaway provoked under test being at all times controllable.

Rough surfaces induce some rear axle tramp when accelerating, a fault doubtless inherited through the rigid axle still employed by Ford, and some up and down movement is also apparent to the rear seat passengers. Accelerating hard from a standstill, 30 m.p.h. was attained in a mean of four runs in opposite directions in 5.82 sec., 60 m.p.h. in 17.5 sec. and 80 m.p.h. in 42.7 sec.; not outstanding figures, these, for a 2.6-litre car, but it should be remembered that dependable long-distance transport on give and take roads is the prior motive behind this car, rather than high performance, which is catered for more by the Zodiac Mk. III.

The Girling braking system, comprising 9¾ in. discs at the front and 9 in. drums at the rear, with servo assistance, proved most effective, being unaffected by adverse conditions or fade, and stopping the car from 30 m.p.h. in a distance of 31 feet at a maximum pedal pressure of 75 lb. The handbrake, too, works well, holding the car on a 1 in 4 gradient.

Driving at night proved the headlights to give excellent vision; dipping is controlled by a long pedal which gives the driver's left foot something to do, while a flasher button is located in the end of the direction indicator lever. The screen wipers, with double-edged blades, cover a broad area of screen, withstood motorway speeds and strong sidewinds without faltering, and had enough pressure to wipe off mud.

Interior equipment

THE interior treatment of the Zephyr Six Automatic is bright and cheerful to the point of flamboyance. The seats are in dual tone vinyl matching the body finish, and have a faintly luminous sheen, as do the top surfaces of the dash, and this reflects rather disconcertingly on to the windscreen, even in daylight. Overlapping metal edging on the simulated walnut facia betrays its press shop origin, while the glove compartment on the left is somewhat crude, the interior being unlined, and the metal lid having sharp edges on the inside, and not always opening easily. There is a broad, deep parcels tray, the top of the facia is padded, the instrument panel is well hooded, and padded sun visors are fitted. The door release catches, cunningly hidden beneath the arm rests, were rather stiff on the test car. Heater equipment in the Zephyr is extremely efficient in the usual Ford style, a simple rotating control on the dash bringing quick and adequate, sometimes devastating, warmth. The demister was less effective under very humid conditions.

Beneath the very wide, counterbalanced bonnet, the engine is commendably accessible for a modern car, removal of the large air cleaner laying the carburetter side ready to hand. Externally, the car is attractive in a slightly overpowering sort of way, with its aggressive nose and heavy stern. The slim screen and window pillars are both attractive and practical, affording the maximum of light and vision, but the broad, high bonnet makes placing the car accurately between narrow gates rather difficult.

Considering the wheelbase of 8 ft. 11 in. and the overall length of 15 ft., however, the back seat leg room is niggardly, and blame for this can only be laid on the present cult for huge luggage boots. "Vast indeed is the boot space" says the Ford catalogue, and vast, indeed, it is, measuring 21¾ cu. ft. overall, and housing the spare wheel and luggage for six people, all of which would be praiseworthy were it not at the expense of the rear seat passengers' comfort. As it is, their shins all too easily meet the unsympathetic lower aft edge of the front seat.

The fuel tank holds 12½ gallons, and the filler cap is located centrally at the rear, being concealed by the hinged number plate. Fuel consumption over a distance of over 1,200 miles worked out at 16.1 m.p.g., much of this mileage being covered at high speeds, with the car driven hard. Even so, it compares unfavourably with the higher-performance Zodiac Mk. III, with manual gearchange, which achieved a consumption of 19.5 m.p.g., and the lower figure must be partially regarded as one penalty of automatic transmission, which tends to be more wasteful at lower speeds than manual control.

Several items of equipment which should be regarded as essentials to motoring today are omitted from the standard specification, but are available as extras. These include the heater and demister, and the screen washer. Individual, fully reclining seats are also available, and it is probable that the man who is ready to pay £96 13s. 4d. for the benefits of automatic transmission will specify these additional aids to creature comfort and safer motoring.

Withal, this is a sound, rugged and willing performer, ideal for the big mileage man who demands comfort and dependability without having to break the £1,000 barrier to obtain it.

Under-bonnet accessibility is above average for a modern design; the well-proven six-cylinder overhead valve engine gives smooth silent performance at all speeds.

Coachwork and Equipment

Starting handle	None
Battery mounting	Under bonnet
Jack	Triangular screw type
Jacking points	Two each side under door sills
Standard tool kit	Jack and wheelbrace
Exterior lights:	Two head, two side/flashers, two tail/stop lamps, two rear flashers, number plate lamp.
Number of electrical fuses:	One (plus one if radio fitted).
Direction indicators	Self-cancelling flashers
Windscreen wipers:	Twin-blade, self-parking, variable speed electric.
Windscreen washers	Optional extra
Sun visors	Two, universally pivoted
Instruments:	Speedometer (with total mileage recorder and decimal trip), fuel gauge, water thermometer.
Warning lights:	Generator, direction signals, oil pressure, main beam, heater fan.
Locks: with ignition key:	both front doors, glove locker and boot.
With other keys:	None.
Glove lockers	One, in nearside of facia panel
Map pockets	None
Parcel shelves:	In front below facia on left; one behind rear seat.
Ashtrays	One front, one rear
Cigar lighters	Optional extra
Interior lights	One courtesy light
Interior heater	Fresh air type as optional extra
Car radio:	Manual or push-button types as optional extras.
Other extras:	Screen washers, individual seats, cloth or hide upholstery, radio, and standard accessories.
Upholstery material:	P.V.C.; cloth or hide as optional extras.
Floor covering	Carpet
Exterior colours standardized	12 single colours
Alternative body styles	None

Maintenance

Sump	6½ pints, S.A.E. 20W (plus 1½ pints in filter)
Gearbox/torque converter	15 pints "A" S.A.E. 10-20
Rear axle	2½ pints, S.A.E. 90
Steering gear lubricant	S.A.E. 90 E.P. oil
Cooling system capacity	21 pints (2 drain taps)
Chassis lubrication	By grease gun every 5,000 miles to 12 points
Ignition timing	8° b.t.d.c.
Contact breaker gap	.015 in.
Sparking plug type	Champion N5
Sparking plug gap	.025 in.
Valve timing:	Inlet opens 17° b.t.d.c. and closes 51° a.b.d.c. Exhaust opens 49° b.b.d.c. and closes 19° a.t.d.c.
Tappet clearances (cold):	Inlet .014 in. Exhaust .014 in.
Front wheel toe-in	.06-.09 in.
Camber angle	1°-2°
Castor angle	0°-1°
Steering swivel pin inclination	6° 17'-7° 17'
Tyre pressures	Front 22 lb. normal, 28 lb. motorways. Rear 22 lb. normal, 28 lb. motorways.
Brake fluid	Girling
Battery type and capacity	12v., 67 amp.-hr.

MAKE: Ford **TYPE:** Zephyr 6 Automatic
MAKERS: Ford Motor Co. Ltd., Dagenham, Essex.

The Motor

ROAD TEST • No. 12/63

TEST DATA:

World copyright reserved; no unauthorized reproduction in whole or in part.

CONDITIONS: Weather: Windy (25 m.p.h. with 40 m.p.h. gusts), occasional rain. (Temperature 45°–50°F., Barometer 29·00 in. Hg.) Surface. Damp tarmacadam. Fuel: Premium grade pump petrol (98 Octane by Research Method).

MAXIMUM SPEEDS
Mean lap speed around banked circuit 87·4 m.p.h.
Best one-way mile time equals 91·0 m.p.h.

"Maximile" Speed: (Timed quarter mile after one mile accelerating from rest).
Mean of opposite runs 84·1 m.p.h.
Best one-way time equals 87·4 m.p.h.

Speed in gears (automatic operation)
Max. speed in 2nd gear 61 m.p.h.
Max. speed in 1st gear 38 m.p.h.

ACCELERATION TIMES From standstill
0-30 m.p.h.	5·8 sec.
0-40 m.p.h.	8·4 sec.
0-50 m.p.h.	12·4 sec.
0-60 m.p.h.	17·5 sec.
0-70 m.p.h.	28·6 sec.
0-80 m.p.h.	42·7 sec.
Standing quarter mile	21·2 sec.

ACCELERATION TIMES on upper ratios
	Top gear	2nd gear	Kick down range
10-30 m.p.h.	7·6 sec.	5·9 sec.	4·1 sec.
20-40 m.p.h.	8·8 sec.	6·6 sec.	4·9 sec.
30-50 m.p.h.	11·8 sec.	7·3 sec.	6·6 sec.
40-60 m.p.h.	14·3 sec.	9·1 sec.	9·1 sec.
50-70 m.p.h.	17·0 sec.	— sec.	17·2 sec.
60-80 m.p.h.	25·2 sec.	— sec.	27·8 sec.

FUEL CONSUMPTION
Overall Fuel Consumption for 1266·1 miles, 78·55 gallons, equals 16·1 m.p.g. (16·6 litres/100 km).

Touring Fuel Consumption (m.p.g. at steady speed midway between 30 m.p.h. and maximum, less 5% allowance for acceleration) 19·1 m.p.g.
Fuel tank capacity (maker's figure) 12·5 gallons

Direct top gear
26½ m.p.g. at constant 30 m.p.h. on level
25½ m.p.g. at constant 40 m.p.h. on level
23½ m.p.g. at constant 50 m.p.h. on level
19? m.p.g. at constant 60 m.p.h. on level
17 m.p.g. at constant 70 m.p.h. on level
15 m.p.g. at constant 80 m.p.h. on level
13 m.p.g. at maximum speed of approx. 87 m.p.h

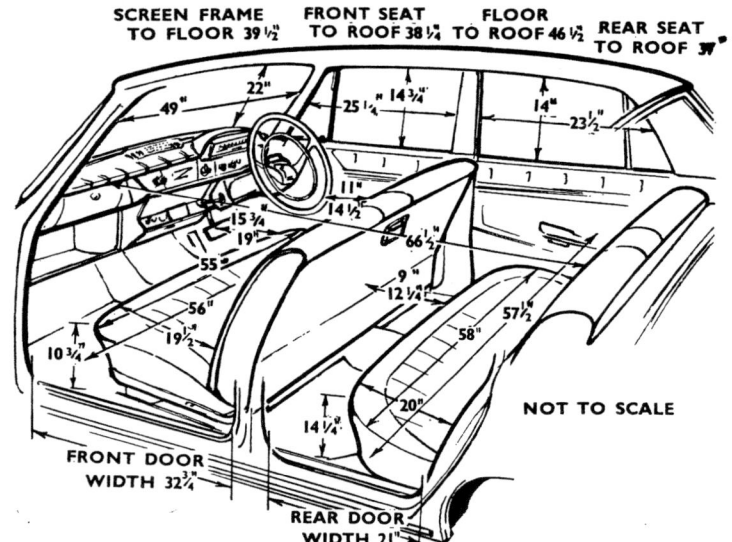

BRAKES
Deceleration and equivalent stopping distance from 30 m.p.h.
0·96 g with 75 lb. pedal pressure		(31 ft.)
0·92 g with 70 lb. pedal pressure		(32½ ft.)
0·79 g with 50 lb. pedal pressure		(38 ft.)
0·34 g with 25 lb. pedal pressure		(88 ft.)

STEERING
Turning circle between kerbs:
Left 35 ft.
Right 33½ ft.
Turns of steering wheel from lock to lock 4½

INSTRUMENTS
Speedometer at 30 m.p.h.	4¼% fast
Speedometer at 60 m.p.h.	6% fast
Speedometer at 90 m.p.h.	5% fast
Distance recorder	2¼% fast

WEIGHT
Kerb weight (unladen, but with oil, coolant and fuel for approximately 50 miles) 24¼ cwt
Front/rear distribution of kerb weight 56¼/43¾
Weight laden as tested 27¾ cwt

Specification

Engine
Cylinders	6
Bore	82·55 mm.
Stroke	79·50 mm.
Cubic capacity	2,553 c.c.
Piston area	49·74 sq. in.
Valves	Overhead (pushrod)
Compression ratio	8·3/1 (7 : 1 optional)
Carburetter	Zenith 36 WIA-2 D/D
Fuel pump	AC Delco mechanical diaphragm
Ignition timing control	Centrifugal and vacuum
Oil filter	AC Delco, Purolator, Tecalemit, full flow
Maximum power (net)	98 b.h.p.
at	4,750 r.p.m.
Maximum torque (net)	134 lb. ft.
at	2000 r.p.m.
Piston speed at maximum b.h.p.	2480 ft./min.

Transmission
Borg-Warner automatic transmission with hydraulic torque converter and 3 speed epicyclic gearbox

Top gear	3·545
2nd gear	5·140
1st gear	8·175
Reverse	7·409
Propeller shaft	Hardy Spicer open
Final drive	Hypoid bevel
Top gear m.p.h. at 1,000 r.p.m.	19·9
Top gear m.p.h. at 1,000 ft./min. piston speed	38·1

Chassis
Brakes Girling hydraulic with vacuum servo; disc front, drum rear.
Brake dimensions Front 9¾ in. dia. discs
Rear 9 in. dia. drums
Friction areas 98 sq. in. of friction lining operating on 330 sq. in. swept disc and drum surface.
Suspension:
Front Independent by Macpherson coil spring/damper strut and bottom wishbone incorporating anti-roll bar.
Rear Live axle and semi-elliptic leaf springs.
Shock absorbers:
Front Armstrong telescopic
Rear Armstrong lever arm.
Steering gear Ford-Burman recirculating ball
Tyres 6·40—13, four-ply tubeless.

This is the first of our attempts to evaluate by means of road usage and comparative data a number of popular British cars. Our objective has been to separate the factual from the opinionated so that the reader may, if he wishes, form his own judgement on a given car without being influenced by our possible prejudices. Where opinions are expressed, we have endeavoured to make them clearly and without resort to double entendre phraseology.

LOOKING AT THE
Ford Zephyr Six

Tester's view

Comfort and Convenience:

The Zephyr Six provides a standard of comfort for five or six passengers that is comparable to that of cars two or three times the Zephyr's price. The wide bench type seats at both front and back are very comfortable and some drivers would find the front seat a little too soft. Leg and headroom is ample in the front and adequate in the rear, though considering the car's overall bulk it is strange that there is not more. The ride comfort is very good indeed and while the sharper road shocks are felt, almost complete absence of pitching more than compensates. The accentuated "nose-dive" under hard braking may be a little disconcerting to the passengers.

Fittings and Controls

One fitting not supplied as standard is a windscreen washer and its absence was a curse throughout the period of the test which took place in late January when the roads were seldom dry. The wipers moved through arcs more suited to a left hand drive car, so what with a rather thick screen pillar and dirty section of windscreen at the right, the driver had a dangerously large blind spot which necessitated leaning to the left when negotiating right hand corners

The output of the heater was really excellent and was capable of de-icing the windscreen in just two or three minutes. Unfortunately the control which regulated the heat flow had insufficiently sensitive adjustment and it was very difficult to obtain an ideal heat flow. The demist—defrost switch was rather out of reach at the left, as was the booster switch. Other switches were conveniently placed, though there was not much room between the

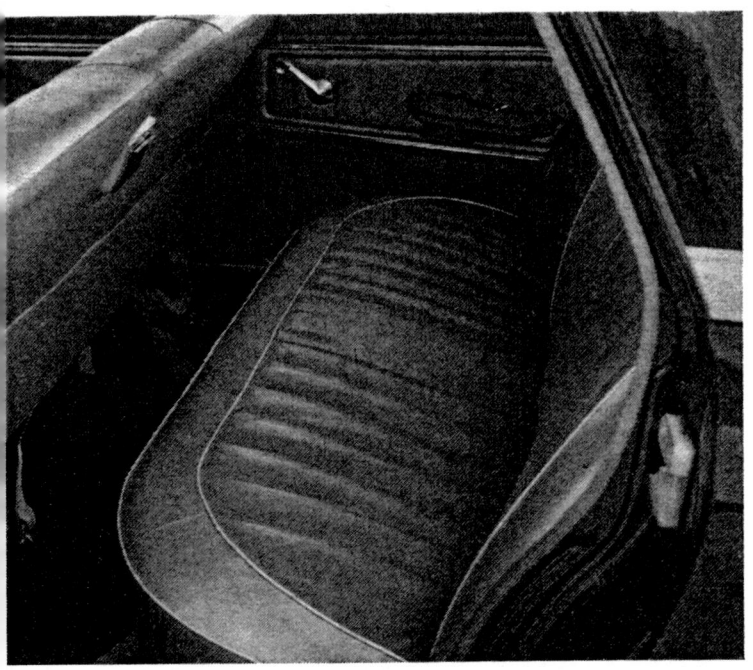

Spacious rear seat allows three adults to sit abreast in comfort. Leg and headroom are both adequate

Large boot with unobstructed floor area. A vertically-mounted spare wheel and larger tool kit would be further improvements

large steering wheel and the door for a heavily clad arm to reach the lighting switch. The flasher incorporated with the traffic indicators is a useful standard fitting.

The four speed all-synchromesh gearbox is operated by a steering column change which is very good indeed, having fairly short travel and a rather direct feel about it. Engagement of reverse is not simple, mainly because the necessary movement (a pull outwards to the left) is a difficult one physically and one imagines that many women would have a struggle. Pedal layout can scarcely be faulted.

Handling

The prevailing weather gave us little chance to get a proper indication of the ultimate roadholding of the Zephyr but presuming it is commensurate with its behaviour in the wet it must certainly be very impressive for a car of this type. Even at relatively high cornering speeds the Six goes precisely where it is pointed. The excess of power means that controllable oversteer can usually be set up but it was noticed that cambers could cause a surprising degree of understeer. Most drivers would find the Zephyr's steering close to neutral. Despite its comparatively low gearing the steering is very heavy at low speeds.

Poorly arranged wiper arc which leaves unwiped area beside the windscreen pillar. The same for left-hand drive cars?

Performance

Its performance is possibly the most pleasing thing about the Zephyr, for the six-cylinder 98 bhp motor gives the bulky saloon really brisk acceleration. The Zephyr is well able to outsprint many sports cars and generally the performance belongs to a much more expensive vehicle. The power is transmitted to the road most effectively via the rigid rear axle and wheelspin is only induced in the dry by insensitive use of the throttle.

During our tests we found the maximum speed to be just under 90 mph, and 80 mph cruising did not seem unreasonable. The brakes matched the performance and better brakes than the servo assisted Girling discs and drums are difficult to imagine. Pedal pressure was light but sufficiently sensitive to allow for quite rapid stops on icy surfaces.

Summary

There is no doubt that the Zephyr Six more than adequately fulfills its purpose, i.e. to be a large but comparatively cheap family car. Accepting its comfort and high performance as bonuses one must conclude that the Zephyr Six is excellent value for money. Several foreign cars of

MAKE	PRICE £	Overall size ft in	Interior width Front in	Interior width Rear in	Legroom Front in	Headroom Rear in	Ground Clearance in	Turning Circle ft in	Kerb Weight cwt	Approx Boot Size cu ft	Brakes Swept Area sq in	Fuel Tank gals
FORD ZEPHYR 6	837	15 1.25	56	58	19	7	35.0	6.80	37 10	25.0	22	330	12.0
VAUXHALL VELOX	822	15 1.00	59	59	20.5	9	34.5	6.50	36 9	24.4	16	316	10.7
STANDARD LUXURY 6	871	14 3.50	54	52	18.0	8	34.0	7.25	37 8	23.5	13	283	12.0
WOLSELEY 16/60	839	14 6.50	50	56	17.0	7	33.5	5.90	37 0	22.2	12	212	10.0
SINGER VOGUE	828	13 9.50	53	52	18.0	9	35.0	6.50	36 0	21.5	16	298	10.5

March, 1963 Sporting Motorist

comparable comfort and performance but with a much higher price tag, could be named to lend weight to this statement.

Admittedly, it is all too obvious that the Zephyr is built to a price, but it is easy enough to forget the poor standard of finish and unattractiveness of the interior when the value is so good.

The car's bulk can be a little embarassing in Britain's crowded cities and while best use is not made of the overall dimensions the great capacity of the boot can be a real boon, and the six occupants can be quite comfortable.

The Zephyr Six is a touring car capable of transporting six people comfortably and quickly. Yet by reason of its splendid performance and good roadholding it can be a delight to own and drive, and that it can be bought for as little as £837 make it a most desirable motor car.

Family man's view

Comfort and convenience

The Zephyr Six seems to me to be almost the ideal for the man with a growing family, a limited pocket and a taste for a powerful car. Not only were my family of four

The stretch for the heater controls (knob and, below, switch) to the left of the picture can be gauged

able to make themselves really comfortable in the spacious interior of the Zephyr, but there was room for an enormous amount of supplementary bits and pieces such as pushchairs, carry-cots and the like in the cavernous boot. There were no complaints about the comfort of the seats from the family, but the driving position I found slightly disturbing on a big car because I could not see the nearside wing. As a result of this I found all the time that I expected the Zephyr, which is, after all, a big car, to be even bigger than it is. Manoeuvring in confined spaces and parking are quite a task in the Zephyr if one is used to a smaller car. The steering takes a lot of winding, the boot is rather long and the width of the car, which is such a boon for the occupants in other ways, becomes a bit of an embarrassment.

Fittings and controls

While basically well designed the Zephyr did seem to have a number of items among its fittings and controls which could be improved. The painted metal strip disguised to look like wood-work on the dashboard seemed quite incongruous and unnecessary. The glove locker was rather inaccessible and the catch on it did not work properly; the ashtray did not fit well, and I had the feeling

Instruments and controls are well grouped around the steering column, although when the door is closed operation of the light switch (extreme right) can be hindered by the narrow gap between steering wheel and window winder

Forward adjustment of the seat brings wheel-in-the-midriff driving position, but knee room for pedal manipulation remains good

ENGINE					TRANSMISSION		PERFORMANCE			
No of cylinders	Max power	Max torque lb ft	Cooling	Position	Gears/ Drive	Mph per 1000 rpm	Fuel consumption mpg	Acceleration 0-60 sec	Max Speed	
6 2553 cc	98 at 4750 rpm	134 at 2000 rpm	water	front	4 rear	20.3	24	14.1	89	
6 2651 cc	95 at 4600 rpm	138.5 at 1600 rpm	water	front	4 rear	19.6	20	15.8	93	
6 1998 cc	82 at 4500 rpm	113 at 2500 rpm	water	front	4 rear	16.2	21	19.7	85	
4 1622 cc	61 at 4500 rpm	90 at 2100 rpm	water	front	4 rear	16.6	25	28.0	70	
4 1592 cc	62 at 4400 rpm	86.3 at 2500 rpm	water	front	4 rear	16.2	28	22.5	83	

The cars detailed side are those whi[ch] consider are compara[ble in] price and purpose [to the] car under test. Th[ere is] that all the cars are [listed] merely indicates that [there] are no full size saloons of foreign [make] in this price bracket.

The figures give[n are] taken from a varie[ty of] sources, and di[fferent] methods may have [been] used for arriving at [them.] We regret, therefor[e, that] while we are asse[rting] our own data, some [of the] comparative details [should] be treated with rese[rve.]

Sporting Motorist   March, 1963

The quarter light is of poor design, being stiff to operate and conducive to wind noise whether open or shut

Rear view of the Zephyr gives a good impression of its width, shows also purposeful appearance and good glass areas

that the upholstery material would look shabby after quite a short space of time. Most of the controls came quite well to hand although it was necessary to reach rather a long way for the heater knobs. The heater itself, incidentally, is among the most powerful I have ever experienced although the distribution of air around the seat could be improved by more vents. At present the left leg gets very hot while the right remains chilled. Quarter-lights are always useful to help ventilation when the heater is on, but those on the Zephyr were so stiff it was practically impossible to open them. The pedals were all very well positioned and light in operation, the brakes being particularly powerful with lightness and, despite being drum variety, never showing any signs of fade during normal driving. The steering column gearchange was excellent of its type, having no free play and a quick, easy movement. The seat adjustment, which is so often a nuisance on cars with a bench seat, worked very well and there was an exceptionally large movement from the front to the back of the runners.

Handling

The Zephyr Six seemed to handle very well, although the sort of conditions under which I drove the car were not conducive to flinging it around corners. There was ice or hard-packed snow underwheel most of the time. Despite fairly soft suspension which gives a pleasant ride over rough and rutted surfaces, there did not seem to be an undue amount of roll on corners and the steering stayed pleasantly positive with a trace of understeer throughout. Very few road shocks were transmitted through the steering and one felt in thorough control of the car even on the difficult surfaces encountered. With the large amount of power in hand it was all too easy to spin the rear wheels on frozen surfaces and a delicate throttle control was required.

Performance

Besides its roominess the performance of the Zephyr is the other feature which really shines. Acceleration through the gears is quite vivid right up to 70 mph when it begins to fall off. But perhaps even more remarkable is the extreme flexibility of the engine, for it is possible to go down to 20 mph and accelerate hard in top gear without losing any smoothness and with a very smart pickup. Braking too was exceptionally good, light pedal pressures producing really rapid stops and the drums giving an instantaneous bite which has become somewhat unfamiliar after driving a car with discs on the front.

Summary

All in all I found the Zephyr a most well-balanced car, ideally suited for a family of four or five. Its main shortcomings I thought were in the quality of some of its accessories and the general standard of trim, while its outstanding feature, after the amount of space it provides for the money, is the really vivid performance which will allow dear old dad to give some of the sports car drivers a very good run for their money!

SPECIFICATION

ENGINE:
Six cylinders; bore 82.55 mm (3.25 in), stroke 79.5 mm (3.13 in). Cubic capacity, 2553 cc. Compression ratio, 8.3 to 1. Maximum bhp (net), 98 at 4750 rpm. Maximum torque, 134 lb ft at 2000 rpm. Overhead valves, pushrod operated. Downdraught carburettor; diaphragm type fuel pump; tank capacity, 12½ gals. Water cooling with pump, fan and thermostat; capacity, 19¼ pints. Pressure lubrication by submerged gear pump; full flow oil filter; sump capacity, 8½ pints. 12V 57 amp/hr battery.

TRANSMISSION:
Single dry plate clutch, hydraulically operated. Four-speed gearbox with synchromesh on all forward gears. Overall gear ratios: 1st, 11.23; 2nd, 7.97; 3rd, 5.01; top, 3.55 to 1. Steering column gear change. Three-quarter floating, hypoid final drive.

CHASSIS:
Suspension: front, independent with coil springs, double-acting telescopic shock absorbers integral with wheel spindle assembly, and anti-roll bar; rear, longitudinal semi-elliptic leaf springs with hydraulic double acting lever type shock absorbers. Brakes: front, 9½in discs; rear, 9 x 2¼in drums. Recirculatory ball steering, ratio 18 to 1; 17in dia two-spoke, dished steering wheel. 13in pressed steel wheels; tyre size, 6.40-13in.

DIMENSIONS:

	ft	in
Wheelbase	8	11
Track, front	4	5
Track, rear	4	4
Overall length	15	0
Overall height	4	9½
Overall width	5	9
Ground clearance		6¾
Turning circle	36	0
Kerb weight	24 cwt	

PERFORMANCE:
Acceleration through gears:

mph	sec
0—30	4.7
0—60	14.1
0—80	29.6

FORD ZEPHYR 6 AND ZODIAC MK IV

INDEX TO REPAIR OPERATIONS

BODYWORK . . . . .
BRAKES . . . . . .
CLUTCH . . . . .
COOLING SYSTEM . . .
ELECTRICAL SYSTEM . . .
ENGINE . . . . .
FRONT SUSPENSION . . .

FUEL SYSTEM . . . .
GEARBOX . . . . .
IGNITION . . . . .
REAR AXLE . . . . .
STEERING . . . . .
WHEELS AND TYRES . . .

BODYWORK

The body shell is a welded all-steel unit incorporating box section reinforcements to create a structure of exceptional stiffness and light weight. The complete shell in bare metal weighs 530 lb. and has a torsional stiffness of 5,560 lb./ft./degree from end to end. The completed and furnished shell with doors, bonnet and boot lid weighs 1,166 lb. (Zephyr 6) or 1,195 lb. (Zodiac). A box-section frame projects 3 ft. forward of the scuttle and is tied transversely by the front suspension mounting member. The scuttle projects outwards on each side and is welded to the wheel arches, the inner sections of the wheel boxes being welded to the projecting frame rails.

REMOVAL OF DOOR TRIM.—Remove the window regulator handle by inserting a length of wire behind the handle to engage a hook-end under a retaining clip and lever this clip from the handle boss. Then remove the door interior lock knob and the combined armrest and door pull. The trim panel is then levered away from the door panel together with a waterproof sheet.

When replacing the window regulating handle, centralise the wire clip in the boss of the handle with the closed end of the clip towards the opening behind the handle. This is important, otherwise it will not be possible to remove the handle at a later date.

REMOVAL OF DOOR WINDOW GLASSES.—Remove the window regulator handle and trim panel, and take out one crosshead screw, spring and flat washer securing the lower edge of the window glass rear channel to the bottom edge of the door inner panel.

Remove the nut and washer securing the top of the glass rear channel run and lift out through the door access hole. Lever off the door outer belt weatherstrip, and then unscrew and remove the four crosshead screws securing the window glass lower channel to the regulator mounting and withdraw the glass through the door frame. Refitting is the reverse procedure.

REMOVAL OF EXTRACTOR TRIM PANELS.—Lift away the rear seat cushion, remove the two screws, nuts and flat washers securing the rear seat backrest and lift this away. Pull away the door opening finish strip, and then pull away the top end of the rear quarter trim panel to give access to two screws and washers securing the lower edge of the extraction trim panel. If a radio is fitted, remove the four nuts and washers securing the radio speaker and grille to the rear parcel shelf, from inside the boot, and remove the parcel shelf.

Take off the section of trim located below the bottom edge of the rear window weatherstrip to gain access to a crosshead screw securing the lower edge of the extractor trim panel. Pull the front edge of the extractor trim panel from the door aperture flange and remove by pulling it from the securing clips.

Refitting.—Locate the panel in position on the rear quarter panel and press firmly into the securing clips. Coat the front edge of the panel with suitable adhesive and position temporarily around the door aperture to prime both surfaces with adhesive. When the adhesive has become tacky, reposition the front edge of the panel over the door aperture flange. Secure the two crosshead screws in the lower edge of the panel, and replace the section of trim under the bottom edge of the rear window weatherstrip. Replace the parcel shelf, and the radio speaker unit if fitted. Apply adhesive to the rear quarter trim panel and body and when tacky position the trim panel on the body. Replace the door opening finish strips and tap them firmly in position using a rubber headed mallet. The rear seat backrest is then replaced and secured with the nuts and washers.

REMOVAL OF AIR EXTRACTION BOX.—With the extractor panel removed, remove four crosshead screws securing the exterior metal louvre to the rear quarter panel and lift away the louvre, then remove the pop rivet securing the top end of the box. From outside the body, drill out the pop rivets securing the box to the rear quarter panel, and lift away the box from inside the body.

BONNET ADJUSTMENT.—Setting adjustments are provided on the spring loaded hinges and the spring loaded catch post. Vertical adjustment is effected by screwing the catch post in or out as required. Vertical adjustment of the rear end of the bonnet is effected by slacking back the hinge securing bolts and moving the hinges up or down relative to the mounting brackets. Lateral adjustment is effected by slackening the bolts securing the bonnet to the hinges.

The sequence of adjustment is first to slacken the locknuts and screw in the two adjustable rubber bump stops and then close the bonnet and check the gap between the sides of the bonnet and the wing panels, followed by the gap at the rear of the bonnet. Slacken the bolts securing the bonnet to the hinges and move the bonnet until all gaps are equal, and retighten the nuts. Now close the bonnet and check the relative height on the rear end and front end, and adjust as required. Finally close the bonnet and check the fit.

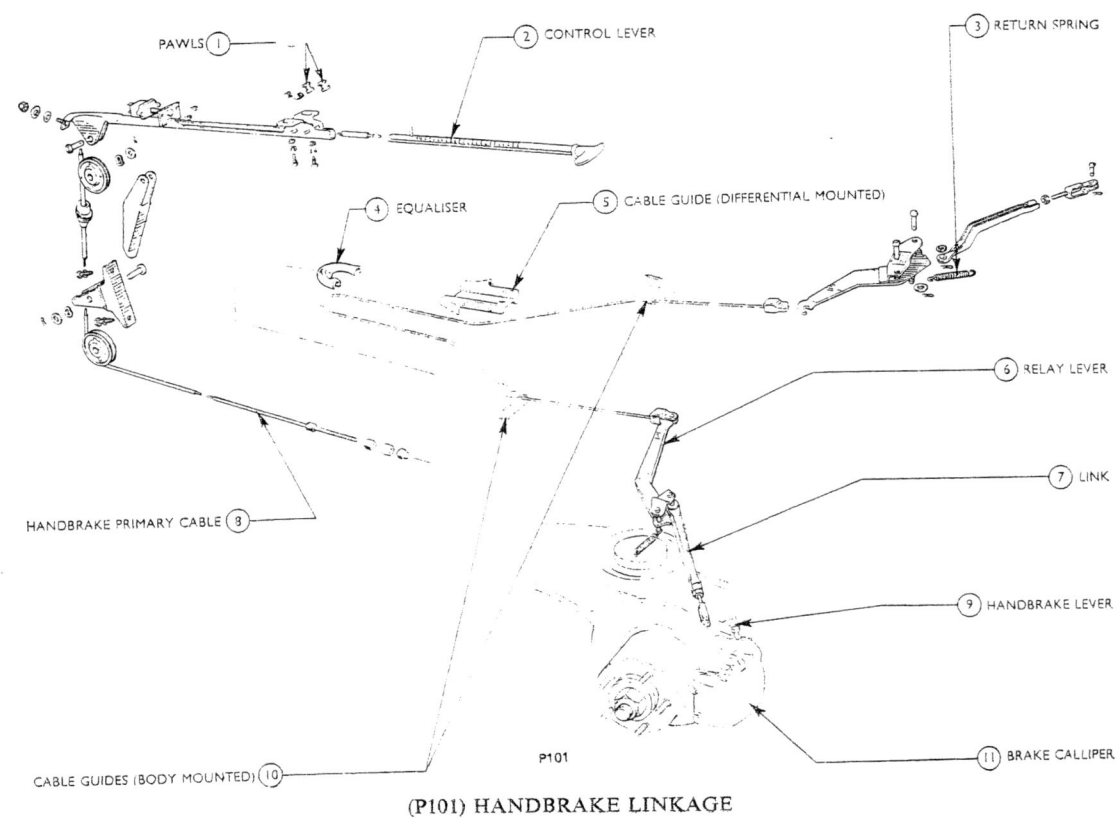

(P101) HANDBRAKE LINKAGE

BRAKES

DATA

Type	Girling hydraulically operated discs with servo assistance and cables to rear callipers from handbrake
Servo type	Girling Supervac 50
Front disc diam.	9·63 in.
Front pad area	5·2 × 4 = 20·8 in. total sq. in.
Rear disc diam.	9·91 in.
Rear pad area	3·50 × 4 = total 14·0 sq. in.
Total swept friction area of discs	353·6 in.

GENERAL.—The brake pedal is linked to a servo with suspended piston to treble the effort applied on the pedal. Braking effort is distributed in the proportion of 65% front and 35% rear to the all-disc installation in which at the front a dual-cylinder calliper embraces a disc which is gripped by four pads. The rear disc brake is of the reaction type with self-adjusting parking brake mechanism.

Replacement of the Handbrake Lever or Primary Cable.—To remove, jack up the front of the car and from underneath detach the primary cable from the equaliser bracket and pull through the guide and pulley. Open the bonnet and remove the nut securing the front end of the control lever and cable assembly to the engine compartment rear bulkhead. Remove two screws securing the rear end of the lever and cable assembly to the facia panel lower edge, push out the floor grommet and withdraw the lever and cable as an assembly.

Remove the bracket and pulley by extracting a spring clip and pin, withdraw the brake handle and detach the cable after removing the ratchet dogs.

Replacement of the Secondary Cable.—Jack up the rear end of the car, release the handbrake, detach the rear ends of the secondary cable from the relay levers on the suspension arms, release the cable from the guide on the differential and remove the equaliser bracket from the rod section of the primary cable.

REAR BRAKE ASSEMBLIES.—These are of the self-adjusting disc type incorporating a swinging calliper. Each calliper is mounted and pivoted on a hinge pin on the rear wheel bearing carrier.

Removing Rear Brakes.—Jack up the car, remove the rear wheel and the splash shield protecting the inside face of the disc. Remove the clevis pin and clip from the link to the cam on the calliper body, detach the brake fluid pipe and fit line plugs to both pipe and calliper.

Remove the stop pin and rotate the cam to allow access to a cap nut on the top end of the hinge pin, taking care not to lift the cam as this will dislodge the handbrake tappet inside the calliper body and if this happens the calliper will have to be completely stripped down to refit this tappet.

Use a hexagon key on the upper end of the hinge pin and a ring spanner on the lower end in order to screw the hinge pin out of the lower seat. Withdraw the pin and lift away the calliper.

Dismantling the Calliper.—Remove two spring locking nuts and detach the cover together with a large sealing gasket located behind the cover, lift off two small rubber sealing rings from the two nuts and remove the two nuts securing the steel spring and beam to the studs. Lever the spring over the studs so that the lever, strut and beam will fall away from the mechanism. Lift away the beam and two sleeves and remove the 'S' type spring. Unscrew the ratchet wheel located between the two studs so that it is free of the winder and remove the wheel and winder separately. Use a hexagon key to remove the base plate securing screw in order to free the base plate.

Detach the handbrake tappet and hydraulic piston. If necessary the handbrake lever can be rotated so that it is clear of the stop and then pulled out of the calliper body. There is a rubber sealing ring fitted inside the lever bore, which should be retained for replacement when re-assembling.

Rear Brake Pad Replacement.—With the wheels removed, lever down the tab washer on the bolt retaining the inner pad guide to the top of the calliper body, remove this bolt, tab washer, guide plate and anti-rattle spring which bears on the outer pad, then slide the pad down below the lower guide plate and remove from the top. Swing the calliper towards the rear and pull the outer pad off the drag pins. It may be necessary to slacken the drag pins to enable worn pads to be moved inwards enough to clear the ends of the pins.

Wind the automatic adjustment back into the body of the calliper by turning the clip on the end of the piston. Fit the new pads (outer first) making sure that they slide into their correct positions. Note that the thick edge of the pad should be towards the rear whilst the thick edge of the inner pad should be towards the front. The clip on the piston must locate behind the rear edge of the inner pad and the retaining bolts must locate in the outer pad backing plate.

Fit the guide plate and anti-rattle spring which is located along the top of the guide plate so that it bears on the outer pad, and secure with a bolt and tab washer. Make sure that the cut-outs in the guide plate and anti-rattle spring engage with a peg set into the calliper adjacent to the rear edge of the inner pad.

CLUTCH

DATA

Type	Single dry plate, diaphragm operated
Fluid type	Amber ME-3833-F
Master cylinder diam.	0.7 in.
Operating cylinder diam.	1.00 in.
Clutch disc outer diam.	9 in.
Damper spring colour	Mauve/red
Pressure plate outer diam.	9½ in.
Pressure plate identification	Red paint spot
Pressure plate to flywheel bolt torque	12–15 lb./ft.

ADJUSTMENTS.—A spring inside the operating cylinder keeps the piston in contact with the clutch operating pushrod, thereby preventing any clearance and making routine clutch pedal adjustment unnecessary.

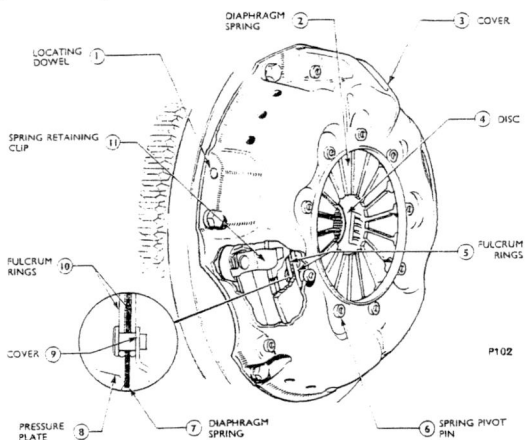

(P102) DIAPHRAGM SPRING CLUTCH

Maintenance of the clutch follows that normally applied to diaphragm clutch assemblies, access to the clutch being obtained after the gearbox has been removed. It should be noted that the flywheel and ring gear are dynamically balanced to close limits, and any remaining heavy point is indicated by a paint mark on the flywheel. There is a similar mark on the clutch unit, and when assembling the clutch to the flywheel, locate this paint mark diametrically opposite to that on the flywheel.

The clutch is located by three dowels and retained by six bolts and spring washers. The clutch pilot bearing is a sealed ball race, and the flywheel has to be removed in order to extract the old race and fit a new one.

COOLING SYSTEM

DATA

Water pump	Centrifugal-type, belt-driven from crankshaft
Thermostat	Wax capsule-type, in intake manifold
Nominal opening temperature	Starts to open 185/192°F; fully open 212°F
Fan	F/L 4-blade 14.120 in. diam.
Drive ratio, fan : engine	1 : 1

GENERAL.—As the radiator height is kept to a minimum, a separate header tank is mounted on the left-hand cylinder bank between the engine coolant outlet and the radiator, and incorporates the filler cap.

In production the cooling system is filled with a 50% solution of anti-freeze, Ford Part No. M97B18-C, which when correctly mixed has a specific gravity of 1.08 at 60°F. This coolant can remain in the engine for two years, or 36,000 miles, and any rust formation or discolouration of the clear green colour indicates that the coolant has reached the end of its useful life, and should be renewed.

WATER PUMP REMOVAL.—The pump is on the right-hand side of the block, separate from the fan. A repair kit is available consisting of shaft and bearing assembly, rubber slinger, pump seal, impeller and gasket. Pump shaft and double ball bearing are serviced as an assembly and should not be dismantled.

Drain the system, retaining the coolant if required for re-use, remove the fan belt, disconnect the radiator lower hose and remove lower hose from water pump. Take off the water pump to automatic choke hose. Unscrew bolts securing pump to the cylinder block, noting that one bolt is trapped by the pump pulley and is lifted away with pump assembly.

FAN BELT ADJUSTMENT.—The correct tension is such that when the belt is pushed and pulled at a point mid-way between the generator or alternator drive pulley and the fan pulley, the total movement is ½ in. Tensioning is carried out in the usual manner of easing the generator or alternator away from the engine, locking up the mounting bolts and adjusting bolt securely after tension has been obtained.

Radiator Removal.—Drain the cooling system, slacken the drain cocks at the bottom of the radiator and on the cylinder block behind the oil filter. Detach the top and bottom hoses and pull off the flexible overflow pipe from the filler pipe on the header tank. Unscrew the four bolts with spring and flat washers, securing the radiator to the front panel, and lift the radiator out of the engine compartment. Capacity of the cooling system for the 2.5 litre engine is 20.8 Imp. pints and for the 3 litre engine 21.8 Imp. pints, and the cap pressure is 13 lb. sq. in.

ELECTRICAL SYSTEM

DATA

Battery	
Type	12-volt Negative earth
Capacity	53 amp. at 20 hr. rate
Generator	
Type	12-volt two-brush
Cut-in speed (generator r.p.m.)	1260
Maximum charge	25 amps.

Brush length	0·7 in.
Fan belt tension (total free movement)	½ in.
Regulator	
Cut-in voltage	12·6–13·4 volts
Armature to core air gap	0·035–0·045 in.
Alternator	
Type	Lucas 11 AC
Nominal voltage	12
Output	43 amps.
Brush length, new	0·625 in.
Replace at	0·156 in.
Starter Motor	
Type	Pre-engaged
Amperage drawing, normal	250 amps.
Minimum brush length	0·25 in.
Brush spring pressure	40 oz.
Starter Motor (Alternative)	
Amperage drawing normal	260
Minimum brush length	0·3 in.
Brush spring pressure	32 oz.

ENGINE

DATA

Type	6 cylinder o.h.v. 60° vee
Bore, 2·5 and 3 litre	3·687 in.
Stroke 2·5 litre	2·376 in.
3 litre	2·851 in.
Cubic capacity 2·5 litre	121·8 cu. in. (1996 c.c.)
3 litre	152·2 cu. in. (2495 c.c.)
Compression ratio:	
2·5 litre (High)	8·9 : 1
3 litre (High)	9·1 : 1
2·5 and 3 litre (Low)	7·7 : 1
Firing order	1-4-2-5-3-6
Camshaft	
Bearing type	Steel back, white metal bushes
Journal diam.:	
Front	1·8737–1·8745 in.
No. 2 intermediate	1·8137–1·8145 in.
No. 3 intermediate	1·7537–1·7545 in.
Rear	1·7387–1·7395 in.
Bearing clearance	0·0008–0·0026 in.
End float	0·003–0·007 in.
Thrust plate thickness	0·210–0·212 in.
Connecting Rods	
Big end bearing material	Steel back copper/lead liners
Big end diam.	2·5210–2·5215 in.
Crankpin to bearing clearance	0·0007–0·0025 in.
End float	0·004–0·010 in.
Crankshaft	
Main bearing journal diam.:	
Blue	2·5006–2·5010 in.
Red	2·5010–2·5014 in.
Green	2·4906–2·4910 in.
Yellow	2·4910–2·4914 in.
Main bearings	Steel back copper/lead
Clearance	0·0005–0·0018 in.
Crankpin journal diam.	2·3761–2·3769 in.
Crankshaft end float	0·003–0·011 in.
Thrust washers	Steel backed copper/lead or aluminium/tin split washers
Thrust washer thickness	0·091–0·093 in.

(P103) SECTIONAL VIEW OF VEE 6 (3 LITRE) ENGINE

Pistons
Upper compression, ring gap	0·010–0·020 in.
Lower compression, ring gap	0·010–0·020 in.
Oil ring	0·010–0·015 in.
Oversize rings available	0·030, 0·045, 0·060 in.

Valves
Valve seat angle	44° 30′–45°
Timing, with inlet clearance at 0·018 in. and exhaust at 0·026 in.	
Inlet opens	20° b.t.d.c.
Inlet closes	56° a.b.d.c.
Exhaust opens	62° b.b.d.c.
Exhaust closes	14° a.t.d.c.
Valve clearance (hot), inlet	0·010 in.
exhaust	0·018 in.

Torque Wrench Data
	lb./ft.
Main bearing cap bolts	55–60
Connecting rod bolts	30–35
Cylinder head bolts	65–70
Flywheel or drive plate bolts	45–50

GENERAL.—The engine has its cylinders arranged in a 60° Vee formation. Cylinder bores are machined directly in the block which incorporates four main bearings. Crankshaft end float is controlled by thrust washers fitted on each side of the centre main bearing. The camshaft is driven at half engine speed by a fibre gear meshing directly with the crankshaft gear.

Valve rocker arms are mounted on studs pressed into the cylinder heads and are retained by spherically faced fulcrum seats and self-locking nuts. Valve clearances are adjusted by these self-locking nuts. Valve springs are close coiled at one end, and this end must be adjacent to the cylinder head when fitted.

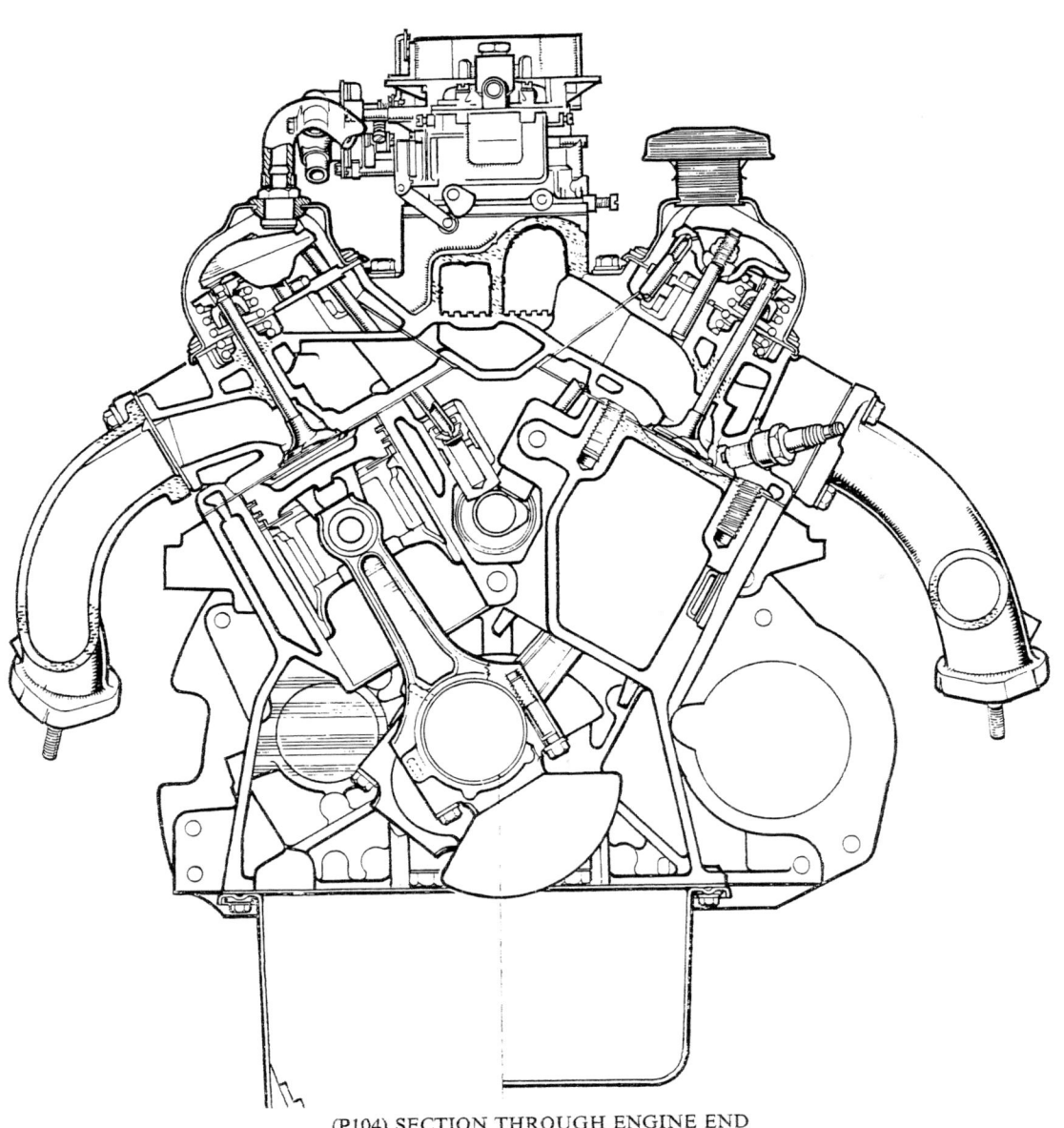

(P104) SECTION THROUGH ENGINE END

REMOVAL OF THE ENGINE.—Disconnect and remove the battery, unbolt and remove the bonnet, drain the cooling system by opening the drain plugs located in the bottom of the radiator and on the left-hand side of the engine. Remove the spare wheel and air cleaner. Disconnect top and bottom hoses at the radiator, unbolt radiator securing bolts and lift out radiator.

Disconnect all electrical connections to the engine and the starter motor leads, remove the fan blade and boss assembly, disconnect fuel supply and return pipes, the servo unit vacuum pipe at the inlet manifold, and, where automatic transmission is fitted, the vacuum connection.

Disconnect heater hoses at bulkhead, also throttle linkage and remove the starter motor and cable. Unbolt and disconnect the exhaust manifolds and then jack up the car and securely support on stands. Remove the flywheel shield, and with automatic transmission, disconnect the converter from the drive plate. Unscrew and remove the clutch housing bolts, and support the gearbox on a jack. Remove generator or alternator and fan belt, and support the engine with suitable lifting tackle. Remove the two bolts and four nuts securing the engine mounting brackets, and lift the unit upwards out of the car.

DISMANTLING.—With the engine mounted on an engine stand, remove the exhaust manifolds, disconnect the high and low tension leads and vacuum pipe, and remove the distributor, sparking plugs and coil. Detach the header tank, carburetter and fuel pump, remove the thermostat housing, water pump, crankcase ventilation tube, oil filler and clutch unit.

Removal of Cylinder Heads.—Take off the rocker covers, unscrew the bolts securing the inlet manifold and remove. Detach rocker arms keeping them in their correct order together with the fulcrum seats. Lift out the pushrods, again keeping them in their correct order for re-assembly. Unbolt and remove the pushrod guide plates, unscrew the cylinder head bolts evenly and lift off the head.

Removing Connecting Rods.—Reverse the engine, unbolt and remove the sump, unbolt and remove the oil pump and extract the pump drive shaft. Unscrew the big end bolts and withdraw the bearing caps. Completely remove the big end bolts, and push the pistons towards the top of the bore, withdrawing them as assemblies. It may be necessary to scrape away hard carbon from around the tops of the bores to allow the pistons to slide out.

Removing Camshaft.—Take off the camshaft pulley using a suitable drawer tool, unbolt and remove the front cover and drive out the oil seal. Draw off the camshaft gear, and note that the fuel pump eccentric is retained by the gear centre bolt. Remove the front cover backplate and the camshaft thrust plate. Withdraw camshaft carefully to ensure that the lobes on the shaft do not damage the bearing surfaces.

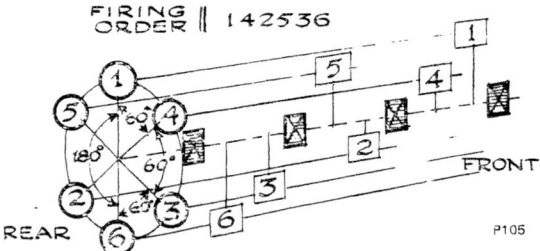

(P105) LAYOUT OF VEE 6 ENGINE FIRING ORDER

At the rear of the engine, withdraw the flywheel, or if automatic transmission is used, withdraw the reinforcing plate, drive plate and spacer, and then detach the crankshaft rear oil seal carrier. Unscrew each main bearing securing bolt in turn, remove the bolts and lift off each cap, removing the thrust washers located on each side of the centre main bearing. The crankshaft can now be lifted out complete with the front gear wheel.

REASSEMBLING THE ENGINE.—The sequence of reassembly is the reverse of that for dismantling, but note the following. When checking the oilways and galleries do not use sealing compound on the threads of the plugs. Refit main bearings in their correct locations, making certain that the tongues in the shells engage in their locations, and that the shells with oil grooves are fitted into the cylinder block while those without are fitted to the caps.

Locate the thrust washers on each side of the centre main bearing with the oil grooves facing the crankshaft flange. Fit the bearing caps in their correct positions with the arrow mark pointing to the front of the engine. Check the end float with feeler gauges, and if necessary fit oversize thrust washers to take up excessive end float. Fit a new rear crankshaft seal to the carrier, and use a centralising tool in the rear seal carrier, leaving this tool in position until after the carrier bolts have been tightened.

With the flywheel secured in position, check the run-out at a radius of $3\frac{3}{4}$ in., and make sure that it does not exceed 0·007 in. total indicator reading. When replacing the camshaft gear, align the camshaft and crankshaft gear timing marks, press the gear right home, and then check the backlash between the gears at four equally spaced points. It should be between 0·004 and 0·007 in. for a new gear, but if the gear is well impregnated with oil, then the minimum backlash should be 0·002 in.

Camshaft end float must be checked with a dial indicator, the camshaft being pulled and pushed to obtain movement readings. The end float should be between 0·003 and 0·007 in. When refitting the crankshaft pulley, align the pulley on to the key and push the pulley home. Final drawing up is done with the centre bolt and washer tightened to 40–45 lb./ft. torque. When fitting the pistons, the 'F' mark on each piston must face towards the front of the engine.

When refitting the valves to the cylinder head place each valve in its correct position, and then relocate the valve springs and retainers over the stem together with the oil seals, compress the springs and refit the split collets. With the cylinder head and a new gasket in position the cylinder head bolts are tightened in the following sequence:

```
7  3  1  5
8  4  2  6   Front
```

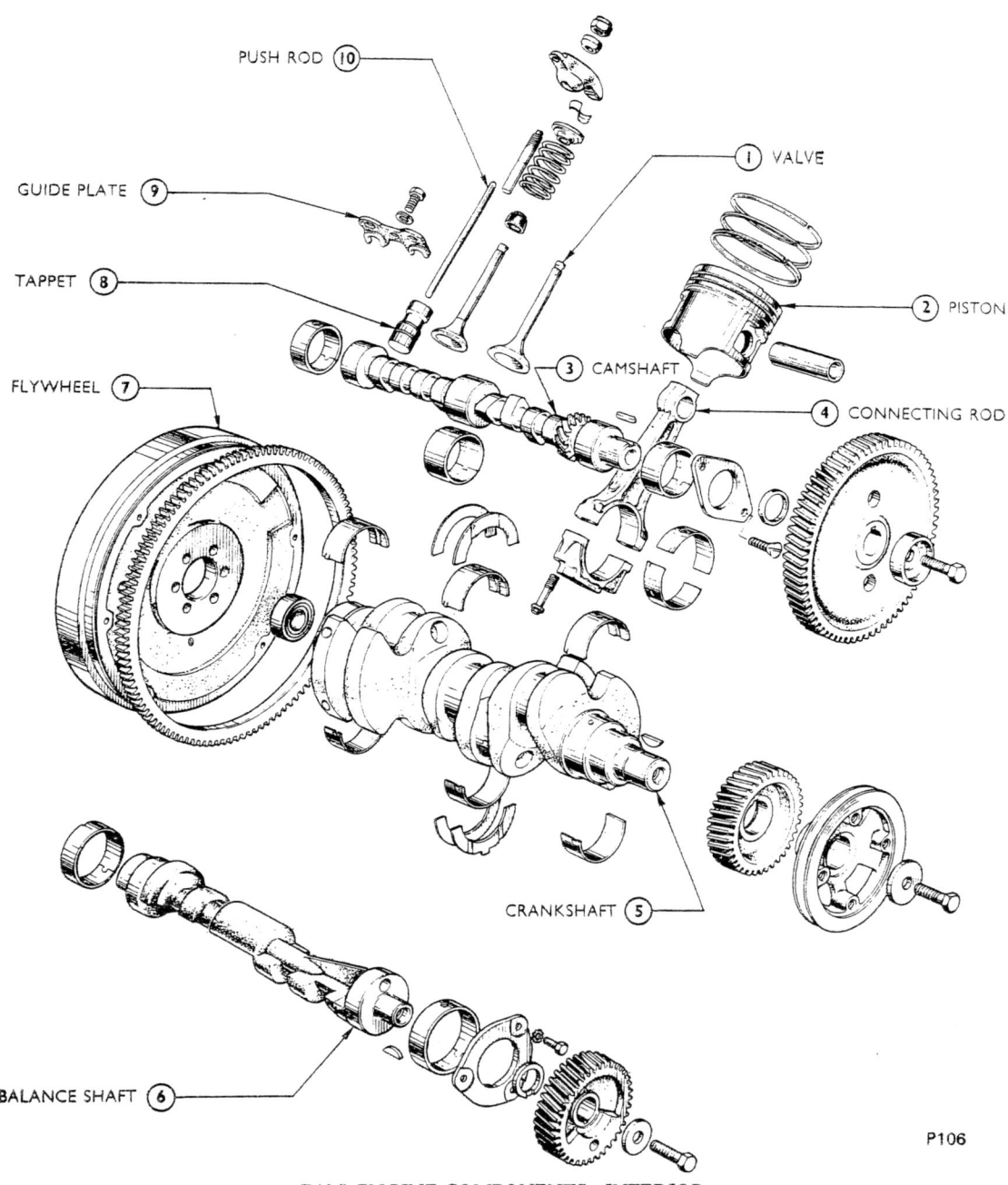

(P106) ENGINE COMPONENTS—INTERIOR

To check and set the valve tappet clearances, turn the crankshaft until the valves are in the following positions.

Valves open	Valves to adjust
1 and 6	10 and 7
3 and 11	5 and 4
2 and 3	9 and 12
7 and 10	6 and 1
4 and 5	11 and 8
9 and 12	2 and 3

To adjust, insert a feeler gauge blade between the rocker pad and valve stem, turn the rocker arm securing nut until the clearance required is attained, making sure that the rocker is correctly seated.

Apply a sealing compound across the joints between the inlet manifold and the cylinder heads. Fit the rocker cover with the oil filler to the left hand bank of cylinders and the cover with the emission valve on the right-hand bank.

When replacing the distributor, time it so that when the mark on the crankshaft is adjacent to 12° b.t.d.c. on the vee 6 engine with high compression or 8° b.t.d.c. on the vee 6 engine with low compression, with No. 1 cylinder on compression, the points are just opening, and the rotor pointing towards No. 1 distributor electrode. To facilitate this location align the recessed end of the distributor gear pin with the notch in the base of the body before actually fitting.

LUBRICATION SYSTEM.—The engine is lubricated by a forced feed system, the oil being circulated by an eccentric bi-rotor or sliding vane type of pump mounted in the crankcase on the left-hand side of the engine. Sump capacity is 8 Imp. pints to which a further 1½ Imp. pints must be added for a dry filter.

The oil filter is mounted on the left-hand side of the engine and is retained by a threaded insert into the block. It may be necessary to use a strap tool around the top of the filter in order to unscrew it. The filter is completely discarded, a new unit being screwed on to the insert until it contacts the mounting pad, and then given a further half turn.

FRONT SUSPENSION

SUSPENSION DATA

Type	Independent, Macpherson strut
Negative castor	—0° 2′ to 1° 02′
Camber	1° 03′ to 2° 03′
King pin inclination	5° 57′ to 6° 56′
Toe-in	0·26 to 0·32 in.

GENERAL.—The system follows the principles used on all British Ford cars employing vertical shock absorber units surrounded by coil springs. A device is incorporated in the stabiliser bar to track control arm mounting consisting of a pair of plastic bushes fitted on the bar with the track control arm sandwiched between them. The function is to permit a small amount of fore and aft movement of the road wheel to reduce the shock loading on the steering linkages when the road wheel strikes an obstruction in the road surface.

When repairs are being carried out to any part of the front suspension units, proper spring clips must be fitted to the coil springs otherwise personal injury may result when dismantling and reassembling.

Front Hub and Brake Disc Removal.—Jack up the front of the car, remove the road wheel and the hub dust cap. Detach the brake fluid pipe from the bracket on the suspension leg, release the tabs from the two calliper mounting bolts, unscrew the bolts and lift off the calliper assembly. Note that it is not necessary to remove the brake pads from their location. Support the calliper so that no strain is put on the hydraulic pipes, which need not be uncoupled.

Withdraw the split pin from the hub nut, withdraw the adjusting nut retainer, nut, thrust washer and outer bearing cone. The hub and disc are then drawn from the spindle.

REMOVING A SUSPENSION UNIT.—Fit spring clips to the coil spring and secure the safety strap. Jack up the front of the car, detach the brake fluid pipe from the bracket on the suspension leg, lift the bonnet and remove the upper bearing plastic cover.

Unscrew the three bolts and remove together with a spring and a plain washer, securing the top of the suspension unit to the underside of the apron panel. Remove three bolts attaching the lower end of the suspension unit to the steering and track control arms, and then move the unit downwards out of its location.

Removing the Stabiliser Bar.—Fit the spring clips to the coil springs and secure the safety strap. Jack up the front of the car and bend back the tabs and remove the four bolts securing the two attachment clamps. Withdraw the split pins and unscrew the stabiliser bar nuts securing the bar to the track control arms. Remove the nuts, large washers and large bushes. The bar is then pulled forward to remove. Withdraw the second large bush, sleeve and large washer from the ends of the bar.

When replacing, make sure that the washer is of the correct type, since it is different from the one fitted on the rear under the securing nut.

Renewing a Track Control Arm Joint.—Relieve the staking and prise out a plug from the ball joint housing. Fit in a tool to depress the spring. Remove the circlip, spring retainer, spring, lower bearing retainer, lower bearing, stud and stud upper bearing.

When fitting a new plug in the ball joint housing, this must be done with a tube over the top hat section and expanding the outer edge of the plug into the track control arm. The plug is made with a sharp periphery so that after fitting, this periphery will form a grease-tight joint with the track control arm body.

FUEL SYSTEM

FUEL SYSTEM DATA

	2½ litre	3 litre
	Carburetter	
	Zenith 38IVT	Weber 40DFA-1
Venturi diam.	29 mm.	28 mm.
Secondary venturi	—	4·5
Main jet	120	180
Compensating jet	100	—
Idling jet	55	60
Accelerator pump jet	70	50
Idling jet air bleed	1·4	200
Air correction jet	—	185
Fast idle setting (std)	0·8–0·9 mm.	0·75–0·8 mm.
with automatic transmission	1·2–1·3 mm.	0·8–0·9 mm.
Fuel pump, delivery pressure		2¾–4½ lb./sq./in.
Inlet depression		8·5 in. Hg.

The fuel system is of the recirculatory type in which a pipe is included to return excess fuel from the carburetter to the tank. Fuel is drawn from the tank to a reservoir secured to the underside of the left hand wheel arch, and from this it is drawn into the fuel pump and so to the carburetter.

ZENITH CARBURETTER—Carburetter Adjustment.—Check that the air cleaner is clean, and make the adjustment against a vacuum gauge. This can be fitted by removing the blanking plug from the inlet manifold and fitting a gauge adaptor. The engine should be brought up to normal running temperature, and adjustment made by screwing in the throttle stop screw until a fast idle speed is attained, and then turning the volume control screw to obtain the maximum vacuum reading on the gauge. Readjust the idling speed as required and continue adjusting until the maximum vacuum reading is maintained at a reasonable slow running speed.

Choke Adjustment.—In the fast idle position for cold starting, the plate should be open 0·8–0·9 mm. this distance being taken between the edge of the throttle plate and the carburetter body, with the fast idle adjustment screw on the top step of the fast idle cam.

The choke plate vacuum pull-down should be set at 4·5–5·0 mm. when measured between the lower edge of the choke plate and the body. The setting is obtained by depressing the vacuum piston to its full extent while holding the choke plate towards the closed position.

Alterations to the setting can be made by loosening the crankpin retaining nut on the choke spindle, turning the crankpin and retightening the retaining nut. With the choke plate held open, slight movement of the throttle lever will release the fast idle cam and the adjustment screw should then be positioned on the first step. If this position is not taken up, adjustment is made by bending the choke lever fast-idle cam abutment stop.

Acceleration Pump Stroke Adjustment.—Adjustment is made by relocating the accelerator pump link in the operating lever. In hot climates the link should be positioned in the outer hole, whilst in cold climates the link should be fitted to the inner hole, thus making for a longer stroke of the accelerator pump.

REMOVAL OF CARBURETTER.—Remove the air cleaner and drain the cooling system, disconnect the hoses to the automatic choke housing, and the throttle linkage at the carburetter. Detach the fuel and vacuum pipe connections, and then disconnect the engine ventilation tube and the float chamber ventilation tube. Unscrew the flange nuts and remove the spring washers, and carburetter together with gaskets and spacer.

Dismantling.—Disconnect the pump control arm, and the fast idle relay lever. Remove the float chamber cover and the two halves of the body and detach. Remove an 'O' ring from around the choke tube. Withdraw the float pivot pin to lift off the float assembly, and withdraw the needle valve. Unscrew the two screws securing the choke plate to its spindle, and remove the thermostatic spring and water housing as a unit.

Remove the three screws securing the automatic choke housing and spindle, unscrew the crankpin retaining nut and withdraw the choke spindle. Detach the gasket and washer and disconnect the fast idle cam from the choke lever. Unscrew the sleeve nut and remove the choke lever from the spindle. Unscrew the vacuum piston retaining screw and lift out the piston, then unscrew the pivot bolt and remove the fast idle relay lever and washers.

Unscrew the needle valve housing and washer and the screw on each side of the choke tube, and remove the emulsion block and its gasket. Withdraw the accelerator pump piston unit. The following jets are removed from the emulsion block using a well-fitting screwdriver:—Main and compensating jets from the lower section, idling jet and accelerator pump non-return valve from the upper section.

Unscrew the brass plug in order to remove the accelerator pump jet. Remove the economy valve housing, diaphragm, two gaskets and the spring. The part-throttle air bleed screw can then be unscrewed and removed.

Remove the accelerator pump lever, unscrew the brass nut with a shakeproof washer from the pump shaft and remove the operating cam. Detach the circlip and withdraw the shaft and brass collar. Take out the volume control screw and throttle stop screw. Remove the throttle lever, stop plate and washer and unscrew the two screws securing the throttle plate to its spindle to withdraw the spindle.

WEBER CARBURETTER.—This instrument is a dual barrel, vertical downdraught unit with a fully automatic choke for cold starting.

Slow Running Adjustment.—Before starting adjustment check that the air cleaner is clean, and that the throttle idling systems are in balance. If necessary, screw both volume control screws right home and then back off each 1½ turns. Tune the engine against a vacuum gauge which can be fitted by removing the blanking plug from the inlet manifold and screwing in a gauge adaptor tube.

Bring the engine up to normal operating temperature, and adjust the first throttle stop screw until the engine is running at 580–620 r.p.m. and then turn the two volume control screws clockwise or anti-clockwise to ensure the maximum vacuum reading, making sure that both screws are turned an equal amount to maintain balance. Continue by adjusting the idling speed and volume control screws to maintain the maximum vacuum reading.

Choke Adjustment.—In the fast idle position, the throttle plate should be open 0·75–0·8 mm., measured between the edge of the plate and the body on one barrel, both barrels having been previously synchronised, with the fast idle adjusting screw on the top step of the fast idle cam.

The choke plate vacuum pull-down is set at 2·5–3 mm. measured between the lower edge of the choke plate and the body, and this setting is obtained by removing the water housing and moving the shaft inwards to the end of its travel while holding the choke plate towards its closed position. Alteration to this setting is made by moving the adjustable stop to alter the travel of the shaft.

The choke operating temperature is governed by the tension of the coiled thermostatic spring and is pre-set, alignment marks being incorporated on the automatic choke and spring housings to assist in correct reassembly. Minor adjustment can be made if the operating temperature is too high, by slackening the clamping screws and turning the housing clockwise to slightly lower the operating temperature.

Pump Stroke Adjustment.—Two positions are provided, numbered 1 and 2, these numbers being cast on the pump cover adjacent to their respective holes. Normal summer temperature requires the use of No. 1 hole. To adjust the setting, drive out the pivot pin from the plain end with a suitable punch, insert the plain end of the pin into the other set of holes and drive the pin into the cover until the serrations are flush with the casing.

THROTTLE LINKAGE.—If the throttle does not open or close fully, adjust as follows: Disconnect the assembly at the throttle ball joint, check the initial settings of the accelerator and floor stops. Adjust these if necessary to ¼ in. and 1 in. respectively from the stop to the bracket and from the stop to the locknut washer.

Set the automatic choke to the idle position by manually turning the fast-idle cam clear of the adjusting screw, and with the accelerator pedal against the return stop, adjust the length of the connecting rod to suit the gap between the throttle shaft and relay lever. Tighten the locknuts and snap into position.

Depress the accelerator pedal and adjust the floor stop until the full throttle position is reached, and lock up with the nut. Check the pedal movement to make sure that full throttle and idle positions are obtained. If it is found that the full throttle position cannot be obtained up to this point, and that all adjustment is taken out of the pedal floor-stop, then the pedal return-stop should be screwed further into the bracket and the re-adjusting procedure carried out again.

GEARBOX

GEARBOX DATA

Ratios
First	3·163 : 1
Second	2·214 : 1
Third	1·412 : 1
Top	Direct
Reverse	3·346 : 1
Countershaft end-float	0·008–0·020 in.
Thrust washer thickness	0·061–0·063 in.
Number of rollers	44
First gear end-float	0·010–0·017 in.
Second gear end-float	0·005–0·009 in.
Third gear end-float	0·005–0·016 in.
Gearbox oil capacity	3¼ Imp. pints
Extra when overdrive fitted	¼ Imp. pint

COLUMN CHANGE ADJUSTMENT.—All bushes in the linkage are of polyurethane and do not need lubrication. To make adjustments, place the gear lever in the neutral position in the third and top plane, slacken the adjusting nuts at the end of the gate selector cable underneath the brake servo unit and by screwing up the adjusting nut, obtain a gap of 0·68 in. between the arm to the inner tube

(P108) SECTION THROUGH FINAL DRIVE

(P107) SECTION OF FOUR-SPEED GEARBOX

and the end of the outer tube. Lock up the adjusting nuts against their brackets and check the setting.

FLOOR CHANGE ADJUSTMENT.—Hold the gear lever towards the first/second gear plane so that there is a 0·050 in. gap between the tip of the gear lever and the insert in the gear selector pivot pin. Push the gate selector lever located on the top of the housing fully towards the front of the gearbox and screw up the adjusting nut at the front until it just touches the spring but does not compress it. Tighten up the rear adjusting nut to 50 lb./in. torque.

REMOVAL OF GEARBOX.—Disconnect the battery, remove the air cleaner and disconnect the throttle linkage. With column change, disconnect the gate selector cable and pivot arm from beneath the brake servo. With floor change, remove the centre console completely, detach the lower gaiter from around the gear lever, slacken the lock bolt on the lower end of the lever, remove the large through bolt on which the lever pivots, and lift out the lever.

From underneath the car remove the bolts securing the starter motor and move the motor to one side. On column change only, disconnect the two rods joined to the gear selector cross-shaft and remove the cross-shaft. If an overdrive or reversing light is fitted, suitably mark the wires and disconnect from the switch.

Remove the clutch operating cylinder from the clutch housing by unclipping the circlip. Unscrew the four bolts securing the propeller shaft to the rear drive pinion, and withdraw the shaft. Unscrew the speedometer gear retaining bolt from the extension housing. Disconnect the exhaust manifold pipes, and fit a jack underneath the sump.

Unscrew the centre bolt securing the cross-member to the gearbox together with the two self-locking nuts and bolts securing the member to the body. Remove the six bolts securing the gearbox to the clutch housing, support the gearbox and slide it carefully towards the rear of the car, lowering the jack under the sump as required to permit the gearbox to clear the underside of the body shell.

IGNITION

IGNITION DATA

Static advance (H.C.)	12° b.t.d.c.
(L.C.)	8° b.t.d.c.
Breaker spring tension	18–24 oz.
Dwell angle	35° ± 3°
Rotation	Clockwise when viewed from above
Breaker points gap	0·014–0·016 in.

TIMING THE IGNITION.—The static advance before top dead centre is when No. 1 cylinder is on compression stroke and the notch on the crankshaft pulley is in line with the timing mark on the front cover. To adjust without the use of a timing light, bring No. 1 cylinder to compression and align the timing marks, to give the initial timing position.

Check that the fourth line on the timing scale, counting from the diaphragm housing, is in line with the distributor body. Remove the distributor cap, slacken but do not remove the body retaining bolt and move the whole distributor body until the contact breaker points are just opening, with the rotor adjacent to No. 1 plug lead. Tighten the bolt and refit the cap.

Readjustment may be necessary on road test, and this is carried out when the engine is at its normal running temperature. Accelerate in top gear on a wide open throttle from 20–45 m.p.h. If heavy pinking occurs, retard the timing until just the faintest trace of pinking can be heard under these conditions of acceleration.

REAR AXLE

REAR AXLE DATA

Axle ratio	3·9 : 1
Number of teeth on crown wheel	39
Number of teeth on pinion	10
Crownwheel and pinion backlash	0·004–0·006 in.
Pinion bearing pre-load	12–15 lb./in.
Differential bearing pre-load	0·004 in.
Pinion thrust washer thickness	0·030–0·032 in.
wear limit	0·027 in.
Oil capacity	3 Imp. pints

GENERAL.—The rear drive unit is mounted between two rear suspension cross-members which are bolted to the body by rubber insulators. A hypoid crown wheel and pinion with a two-pinion differential are mounted within a cast iron differential housing. Adjustments follow the normal practice for hypoid rear axle assemblies.

REMOVING THE REAR DRIVE UNIT.—Jack up the rear of the car and jack up one of the suspension arms, using a piece of wood between the arm and jack. Make sure that the handbrake is 'off' and detach the brake cable from the lever pivoted on the rear suspension arm. Remove the pivot pin and return spring securing the handbrake lever, pull the lever towards the rear, lift it upwards and place it out of the way on the suspension arm.

Fit the spring clip tool to the suspension coil spring. Free the shock absorber from its lower mounting and lower the jack so that the coil spring can be removed. Remove the spring seat and rubber insulation pads from the top and bottom spring locations, and repeat the above series of operations for the other side of the car.

Disconnect the inlet pipe from the three-way

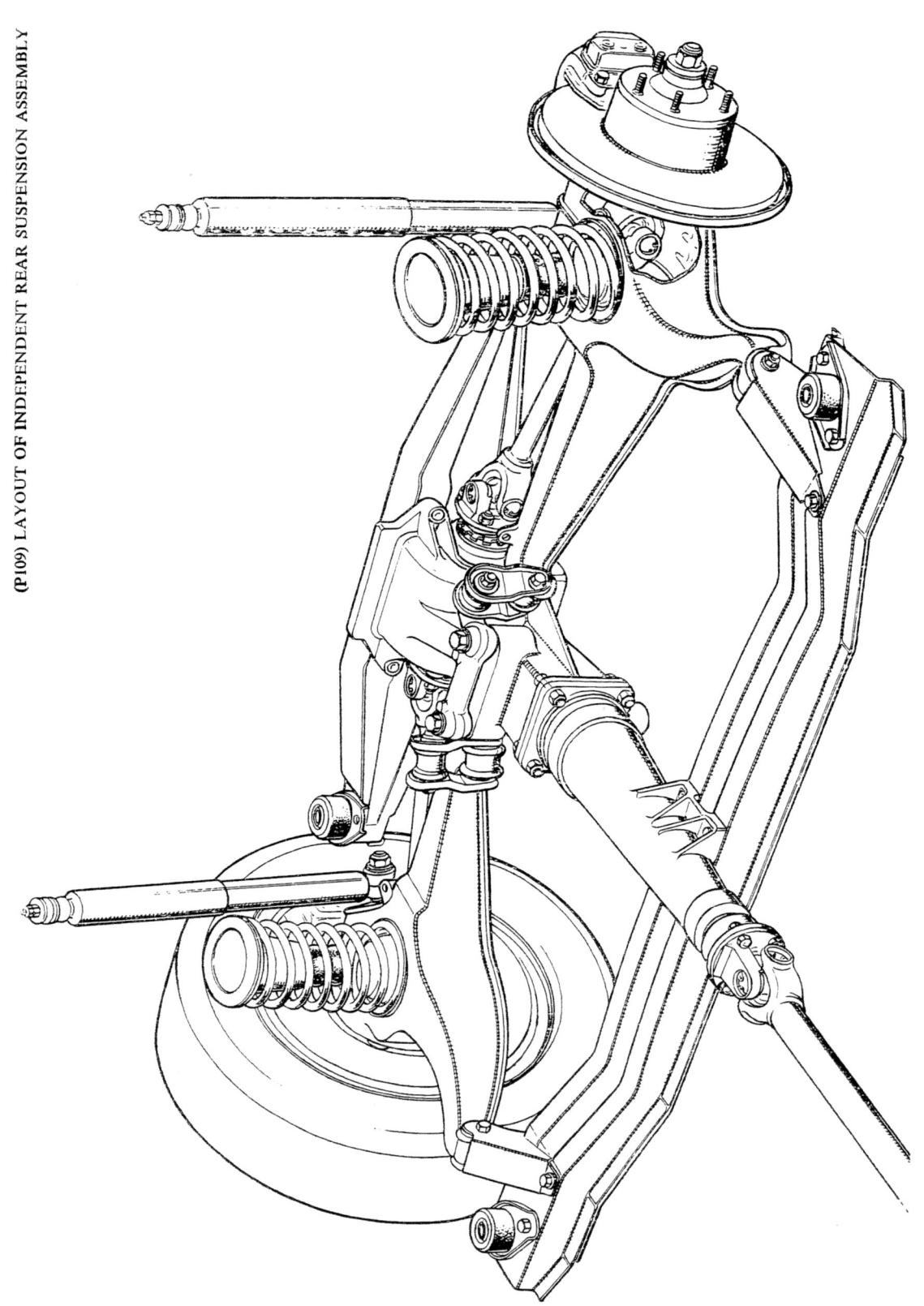

(P109) LAYOUT OF INDEPENDENT REAR SUSPENSION ASSEMBLY

brake pipe union fitted on the underside of the floor pan, fit plugs, and disconnect the union from the floor. Remove the handbrake cable guide from the differential extension housing and feed the cable forward so that it clears the rear suspension forward cross-member. Mark the mating flanges of the drive shaft and pinion and disconnect. Release the exhaust system clamp joint, unhook the exhaust from the 'O' rings and remove the pipe.

Place a trolley jack under the differential unit, remove the two nuts securing the cross-member to the underside of the car, remove the nuts securing the front cross-member bracket to the body side rails, lower the trolley jack and bring the whole drive assembly with the suspension units from under the car.

To remove the differential unit from the suspension, unscrew and remove the four bolts at both the front and rear cross-members, remove the two bolts at the shackle mounting bracket location, mark the flanges of the drive shafts, and remove the four bolts securing each half-shaft and lift these out of the way. The differential unit can now be removed.

REMOVAL OF DRIVE SHAFTS.—With the rear of the car jacked up, remove the splash guard protecting the face of the brake disc, extract the pin and clip securing the handbrake lever relay to the cam on the calliper body, and remove the locking nut cap from the top of the hinge pin after the stop pin has been unscrewed to allow the cam to be rotated. Use a hexagon key on the upper end of the hinge pin and with an open-end spanner, screw the hinge pin out of the lower seat and withdraw.

Pull the brake calliper from its mounting and support so that no strain is imposed on the flexible pipe. Remove the hub nut and spacer and pull off the hub and disc assembly using a puller tool. Unscrew four bolts securing the hub carrier to the suspension arm and detach the carrier. Mark the mating flanges of the drive shaft inner universal joint before unscrewing the four nuts. Pull shaft off its flange and withdraw.

Note: It is necessary to remove the rear portion of the exhaust system when taking out the drive shaft from the exhaust side of the car.

Renewing Hub Seals.—To renew the rear wheel hub seals and fit new bearings, jack up the rear of the car and remove the brake callipers and disc. Use a pointed tool to lever the grease seal from the inner end of the bearing bore. Position the carrier, flange-side downwards, over the jaws of a bench vice which are opened wide enough to allow the bearing to pass between them. With a suitable bearing punch, knock the bearing out of the carrier. The outer grease seal can now be pushed out of the bearing bore. When replacing, position the carrier on a press bed with the flange upwards, and press the bearing into position. Fit new grease seals to each side of the carrier.

STEERING

STEERING DATA

Type	Recirculating ball
Lubricant capacity	0.7 Imp pint
Ratio	20.6 : 1
Steering shaft bearing adjustment	Shims
Steering shaft bearing pre-load	0.003 in.
Rocker shaft adjustment	Adjusting stud and locknut
Rocker shaft pre-load:	
Measured at steering wheel rim	1¼–1½ lb.
Measured at flexible coupling	8–10 lb.

REMOVING AND DISMANTLING STEERING BOX.—The steering box is connected to the column through a flexible coupling in which a fail-safe device is incorporated. As the steering gear is not integral with the column it can be removed after disconnecting the flexible coupling and the drop arm, and removing the mounting bolts.

To Dismantle.—Unscrew the double hexagon-headed bolt securing the flexible drive, remove the four bolts retaining the top cover plate, and drain the lubricant, keeping the rocker shaft in engagement with the nut. Lift the rocker shaft out of the steering box and if necessary withdraw the thrust button, two coil springs and the spring seat from recess in top of shaft.

Slide the slotted roller from the peg on the steering nut, unscrew the four bolts and spring washers from the rear cover, pull off the thin oil seal retainer plate, the oil seal housing and the seal. Discard the seal. Remove the shim pack from the rear face of the box and withdraw the bearing spacer. Pull the shaft rearwards to dislodge the upper bearing, noting that there are ten balls in this bearing.

Lift the steering shaft complete with the nut through the opening in the top of the box. Withdraw the ten balls from the lower bearing and remove the bearing cup.

Unscrew the nut from the steering shaft and remove the 27 balls noting that the balls fitted in this assembly are not all the same size, so that they should not be mixed. Those fitted to the upper and lower shaft bearings are $\frac{9}{32}$ in. diameter, while those fitted in the steering nut are $\frac{5}{16}$ in. diam. Remove and discard the rocker shaft oil seal.

Remove rocker shaft bushes if they appear worn, by tapping with a suitable thread and using screwed rod and drift or extension piece.

When installing new bushes, ensure that the open end of the oil groove faces towards the steering shaft. Use a standard 1·00 in. reamer to ream out the two new rocker shaft bushes, the internal finished size being 1·00–1·001 in.

(P110) EXPLODED VIEW OF STEERING GEAR AND COLUMN

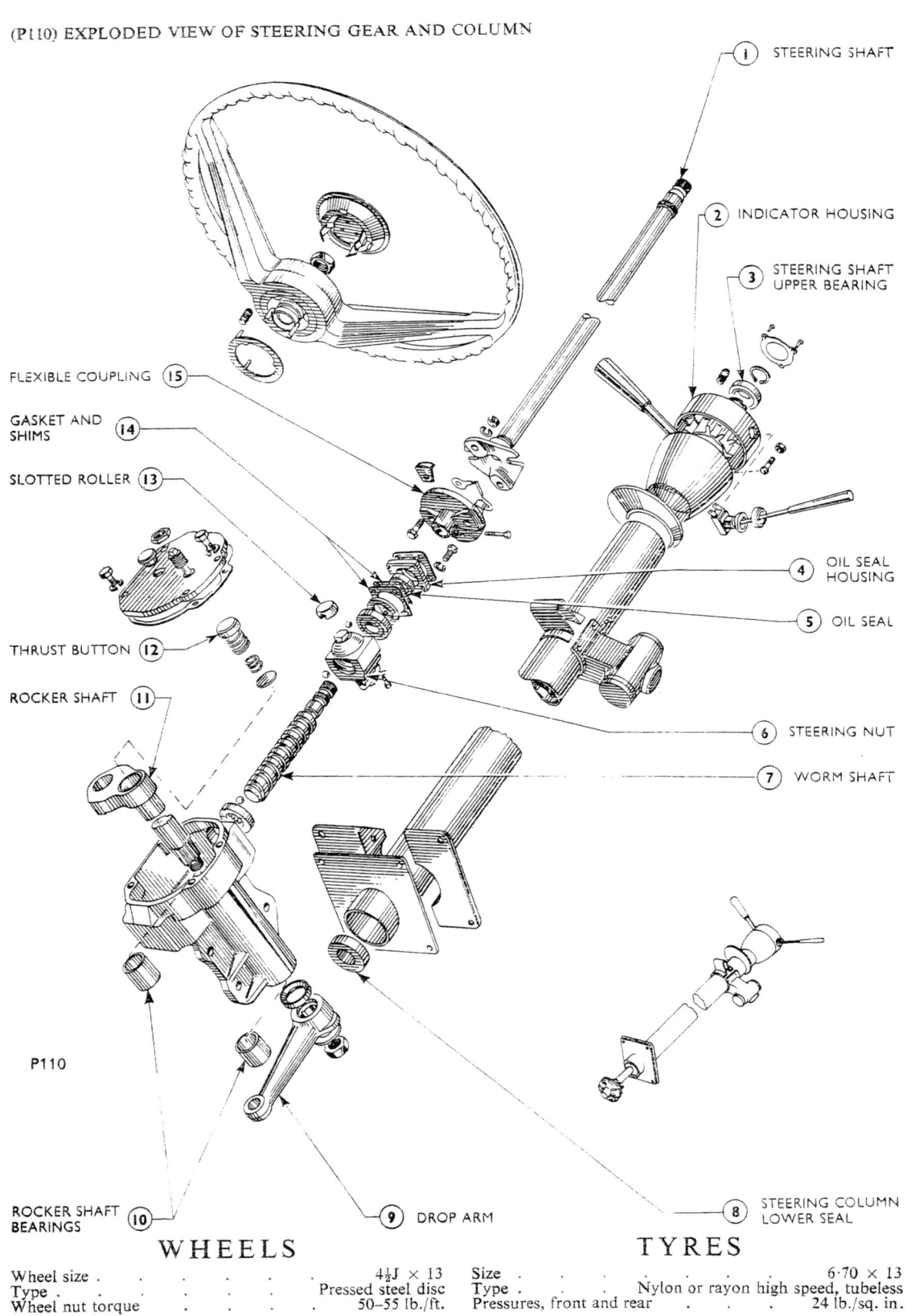

1. STEERING SHAFT
2. INDICATOR HOUSING
3. STEERING SHAFT UPPER BEARING
4. OIL SEAL HOUSING
5. OIL SEAL
6. STEERING NUT
7. WORM SHAFT
8. STEERING COLUMN LOWER SEAL
9. DROP ARM
10. ROCKER SHAFT BEARINGS
11. ROCKER SHAFT
12. THRUST BUTTON
13. SLOTTED ROLLER
14. GASKET AND SHIMS
15. FLEXIBLE COUPLING

WHEELS

Wheel size	4½J × 13
Type	Pressed steel disc
Wheel nut torque	50–55 lb./ft.

TYRES

Size	6·70 × 13
Type	Nylon or rayon high speed, tubeless
Pressures, front and rear	24 lb./sq. in.

71

"... *smooth, very quiet and effortless ... at its best when driven in a moderate and restrained manner ...*"

Number 29 MOTOR TESTED 1070 MILES

FORD ZEPHYR SIX ESTATE

PRICE
£922 plus £192 12. 11d.
purchase tax equals £1,114 12s. 11d.
overdrive £51 7s. 1d. extra.

How they run ...

MAXIMUM SPEED (m.p.h.)

Car	Speed
Ford Zephyr Six Estate £1,166	~88
Vauxhall Cresta Estate £1,306 (Velox £1,203)	~91
Citroen Safari £1,698	~91
Fiat 2300 Estate £1,426	~94

FUEL CONSUMPTION (m.p.g.) — ● OVERALL ○ TOURING

Car	Overall	Touring
Ford Zephyr Six Estate	~19	~22
Vauxhall Cresta Estate	~18	~24
Citroen Safari	~21	~27
Fiat 2300 Estate	~18	~25

ACCELERATION (seconds) — ● 0–50 ○ 20–40 IN TOP

Car	0–50	20–40 in top
Ford Zephyr Six Estate	~12	~11.5
Vauxhall Cresta Estate	~11	~8
Citroen Safari	~12	~17
Fiat 2300 Estate	~10.5	~10

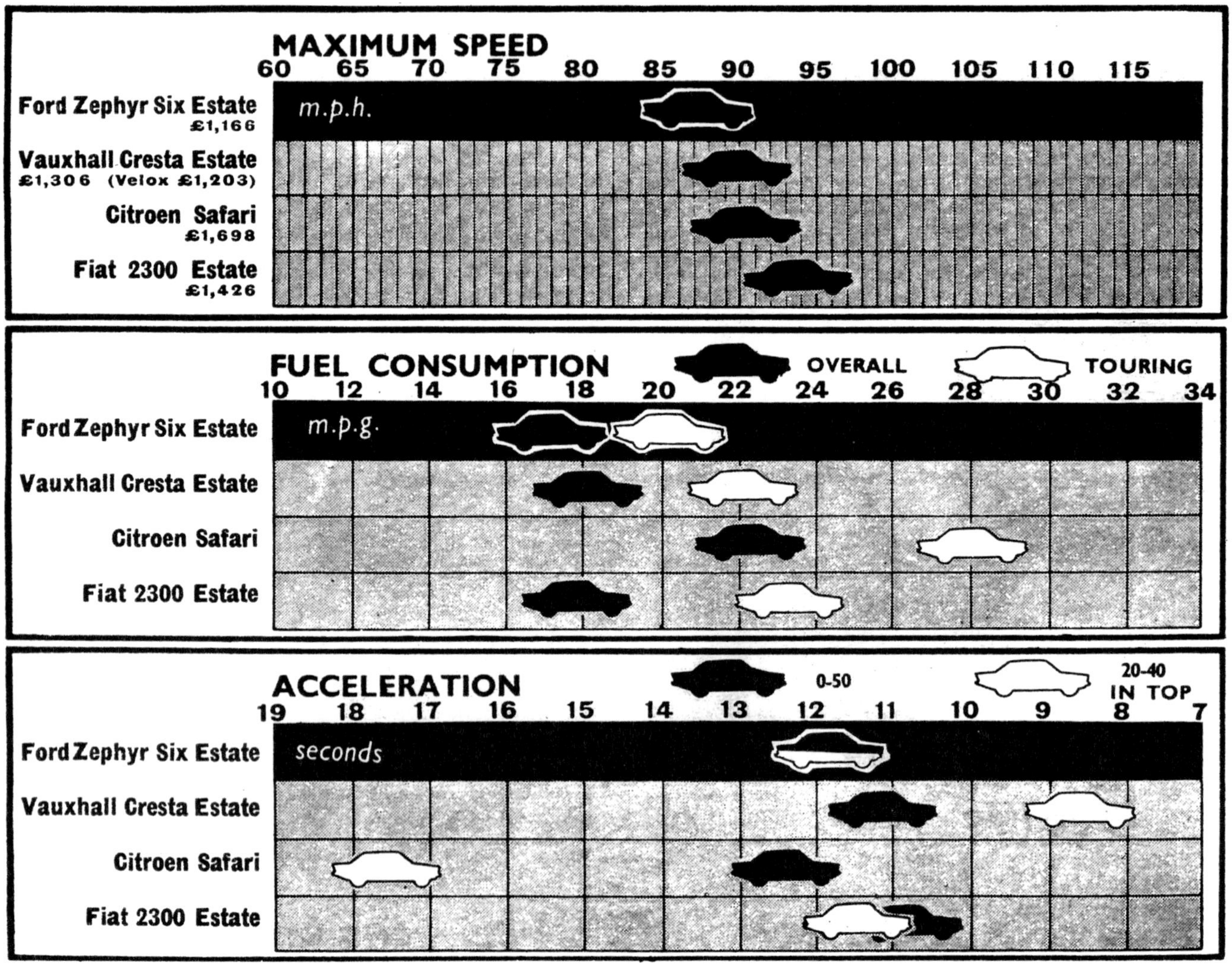

"... no trace of the 'added-on' look which distinguished so many earlier converted saloons".

IN Europe there is a curiously well-defined class of large estate cars which differ from their smaller competitors, not so much in luggage-carrying capacity, as in engine power and width; an additional inch or two on the track makes three-abreast seating practical as opposed to possible. Of this group, the Zephyr 4 is the cheapest; its own sister car the more powerful Zephyr 6 comes next. As usual, the conversion adds a good deal to the price of the standard saloon—in this case nearly £280.

Abbotts of Farnham have made a particularly neat job of the re-styling and, although the saloon body remains practically unaltered below the waistline, there is no trace of the "added-on" look which distinguished so many earlier converted saloons; the appearance is elegant and the rear-end treatment is rakish rather than bluff. The Zephyr has the usual estate-car advantages of a very large flat floor with the rear seat folded away; easy convenient loading through a one-piece top-hinged door, counterbalanced by struts linked to torsion bars below the floor; and the ability to carry very long objects on occasion. With both front and rear bench seats in use its luggage accommodation is not exceptional, since the floor level is rather high and the loading height at the rear-door opening is only a little over 2 ft.

Mechanically, the Zephyr is remarkably smooth, quiet and effortless, a description which applies as much to the all-synchromesh four-speed gearbox as to the six-cylinder engine. Even in the direct top ratio it is slightly overgeared, and we found the optional overdrive fitted to the test car rather superfluous, except for improving the fuel consumption on very long, straight roads or motorways. Easy performance is matched by good brakes and light controls. When pressed unduly hard, particularly on rough roads, the handling remains controllable, but becomes rather untidy; the car is at its best and most comfortable when driven in a moderate and restrained manner, and it is then capable of carrying a very heavy load without the marked deterioration in handling characteristics which afflicts some estate cars.

Performance and Economy

AN OUTSTANDING feature of the Zephyr is its very smooth, quiet, six-cylinder engine. From tickover to peak r.p.m. (4,750) it seems to have no vibration periods at all and only when approaching 5,500 r.p.m. in the lower gears does one become aware of a slight roughness; this is higher than it is ever necessary to go for optimum performance. Hot or cold, it starts immediately and only needs the choke for a short distance after a cold start.

The maximum speed of 91 m.p.h. was measured in direct top, a gear which gives over 20 m.p.h./1,000 r.p.m., so that maximum-power engine speed is only reached in favourable conditions. In overdrive, a considerably lower maximum was recorded and acceleration is distinctly leisurely; this is essentially a gear for constant-speed cruising on long, straight roads. The single-carburetter, over-square engine, less highly tuned than the similar unit in the Zodiac, develops its maximum torque at very low r.p.m., but a high bottom ratio made a restart on the 1-in-3 test hill impossible; the 1-in-4 gradient, however, was dealt with comfortably. Long left-hand corners taken very fast produced signs of engine cutting due to fuel starvation.

Driven hard, the overall fuel consumption of 18·6 m.p.g. may be considered moderate for a big car, especially as mixture grade fuel (94 octane) seemed to satisfy its needs. We used Premium for performance testing as this is specifically recommended in the handbook. At middle-range cruising speeds the consumption graph shows that overdrive will achieve a fuel economy in the region of 10% but, even so, the touring fuel consumption of 21·6 suggests that gentle driving will not pay quite such big dividends as in some cars.

FORD ZEPHYR SIX ESTATE

Components which need regular servicing under the bonnet are all easily accessible. Until recently there were chassis greasing points but these have now been eliminated.

Transmission

THE CLUTCH is light with a comparatively short travel but rather a large free movement. It grips very firmly but lacks feel, so that it is easy to stall the very quiet engine on take-off until one becomes familiar with the car. Little criticism can be levelled at the gearbox—it has quiet gears, effective although not unbeatable synchromesh on all four closely spaced ratios, and a light, positive steering-column gear change.

Our test car was equipped with Borg-Warner overdrive, an optional extra costing £51 with tax. It can be engaged at any speed over 35 m.p.h. simply by releasing the accelerator and pausing momentarily. This means that it can be used in conjunction with any of the forward gears—even bottom at a pinch. When extra acceleration is needed for overtaking, direct drive can be regained by hard pressure on the throttle pedal to operate the kick-down switch. Below 30 m.p.h. the car will freewheel when overdrive is selected; some drivers prefer this in heavy traffic conditions since it makes for very smooth progress, others dislike being entirely dependent on the brakes; by pulling a knob under the facia the overdrive can be locked out of action altogether leaving a perfectly normal four-speed transmission.

In taking performance figures, overdrive was used only in fuel consumption tests and not in acceleration through the gears. Some cars need such a device to achieve quiet, effortless, high-speed cruising, but in the case of the Zephyr engine noise is so low as to fall below the threshold level of other sounds and it is impossible to tell whether the overdrive is in use or not. It would be true to say, there-

Items needing regular routine maintenance are within easy reach under the rear-hinged counterbalanced bonnet. 1 and 2, brake and clutch fluid reservoirs. 3, coil. 4, distributor. 5, oil dip stick. 6, carburetter. 7, oil filler cap. 8, windscreen washer reservoir.

The squab of the back seat folds forward to form a platform 5 ft. 10 in. long. The floor is quite high, but the big rear door lifts well out of the way to make loading easy. Spare wheel is under the floor.

Performance

Test Data: World copyright reserved: no unauthorized reproduction in whole or part.

Conditions: Weather: Dry, warm, gusty wind 10-30 m.p.h. (Temperature 54°-66°F, Barometer 29·5-29·3 in. Hg.) Surface: Dry tarmacadam. Fuel: Premium grade (97 Octane R.M.).

ACCELERATION TIMES

0-30 m.p.h.	...	...	...	4·9 sec
0-40	...	...	...	7·9
0-50	...	...	...	11·1
0-60	...	...	...	16·7
0-70	...	...	...	22·9
0-80	...	...	...	33·4
Standing quarter mile			...	20·3

M.p.h.			O/d Top sec.	Top sec.	3rd sec.
10-30	...	...	—	9·2	6·1
20-40	...	...	—	11·1	6·9
30-50	...	...	—	12·4	7·8
40-60	...	...	19·6	14·2	9·1
50-70	...	...	25·6	17·9	11·2
60-80	...	...	42·0	20·3	16·7

1, heater air control. 2, 3 and 4, radio. 5, heater temperature. 6, choke. 7, fuel gauge. 8 and 11, indicator warning lights. 9, speedometer. 10, mileage recorder. 12, water thermometer. 13, parking light switch. 14, main lighting switch. 15, heater fan. 16, fan warning light. 17, ashtray. 18, gear lever. 19, handbrake. 20, screen wipers and washers. 21, horn ring. 22, oil pressure warning light. 23, main beam warning light. 24, ignition warning light. 25, overdrive lock. 26, ignition/starter. 27, indicators/headlamp flasher. 28, bonnet release.

Trim, equipment and roominess are identical to those of the Zephyr saloon. Both seats will accommodate three people, the front bench having a central folding arm rest.

fore, that its main advantages, to be balanced against initial costs, are the economic ones of slightly better fuel consumption and lower engine wear.

Handling and Brakes

FOR ALL normal purposes the Zephyr is a safe, unobtrusive and effortless car to drive. The steering is light, even for low-speed manoeuvring, and feels much higher geared than the figure of 4¼ turns for an indifferent lock would suggest. The car goes accurately where the driver intends without close attention on his part; strong, gusty sidewinds do not disturb it unduly, and neither understeer nor oversteer effects are prominent. It did, however, seem rather sensitive to white lines and ridges.

It is not a car designed for the sporting fast driver, and any attempt to drive it in such a way reveals less pleasant characteristics, including appreciable roll and tyre squeal and a tendency for the rear axle to hop on bumpy corners. In these circumstances the driver has to work much harder and it becomes more difficult to follow a predetermined line. On wet and slippery roads, adhesion is not as good as with many modern cars, particularly at the back, but mild tail slides can be corrected very easily and quickly.

Girling brakes (disc front and drum rear), aided by a vacuum servo, give powerful, fade-free deceleration with light pedal pressures and no roughness or judder, even when applied at very high speeds, although clumsy use of the pedal emphasizes a tendency to nose-down pitching in rapid stops. A "pull-and-twist" handbrake projecting from the facia is quite convenient to use and will hold the car on a 1-in-3 gradient.

Comfort and Control

GENEROUS interior width and the absence of floor controls make it possible to carry three people comfortably on both the front and rear bench seats, but leg room is provided on a less liberal scale. A driver of average height (5 ft. 9 in.) needs to slide the seat right back to achieve a proper relationship with the pedals, and this leaves barely adequate knee room in the back for long-legged passengers. The driver sits high with a commanding view over the bonnet and the steering wheel is well placed. Both seats

MAXIMUM SPEEDS

Mean lap speed banked circuit...	91·0 m.p.h.
Best one-way ¼-mile ...	96·8
O/d top gear ...	85·0
3rd gear ...	80·0
2nd gear ...	51·0
1st gear ...	36·0
"Maximile" Speed: (Timed quarter mile after 1 mile accelerating from rest)	
Mean ...	88·2
Best ...	92·8

BRAKES

Pedal pressure, deceleration and equivalent stopping distance from 30 m.p.h.

lb.	g.	ft.
25	·25	120
50	·62	48
75	·85	35½
100	·96	31

HILL CLIMBING

At steady speed		lb./ton
Top ...	1 in 11·1 ...	(Tapley 200)
3rd ...	1 in 7·4 ...	(Tapley 300)
2nd ...	1 in 4·7 ...	(Tapley 470)

FUEL CONSUMPTION

Touring ...	21·6 m.p.g.
Overall ...	18·6 m.p.g.
	(=15·2 litres/100 km.)
Total test distance ...	1,070 miles

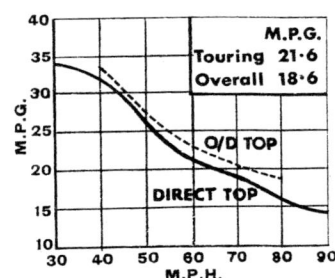

STEERING

	ft.
Turning circle between kerbs:	
Left ...	35¼
Right ...	34¼
Turns of steering wheel from lock to lock	4¼

SPEEDOMETER

30 m.p.h.	8% fast
60	7% fast
90	5% fast
Distance recorder	3½% fast

WEIGHT

	cwt
Kerb weight (unladen with fuel for approximately 50 miles) ...	25
Front/rear distribution ...	52½/47½
Weight laden as tested ...	28¾

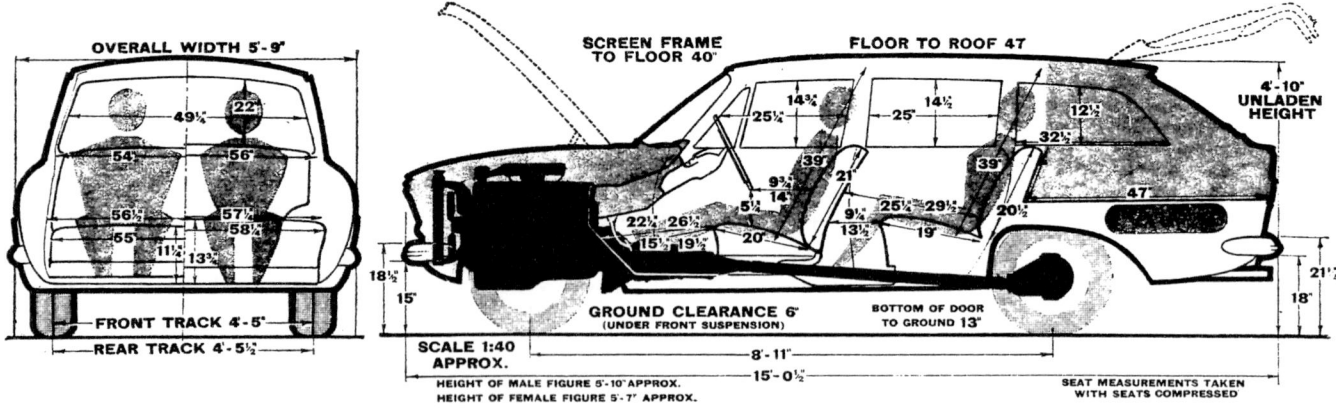

FORD ZEPHYR SIX ESTATE

have comfortably shaped, but very upright, squabs and lack of side-support, common to bench seats, is emphasized by a tendency for the squabs to give way at the edges, so that the driver finds himself pushed towards the door.

Not unnaturally, the ride is at its best with a fairly heavy load; unladen it feels a little lively at the rear although, in fact, there is very little pitching and wavy roads are taken very well. Rough surfaces, however, evoke rattles from the tail door and the rear seat, and a certain amount of shake in the structure detracts from the feeling of solidity.

Wind noise is present at high speeds to an average, although not excessive, extent, even with all the windows shut. Mechanically, the car is extremely quiet and above 50-60 m.p.h. it is practically impossible to hear or feel the engine at all. The front quarter lights can be opened without adding a great deal to the noise level, and this increases considerably the flow of cold air through the ventilating system. As far as it was possible to judge in mild summer weather, the heating system (an optional extra) is extremely powerful.

A large interior mirror, which gives a wide field of vision through the rear window, is supplemented by a wing mirror for occasions when the luggage is piled high in the back. The headlights of our car were out of adjustment but appeared to give a good night-driving beam.

Fittings and Furniture

IN GENERAL, the interior follows that of the Zephyr 6 saloon and the facia panel is identical. For safety, it has padded edges and there is also a flexible moulded surround to the rearview mirror and the sun visors are of soft construction. Below the facia on the passenger's side there is a large parcel shelf; the lockable glove box above it is rather small and sharp-edged, and its lid was sometimes difficult to pull open.

Control knobs are identified by symbols and their positions are easy to learn, but the combined wiper/washer control is not easy to reach round the edge of the steering wheel. By rotating this knob the speed of the wipers can be varied, and they work quietly and effectively even at high speeds. A lever projecting from the steering column on the opposite side from the gear control operates the direction indicators and houses a small button in the end which flashes the headlamps. When the car is parked at night it is possible, by means of a parking switch, to extinguish the near-side tail and side lamps and thus relieve the battery load, this switch also isolates the starter solenoid to prevent the absent-minded owner from driving away in a half-lit condition. It is possible to operate it accidentally when reaching for the bonnet release and the resulting loss of the starter can puzzle the unfamiliar driver.

The spare wheel and tools are recessed below the wooden deck of a rather high rear floor which is covered by a buttoned-down cover of plastic-backed material. The boot of an ordinary Zephyr saloon would probably carry more luggage than could be stacked in the rear of the estate car without piling it so high as to endanger the rear passengers under sudden braking. But when the rear seat squab is folded down on top of the cushion the rear deck length is increased to 5 ft. 10 in., so that it would be possible for two people to sleep in the back. There is a gap of about a foot between this platform and the front seat-back; a stainless-steel tube prevents luggage from sliding over the front edge.

MAKE Ford • MODEL Zephyr Six Estate • MAKERS Ford Motor Co. Ltd., Dagenham, Essex

ENGINE
- Cylinders .. 6
- Bore and stroke .. 82·55 mm. × 79·5 mm.
- Cubic capacity .. 2,553 c.c.
- Valves .. Overhead (pushrods)
- Compression ratio 8·3 : 1 (optional 7 : 1)
- Carburetter .. One Zenith Downdraught 36 WIA-2
- Fuel pump .. A.C. mechanical
- Oil filter .. Full flow
- Max. power (net).. 98 b.h.p. at 4,750 r.p.m.
- Max. torque (net) 134 lb. ft. at 2,000 r.p.m.

TRANSMISSION
- Clutch .. Ford/Borg and Beck 8½ in. s.d.p.
- Top gear (s/m) .. 1·00 (overdrive 0·77)
- 3rd gear (s/m) .. 1·41 (overdrive 1·085)
- 2nd gear (s/m) .. 2·21 (overdrive 1·70)
- 1st gear (s/m) .. 3·16
- Reverse .. 3·35
- Overdrive.. Borg Warner
- Final drive .. 3·545 hypoid bevel
- M.p.h. at 1,000 r.p.m. in:—
- O/d top gear .. 26·5
- Top gear .. 20·4
- O/d 3rd gear .. 18·8
- 3rd gear .. 14·5
- 2nd gear .. 9·2
- 1st gear .. 6·5

CHASSIS
- Construction .. Integral body/chassis

BRAKES
- Type .. Girling (disc front, drum rear) with Bendix vacuum servo.
- Dimensions .. 9¾ in. discs, 9 × 2¼ drums
- Friction areas .. 99 sq. in. of friction lining working on 345 sq. in. swept area of discs and drums

SUSPENSION AND STEERING
- Front .. Macpherson strut type with coil springs and anti-roll bar
- Rear .. Live axle and leaf springs
- Shock absorbers:
- Front .. Armstrong telescopic
- Rear .. Armstrong lever
- Steering gear .. Ford/Burman recirculating ball
- Tyres .. 6·70-13 4-ply tubeless

COACHWORK AND EQUIPMENT
- Starting handle .. No
- Jack .. Screw type
- Jacking points .. 2 each side below doors
- Battery .. 12 volt, 57 amp hr.
- Electrical fuses .. One (plus one for radio)
- Indicators .. Self-cancelling flashers
- Screen wipers .. Self-parking variable speed
- Screen washers .. Optional extra—manual
- Sun visors.. .. 2
- Locks:
- With ignition key Front doors, glove box and boot
- Interior heater .. Optional extra, fresh air type.
- Extras .. Overdrive, automatic transmission, whitewall tyres, etc.
- Upholstery .. P.v.c./Chevron or Saranweave
- Foor covering .. Fitted carpets

MAINTENANCE
- Sump .. 6¼ pints S.A.E. 20/20W
- Gearbox .. 4·3 pints S.A.E. 80
- Rear axle .. 2½ pints S.A.E. 90 hypoid
- Steering gear .. S.A.E. 90 hypoid oil
- Cooling system .. 17 pints (plus 1½ pints for heater) (2 drain taps)
- Chassis lubrication None
- Ignition timing .. 8° before t.d.c.
- Contact breaker gap .. ·014–·016 in.
- Sparking plug type Champion N8 or Autolite A.G. 5–A
- Sparking plug gap ·023–·028 in.
- Tappet clearances (cold) Inlet ·014 in., Exhaust ·014 in.
- Front wheel toe-in 1/16 to 3/16 in.
- Castor angle .. +0° 41′ to −0° 19′
- Tyre pressures .. 24 to 30 lb. all round

what gives the NEW ZODIAC and Zephyr their luxury ride?

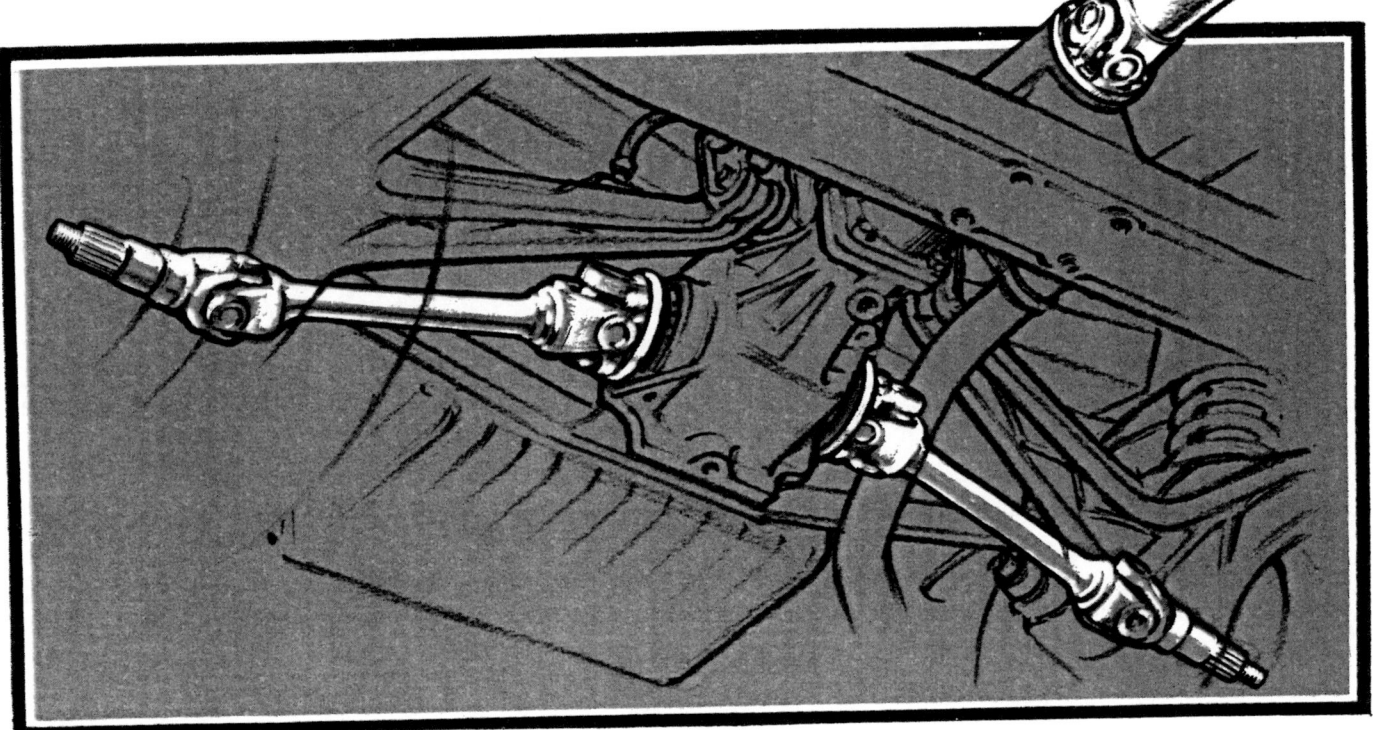

By using B.R.D. transmission equipment on the new "Mark of Distinction" Zodiac and Zephyr cars, Ford Motor Company again confirm their confidence in B.R.D. products manufactured from forgings supplied by GARRINGTONS LIMITED.

The Best from Britain for British cars.

independent rear suspension with B.R.D Rear Axle Drive Shafts and Universal Joints

These independent articulating axles incorporate special joints of small swing diameter, capable of carrying high torque loads. Designed specifically by B.R.D. in conjunction with Ford Motor Company Engineers, they emphasize the lead B.R.D. now hold in independent rear axle design and manufacture.

 LARGEST SUPPLIERS OF LINE DRIVE SHAFTS AND INDEPENDENT REAR AXLES TO THE BRITISH VEHICLE INDUSTRY.
B.R.D. COMPANY LTD
ALDRIDGE STAFFS ENGLAND

The largest manufacturers of Forged Components for the Motor Industry
GARRINGTONS LIMITED BROMSGROVE and DARLASTON

AUTOCAR, 22 April 1966

Autocar ROAD TEST

NUMBER 2076

ZEPHYR 6 Mk IV 2,495 c.c.

AT A GLANCE: New 5-seater replacement for Mark III Zephyr with smooth vee-6 engine. Sensitive fade-free disc brakes on all four wheels. New independent rear suspension behaves better laden than with the driver only on board. High levels of wind and road noise, but engine very quiet. Comfortable seats and lots of room inside, but larger external dimensions and very heavy steering when parking. A worthwhile improvement on the previous model.

MANUFACTURER:
Ford Motor Co. Ltd., Warley, Essex.

PRICES
Basic .. .. .. Not available
Purchase Tax .. .. when these
Total (in G.B.) .. .. pages closed for
                          press. See first
EXTRAS (inc. P.T.)   page of News
Ford push-button radio   and Views later
Ford inertia-reel seat   in this issue.
  belts ..
Bucket seats ..

PERFORMANCE SUMMARY
Mean maximum speed .. 96 m.p.h.
Standing start ¼-mile .. 19·6 sec.
0–60 m.p.h. .. .. 14·6 sec.
30–70 m.p.h. (through gears) 15·8 sec.
Overall fuel consumption .. 19·4 m.p.g.
Miles per tankful 290

FORD (in this country, at least) are not a company to make changes purely for the sake of change. A new Ford model, therefore, is a new car which warrants the fullest treatment we can give it and this issue contains drawings and technical information on all details of the new Mark IV saloons, except its performance on the road; that is the purpose of this test.

We chose what we considered to be potentially the most popular version of the new range, a Zephyr 6 with floor-change manual gearbox and bucket front seats. With its close-to-£1,000 price tag all in, this is the Ford that most firms would choose for their junior executives and for family men with a lot to carry. It is one of the largest cars, size for price, available today.

The Zephyr 6 has a 2½-litre version of the new vee-6 engine with bore and stroke identical with those of the 1700 V-4 Corsair. It develops 112 b.h.p. net at 4,750 r.p.m., which is 14 b.h.p. more than the previous Zephyr in-line six and 3 b.h.p. more than the previous Zodiac. Maximum torque is practically the same as the old Zodiac's with 137·5 lb.ft. at 3,000 r.p.m. The new car has put on a bit of weight—it is larger overall—and turns the scales at 25·8 cwt ready for the road, about 1¼ cwt heavier than the last Zephyr 6 we tested almost exactly two years ago on 10 April 1964.

Bearing these figures in mind, one might expect the new car to perform about as well as a Mark III Zodiac, but it is difficult to verify this because we have only tested the automatic versions in recent years. Compared with the previous Executive Zodiac, the new Mark IV Zephyr is much more sprightly. From rest, 60 m.p.h. is reached ½ sec earlier in 14·6 sec and 80 m.p.h. comes up 3·2 sec sooner in 28·7 sec. Maximum speed was a regular 96 m.p.h. mean for several laps of the M.I.R.A. banked circuit with 102 registered on our electric fifth-wheel speedometer over the most favourable quarter-mile.

In its performance characteristics the new engine feels much like that of the 2-litre V-4 Corsair GT we tested recently. There is a lot of bottom-end punch, and although the engine can be run up to almost 6,000 before valve bounce sets in, it does not pay to go more than a couple of hundred r.p.m. beyond the peak of the power curve (4,750) for maximum acceleration.

During this testing we were impressed with the quietness of the engine, for it never made itself heard except at the very top end; the only noise was the whoosh and roar of well-muffled intake and exhaust. In terms of smoothness there are no noticeable vibration periods, yet the ▶

Autocar Road Test 2076

MAKE: Ford

TYPE: Zephyr 6 Mk IV

Speed range and time in seconds

m.p.h.	Top (3·90)	Third (5·50)	Second (8·63)	First (12·32)
10—30	—	7·4	4·4	3·3
20—40	9·5	6·1	4·4	—
30—50	9·7	6·8	5·6	—
40—60	10·7	7·8	—	—
50—70	12·0	11·6	—	—
60—80	16·5	19·2	—	—
70—70	26·4	—	—	—

WEIGHT
Kerb weight (with oil, water and half-full fuel tank): 25·8cwt (2,896lb–1,317 kg)
Front-rear distribution, per cent F. 57·5; R. 42·5
Laden as tested .... 28·8cwt (3,232lb–1,471kg)

TURNING CIRCLES
Between kerbs .. L, 37ft 5in.; R, 38ft 7in.
Between walls .. L, 40ft 4in.; R, 40ft 7in.
Steering wheel turns lock to lock .. 5·5

PERFORMANCE DATA
Top gear m.p.h. per 1,000 r.p.m. .. 19·4
Mean piston speed at max. power 1,880ft/min.
Engine revs at mean max. speed .. 4,950 r.p.m.
B.h.p. per ton laden 78

OIL CONSUMPTION
Miles per pint (SAE 10W/30) 2,000

FUEL CONSUMPTION
At constant speeds
30 m.p.h. .. .. 30·5 m.p.g.
40 m.p.h. .. .. 28·8 m.p.g.
50 m.p.h. .. .. 26·6 m.p.g.
60 m.p.h. .. .. 23·3 m.p.g.
70 m.p.h. .. .. 20·1 m.p.g.
80 m.p.h. .. .. 17·5 m.p.g.
90 m.p.h. .. .. 14·6 m.p.g.
Overall m.p.g. .. 19·4 (14·6 litres/100km)
Normal range m.p.g. 17-25 (16·6-11·3 litres/100km)
Test distance .. .. .. 872 miles
Estimated (DIN) m.p.g. 18·3 (15·5 litres/100km)
Grade .. .. Premium (96·2-98·6 RM)

TEST CONDITIONS
Weather .. Cloudy with 5-10 m.p.h. wind
Temperature .. .. 6 deg. C. (43 deg. F.)
Barometer .. .. .. 29·7in Hg.
Surfaces .. .. Dry concrete and tarmac

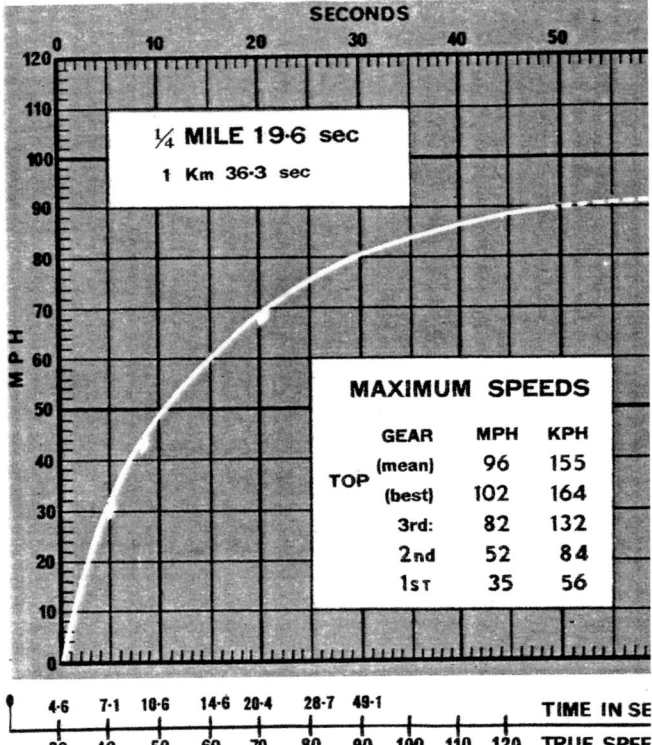

¼ MILE 19·6 sec
1 Km 36·3 sec

MAXIMUM SPEEDS
GEAR		MPH	KPH
TOP	(mean)	96	155
	(best)	102	164
3rd:		82	132
2nd		52	84
1st		35	56

							TIME IN SE
4·6	7·1	10·6	14·6	20·4	28·7	49·1	
30	40	50	60	70	80	90	100 110 120 TRUE SPEE
32	42	51	60	70	79	88	97 INDICATE

BRAKES (from 30 m.p.h. in neutral)
Pedal load	Retardation	Equiv. distance
25lb	0·25g	120ft
50lb	0·58g	52ft
75lb	0·80g	38ft
90lb	1·00g	30·1ft
Handbrake	0·30g	100ft

CLUTCH Pedal load and travel—30lb and 4·5in.

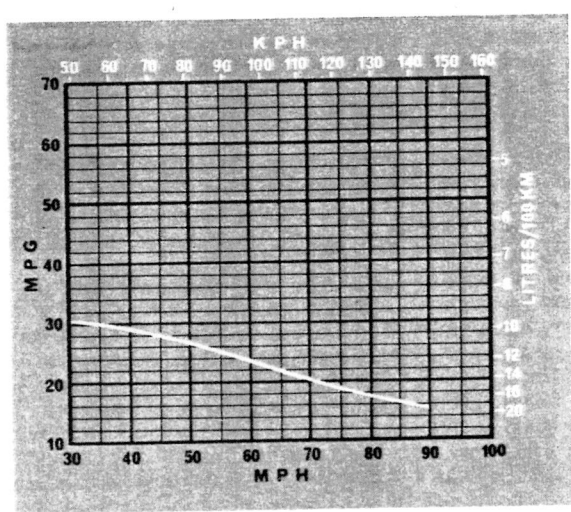

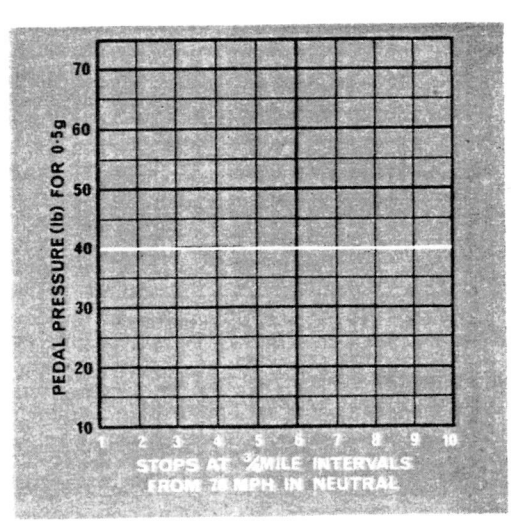

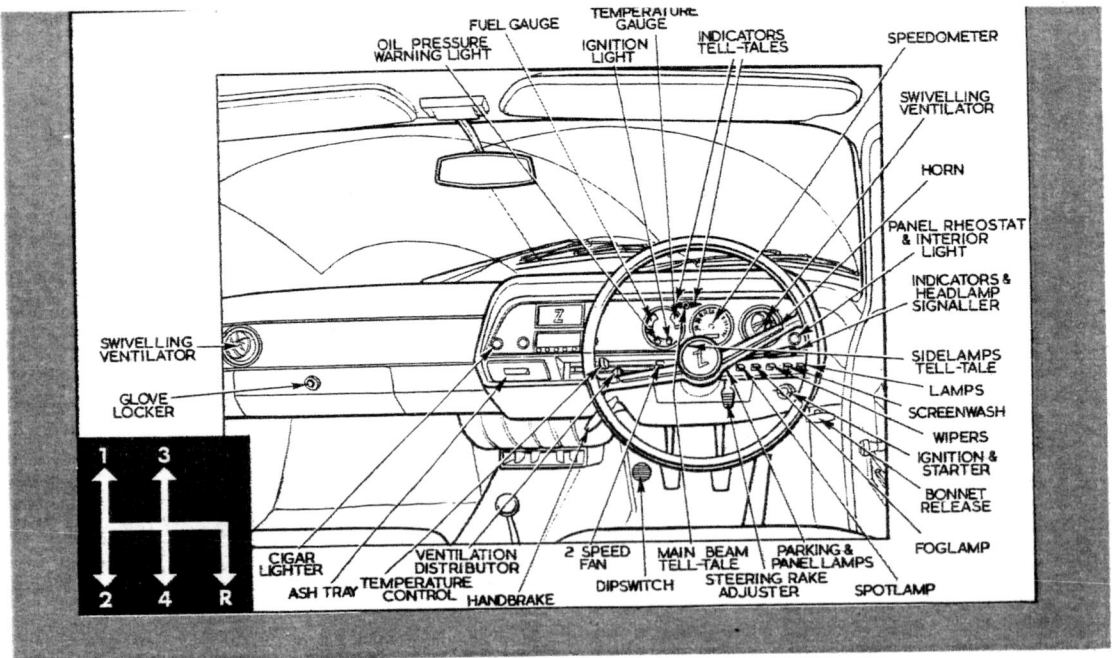

sweetness of a straight six has been lost somehow particularly at the top end of the rev range.

Acceleration figures for each gear show the torque curve to be very flat with almost equal times for each 20-m.p.h. increment. First and second feel rather low compared with third, which has a very flexible range from 10 to 80 m.p.h. if required, although it is better not to go beyond 70 before changing into top. This makes it an ideal ratio for sweeping through the twisty bends of a country lane or surging past the inevitable 30-40-m.p.h. heavy lorries on trunk roads; each time we changed down again into second when baulked, we realized third would still have been adequate.

Gearbox

The gear-change is well up to the high standards set by smaller Fords, and in many ways it works and feels just like that of a GT Cortina. Reverse is over to the right beyond top, with a strong spring guard, and a key to the positions is moulded in the knob. The synchromesh is light and completely effective on all four ratios. The indirect gears run quietly with only a very faint, subdued whine that would never normally be noticed.

Despite being ½in. bigger in diameter and using higher spring clamping pressures, the clutch now needs a pedal load of only 30lb. instead of 50, while the travel has been cut by one inch to 4½in. There is an overcentre diaphragm spring which causes a rather abrupt take-up, but we were able to spin the back wheels on dry concrete without clutch slip. No hot smells or loss of efficiency resulted from easing the car from rest on a 1-in-3 test hill.

Ford still use Girling brakes with servo assistance, but discs are now fitted at the back as well as at the front; the entire system, including the handbrake, is self-adjusting for wear. Tested in neutral from 30 m.p.h., the brakes showed slightly better sensitivity than those of the previous model, with the rear wheels starting to lock at 75lb on the pedal and an easy 90lb giving 1g retardation. During fade tests from 70 m.p.h. there was no loss of braking power at all, quite the opposite in fact, with the driver having to lift off from 45 to 35lb during each stop to maintain 0·5g on the Mintex gauge (our chart shows the mean value of 40lb). There was, however, some slight unevenness as temperatures increased, which made itself felt as a twitching through the steering wheel; occasionally we encountered this on the road as well. Stability during braking was excellent, with barely any slewing.

The handbrake is worked by a T-handle on the left of the steering column under the facia. It is easy to reach with seat belts fastened and will fly off rather noisily by twisting the handle and letting go. Tested on its own from 30 m.p.h. it proved easily able to lock the back wheels (0·3g) and held facing up or down a 1-in-3. However, we were surprised to find that when pulled really hard, as it needed to be, the handle came out a good 6in. beyond its more usual "on" position as something in the mechanism stretched. We would be worried about leaving the car parked like this, in case it caused some permanent set.

In one aspect the new big Ford has stolen a march on its competitors in the 2½-3-litre class by including independent rear suspension in its specification. The system used is a new and unusual one with articulated fixed-length drive shafts and semi-trailing alloy wishbones. It is designed to give controlled camber and toe-in angle changes to the wheels to

The spare wheel is mounted in the nose of the car to leave the boot area clear. Radiator header tank, battery and screen washer bottle are all easy to fill and the dipstick is tucked away near the top radiator hose

Doors open very wide and each has an armrest-cum-door-pull; the interior release handles are recessed into rectangular openings below the window winders. Front-seat backrests are fixed but the steering wheel is adjustable for height

Ford Zephyr 6 Mk IV ...

The boot is deep and roomy with no spare wheel to steal the space from luggage. Its lid is countersprung but there is a high sill to lift cases over

compensate for the weight distribution differences between the driver-only and fully-laden conditions. With passengers in the back it is most effective and the previous tail-swing and poor steering response when carrying a load is effectively eliminated.

In this loaded state there is an initial stable understeering tendency as the corner is entered which decreases towards the apex, so that the car seems to follow round without any further correction. With only two in the front there is a big difference. As the car goes into the turn it feels just the same until the lateral forces reach the tail, which rolls appreciably and causes very definite oversteer. During fast laps of a closed test circuit we lifted the inside rear wheel at this point, and rather than be caught out by sudden breakaway, we preferred to flick the tail round in stages by sawing at the steering wheel.

On ordinary roads, of course, one never reaches this point and the Zephyr can be thrust through fast bends, leaning hard but holding a very stable line. The liveliness of the previous beam axle is all gone, and we were able to patter over a level crossing diagonally without the tail tramping sideways.

Unfortunately, the new Zephyr has more weight in the nose (the spare wheel has been moved up front) and although the steering ratio is slightly lower, wheel effort has increased. We measured 5½ turns between locks on a 38ft turning circle, although practically half a turn of this seemed to be springiness in the mounting of the mechanism. There is a very strong self-centring action which does not decrease much with speed, and manoeuvring to park the car calls for beefy muscular effort. We feel this would be beyond the strength of most women and any family man whose wife likes to drive should seriously consider the optional power assistance.

Despite its extra weight and bulk, the new Zephyr returned an overall fuel consumption of 19·6 m.p.g., which is slightly better than before. Big Fords always seem to have a dip in their steady speed fuel graphs around 70 m.p.h., so our estimated (DIN) figure is for once unrealistically low. On a run we found 20 m.p.g. quite easy to get, although cruising at near 90 m.p.h. gives only 15 m.p.g. At this speed the engine is revving at 4,650 r.p.m., with a very low mean piston speed of 1,830 ft/min, well within its potential.

At speed the Zephyr runs more true than its predecessor, and showed remarkably little deviation when buffeted in gale-force winds across the downs behind Beachy Head. On motorways it runs straight right up to the maximum speed and there is no delay to steering movements when changing lanes.

One of our criticisms of the last Zodiac was the loud wind roar from the front door edges above 75 m.p.h. and despite fixed front quarterlights

Tested before its announcement, the Zephyr 6 was disguised with masking tape over the name plates. There are no over-riders and the twin reversing lamps under the bumper are extra

TOTAL Approx £1,000
PRICE £1,162
£1,180
£1,119
£2,355

HOW THE FORD ZEPHYR 6 Mk IV COMPARES:

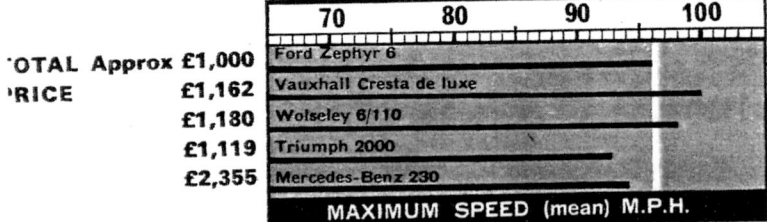

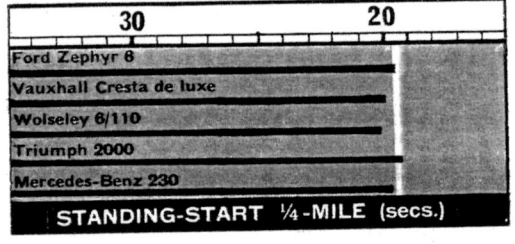

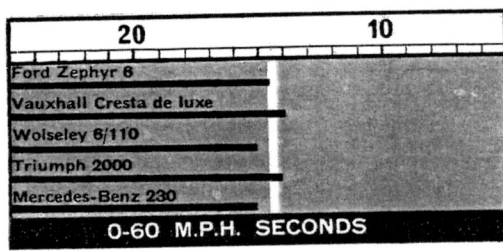

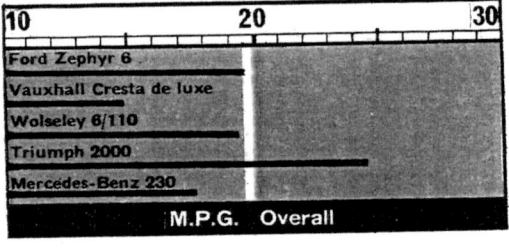

there has been no improvement. With the radio speaker on the rear shelf we had trouble hearing it unless the volume was turned well up for motorways.

Another aspect where the car disappoints is in the comfort of the suspension. The ride is harsh and decidedly noisy, every dip and ridge seeming to thump through the body, first at the front and then the back. Taut springs and firm damping give good resistance to pitching and the Zephyr ran across our close-set concrete waves in a most impressive and level manner. The washboard corrugations were completely ironed out from 40 through to 60 m.p.h., but the *pavé* track caused a lot of rattles and disturbing bangs as the wheels bounced about on the uneven slabs.

The tyres, too, make a lot of noise at times, whining on some types of road dressing and growling deeply on others. All the time it feels as if they have been inflated too hard, and although we started the test at 28 p.s.i. all round for our performance work, there was no improvement when we later let them down to the normal pressure of 24.

For the first time these British Fords are fitted with an automatic starting device on the carburettor and it worked perfectly throughout the test. Hot or cold, one just touched the accelerator, turned the key and the engine started. Always it would pull away smoothly without any hesitation and idled smoothly. Within a mile from leaving home in the morning the heater blows out warm air.

Aeroflow ventilation of a type is fitted to the new Mark IV cars, but it is not as good as the system used on the Cortina and Corsair. There are extractor grilles on the rear quarters which dispense with the need to open a window for a through flow, and face-level ventilators each side of the facia. However, the temperature control proved very insensitive, switching itself suddenly from hot to cold over less than half an inch of its 4·5in. range and spoiling the effectiveness of the sensibly planned distribution valve. On the credit side, back seat passengers receive a good flow round their feet and at the same time those in the front can arrange for a refreshing cool stream to blow at face level.

The optional bucket seats are good, with much better springing than in the past. All the occupants sit high and have good visibility, so there is no disadvantage on this score in having to travel in the back. Lengthening the wheelbase by 8in., plus the shorter engine, have improved legroom by at least as much and the driver can now get well back from the pedals if he has long legs. In the back it is possible to stretch out, cross the knees and move around to prevent getting stiff on long runs.

An innovation is the vertical adjustment for the steering wheel which raises or lowers its rim by 1·5in. and is released and locked by a quick acting lever below the facia on the right.

In front of him the driver sees a small circular speedometer, accurate in the middle of its range and (even more unusual) pessimistic at the top end; there is a total mileage recorder (with 10ths) only, and this too is dead accurate. On the left is a matching dial containing a steady and accurate fuel gauge with water thermometer alongside and two warning lights below. To the right of the column is a row of piano-key switches for the accessories, all labelled and illuminated at night to match the instruments.

Most features of the new Ford show considerable improvements over the Mark III models. It is a bigger car overall, with much more room inside and considerably better and more comfortable furniture. There is a substantial performance increase, better braking, less heavy fuel consumption and the roadholding (especially with the car laden) has been made safer. The comfort of the suspension and general noise level seem less good comparatively, but the price is a competitive one in a very tough sector of the big-car market.

SPECIFICATION: FORD ZEPHYR 6 Mk IV, FRONT ENGINE, REAR-WHEEL DRIVE

ENGINE
Cylinders	6, in 60 deg. vee
Cooling system	Water; pump, fan and thermostat
Bore	93·7mm (3·69in.)
Stroke	60·3mm (2·38in.)
Displacement	2,495 c.c. (152·2 cu. in.)
Valve gear	Overhead, pushrods and rockers
Compression ratio	9·1-to-1
Carburettor	Zenith 38 IVT
Fuel pump	AC mechanical
Oil filter	Full-flow, renewable element
Max. power	112 b.h.p. (net) at 4,750 r.p.m.
Max. torque	137·5 lb. ft. (net) at 3,000 r.p.m.

TRANSMISSION
Clutch	Single dry plate, 9in. dia., diaphragm spring
Gearbox	4-speed, all synchromesh
Gear ratios	Top 1·0, Third 1·41, Second 2·21, First 3·16, Reverse 3·35
Final drive	Hypoid bevel, 3·9 to 1

CHASSIS AND BODY
Construction	Integral with steel body

SUSPENSION
Front	Independent MacPherson struts with co-axial coil springs and dampers, anti-roll bar
Rear	Independent, semi-trailing arms, coil springs, telescopic dampers

STEERING
Type	Recirculating ball
Wheel dia.	16·5in.

BRAKES
Make and type	Girling discs front and rear
Servo	Girling vacuum type
Dimensions	F, 9·6in. dia.; R, 9·9in. dia.
Swept area	F, 214 sq. in.; R, 139 sq. in. Total 353 sq. in. (245 sq. in. per ton laden)

WHEELS
Type	Pressed steel, 5 studs, 4·5in. wide rim
Tyres	Goodyear, Firestone or India tubeless (Goodyear G.8 on test car), 6·70-13in.

EQUIPMENT
Battery	12-volt 53-amp. hr.
Generator	Lucas C40L 300 watt d.c.
Headlamps	2 Lucas sealed-beam 50—40-watt
Reversing lamp	Extra
Electric fuses	10, including circuit breakers
Screen wipers	2-speed, self-parking
Screen washer	Standard, electric
Interior heater	Standard, fresh-air type
Safety belts	Extra, anchorages built in
Interior trim	P.v.c. seats, p.v.c. headlining
Floor covering	Looped-pile carpets
Starting handle	No provision
Jack	Screw pillar
Jacking points	2 each side under sills
Other bodies	None

MAINTENANCE
Fuel tank	15 Imp. gallons (no reserve) (68 litres)
Cooling system	19·5 pints (including heater) (11 litres)
Engine sump	9·5 pints (5·4 litres) SAE 10W/30. Change oil every 5,000 miles. Change filter element every 5,000 miles.
Gearbox	3·25 pints SAE. Change oil after first 5,000 miles only.
Final drive	3 pints SAE 90. No change necessary
Grease	No points
Tyre pressures	F and R, 24 p.s.i. (normal driving); F and R, 28 p.s.i. (fast driving)

This is the automatic version of the new Zodiac. There is a rev counter, separate gauges for fuel, oil pressure, water temperature and battery current, and the speedometer has a trip mileage recorder. Reclining front seats are standard

Zodiac Automatic 2,994 c.c.   DRIVING IMPRESSIONS—By THE EDIT

ONE way of getting to know a new car is to pound it south over the not-always good roads extending from Tunis on the Mediterranean coast of Africa to the edge of the desert proper, and back again. This we did with the new 6-cylinder Fords, covering some 630 miles in two days. The few main metalled roads have long undulating straights with unmade edges; while we were there, they were buffeted by fierce winds. Storms and wind together caused wash-outs where normally dry stream beds crossed the road and there were some sand-drifts. There is practically no traffic, and we were able to hold over 90 m.p.h. for long periods on some desert roads, both Zephyr and Zodiac showing how rapidly they can cover long distances.

Our first car was a Zodiac with automatic transmission, export suspension and tyres blown up to 28 p.s.i. for fast, hot driving. Only recently run-in, it was less lively than we had expected and would not reach 100 m.p.h. The automatic changes were smooth and sweet, and the maximum kick-down speed was only 54 m.p.h. We decided that this car was not representative from the performance point of view and that the hard tyres and stiffer suspension were detracting from the ride and causing vibration through the body. The engine was always smooth and mechanically quiet, such sound as was heard at high r.p.m. seeming to come from the fan and perhaps the air intake. A gentle, easy-going engine, this three-litre was over its power peak and beginning to run out of breath well before the red section of the r.p.m. indicator was reached.

Full throttle acceleration in D1 gave change-up speeds of about 22 and 55 m.p.h. These are below the designed figures, which should be 32-36 and 60-64 as confirmed by other automatic Zodiacs in the group taken to Tunisia. The kick-down speeds at full throttle should be about 2 m.p.h. below the maximum change-up speeds. The gear-selector on our car could have been more positive.

When we changed to a manual Zodiac we found it was faster and accelerated better than the automatic one. It reached 102 m.p.h. quite quickly and pulled really hard in the middle r.p.m. range. In this respect the advantage of the extra half-litre as compared with the Zephyr 6 engine could be felt. Even so, the Zephyr 6 we drove in Tunis h plenty of performance and would a top the 100 m.p.h.

Both Zodiacs and Zephyrs w very stable directionally and neit camber nor ridges along the r edges caused the cars to wander, a the strong winds scarcely affec them. What we at first took directional vagueness proved to an impression gained from the lc geared steering which has a slop feel around the centre point, with much ineffectual movement of steering wheel. Towards the lo the steering quickens and wl taking a positive steering action car controlled quite precisely.

The present sealing of the do and windows is perfectly satisfact for its primary purposes, but thought to be responsible for external wind noise, which becor too loud at high cruising spee Otherwise, the Zodiacs in particu were a lot quieter than the moc they replace.

Comfort is noticeably improv too; the Zodiac seats are thic padded and "dead" sprung so ride was smoother, apart from fact that the new suspension g more level progress. The absenc roll and of sideways movements of tail over rough roads contribute lot to the stability and comfort the occupants. For the first t also there is leg- and foot-room spare in the back of a big Ford.

One or two sections of road Tunisia were still being made and it was over these that the advantages of the i.r.s. beca apparent. The cars held a strai course, hands-off, with no hopp about at the back, with pretty g suspension damping, and at no t did our car bottom (carrying th people and luggage).

Although North Africa was hot three weeks ago, there w sufficient heat and humidity exercise the ventilation system. Be 40 m.p.h. there is little ram ef but the rather noisy booster fan (or very fast) churns the air thro the ducts very well. At hig speeds plenty of fresh ram air fl through the face-level ducts. screen wiper blades are long efficient and gave a clean sweep even pressure at over 80 m.

We finished our days of dri fresh and relaxed, which speaks for the cars. There were no bre downs in over 15,000 miles communal driving and no single used more than one pint of oil du the two days of testing.

Mobil congratulate all concerned in the development of the outstanding new Zodiac/Zephyr Mk. IV range, and are proud to have the approval of Ford of Britain for Mobiloil Special to lubricate and protect these 'Marks of Distinction.'

Mobiloil Special—approved by Ford of Britain

Fred Hart

Chief Engineer, Passenger Cars, Ford Motor Company

Discusses the background of the Mark IV Fords with RONALD BARKER

BARKER: Presumably your mind is already preoccupied with projects for the next decade Mr. Hart; could you give us some idea of this factor of forward planning. When did you start thinking about the Mark IV range just introduced?

Hart: We commenced this project late in 1961 in our advanced design section, which is mainly concerned with packaging of the people and components. After about 2½ years on this we got full programme approval in December 1963.

Barker: How much influence does the American parent exert over the basic engineering concept of each new model—its physical dimensions, engine type and capacity, suspension and so on?

Hart: None directly, but with a number of American directors there must be some transatlantic influence. I think this produces a happy combination of what we need in world markets. All the engineering, though, is based in Dagenham.

Barker: Can you make use of Detroit's facilities if you wish?

Hart: Very much so; we use Detroit considerably. We have full access to all American advance work on new ideas and materials.

Barker: What about their enormous testing facilities?

Hart: Most of the testing is now done in Europe where we have proving grounds very much like those in America. At one time we used the American test grounds at Dearborn and Romeo in Michigan, but now, in addition to our track here in Essex, we have one at Lommel in Belgium.

Barker: How much of the styling is dictated by Detroit and executed there?

Hart: Again, the styling is exclusively Dagenham, but influenced, of course, by world-wide requirements; the Mark IV is typical of this European or international styling; but America feels that, as we have to sell the car, the shape must be exclusively ours. Naturally they would object if they found something particularly poor about it.

Barker: It's a brave design, breaking new ground for a front-engined, rear-drive car, with the virile Mustang look.

Hart: That's a very good description of it; we call it the elegant thrusting look.

Barker: Yet the shorter your engine the longer bonnet you put over it!

Hart: We say here the big car man has power under the bonnet, and the longer the bonnet the stronger this image.

Barker: Where have these cars been tested on public roads outside this country?

Hart: Mainly in Belgium, on circuits combining *pavé*, rough going and hilly country—totalling about 60,000 miles in that area alone. Another 10,000 miles in Belgium, Austria, Germany and Italy on ride and handling and mountain circuits. We did 15,000 miles in Scandinavia, mostly north of the Arctic Circle. For extended durability trials in a hot climate we ran up about 5,000 miles over the dusty mountain roads of Spain. Add some 10,000 miles hammering up and down *autobahnen*, and you have some 100,000 miles overseas.

Barker: Approximately how many prototypes of each model did you make; and how long have they been running?

Hart: Of 20 prototypes, 9 were mechanical ones disguised by Fairlane bodies, but with correct underbodies so that we could get the suspension and other mechanicals correctly related. The first of the nine phase 1 prototypes was ready by October 1963, whereas the 11 phase 2 and phase 3 prototypes, complete to the correct body form, were progressive from the beginning of January 1965.

Barker: How much does it cost to put a new range like this into production from scratch?

Hart: It cost about £28m to produce the first car off on the Mark IV, which is the total figure including the engines. £2m was spent on engineering the car excluding engines, which were developed as a separate project.

Barker: Is pure research on materials and so on included in those estimates?

Hart: Oh, no. What we call the support costs would add perhaps another 100 per cent. My own costs, for instance, and those of other senior people are not included in the basic cost of designing a vehicle.

Barker: Let's take the ace question now—your adoption of independent rear ▶

Placing the spare wheel in the nose is claimed to provide a safety cushion in a head-on accident, as well as keeping the boot free for luggage

Mk IV Fords...

suspension. Did prestige value or engineering considerations take precedence in this decision?

Hart: Engineering every time, for better ride and handling, particularly over rough territories and in Europe, of course, where much motoring is done over indifferent roads, and the independent suspension gives you a big plus. Certainly there is prestige value as well which, if secondary to the engineering reasons, is important because we have competitors like Mercedes and Citroen on the Continent and the 2-litre Triumph here.

Barker: Mind you, a good live axle design is still better than a second-rate i.r.s.

Hart: True, and we at the Ford Motor Company delayed having i.r.s. until we found one that was better than a current beam axle.

Barker: I suppose you've been playing with i.r.s. designs since long before this project?

Hart: Oh, yes; we evaluated just about every type we could find before settling for the semi-trailing link type as used on the Mark IV. It was to overcome the main problem of this layout—friction in the drive-shaft sliding splines restricting the value of the i.r.s.—that led us to fixed length shafts and swinging links or shackles. This allowed the axle to move in the plane we wanted on a free basis—that is, the inner part of the wishbone moves quite freely without restricting the changes of camber and toe-in. In fact, it helps these.

Barker: Is this i.r.s. much more costly than a live axle once you've got it in production?

Hart: It's certainly more expensive, but the quite considerable advantages are well worth it in this class of car.

Barker: Any suspension is a compromise; certain factors such as cost, ease of manufacture and maintenance are more important to you than they are to, say, Rolls-Royce.

Hart: Yes, packaging advantages have to be taken into account. But, again, we haven't found a better i.r.s. than the one we've chosen to employ. It certainly gives us advantages in cost and sheer simplicity. And its durability has been well proven.

Barker: Will the increased tyre section offset the higher rate of wear that usually occurs when a car's cornering power is increased?

Hart: Certainly, and I think a good geometry will help.

Barker: The new car can carry a greater load than the Mark III, I suppose?

Hart: Right, but it is well within the capacity of the tyre; in fact, smaller tyres would carry the weight of the new Zodiac, but the larger section improves the ride as well as the mileage.

Barker: Might we say that they look better, too?

Hart: Of course.

Barker: Your more discerning customers will welcome the wider tracks and longer wheelbase. But surely these assets are also costly?

Hart: The extra length in the track control arms, axle shafts and so on do not amount to much, but the advantages are considerable. The designer, of course, always wants as long a wheelbase and as wide a track as he can have within the confines of the car. A long wheelbase gives him a better

Rear suspension unit is carried on two independent cross-members with widely spaced rubber mounts to the body structure. Inner wishbone arms are shackled

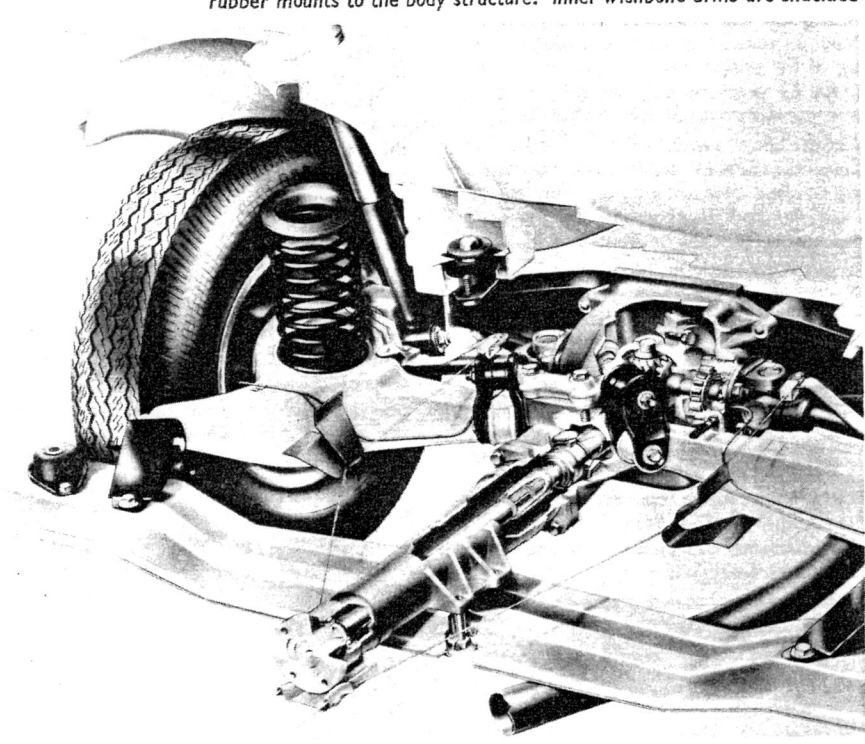

ride with less pitch; a wider track and consequently a wider spring base improves the handling. But of course he must get this within the confines of the car and the styling. Some cars are styled so that the wheels are outside the body limits; others such as this type of saloon look better with the wheels just inside the vehicle's maximum width.

Barker: You must have had road noise problems: How did you deal with these?

Hart: The front suspension now has compliance between the struts and stabilizer bars, allowing the wheels to move fore-and-aft enough to take up road bumps with the minimum noise. We also have P.t.f.e. bushes to allow the struts to slide more easily, and the springs are offset relative to the strut's centre-line to prevent or reduce "striction." So this unit moves freely. The rear suspension is supported in a sub-

Mark IV is extremely competitive in this class of car.

Barker: What is your opinion of radial ply tyres? Do you think they will become universal in time?

Hart: There's no doubt in my mind that they are the tyres of the future, but their manufacturers have still some way to go. Lack of uniformity in this tyre still creates problems, such as lateral shake. But their advantages in tread life, fuel economy and vehicle handling are much to be desired.

Barker: And noise?

Hart: Well, I'm not too sure about this. You can fit radial ply tyres to some cars and get wonderful results; in others the suspension had to be designed in conjunction with them.

Barker: When driving the Mark IV, I noted particularly good turning circles, so helpful when parking a large

Barker: True, few have achieved a good turning circle with f.w.d.

Hart: We thought we could achieve almost all that f.w.d. had to offer for less cost with i.r.s.

Barker: Why do you need such a large steering-wheel, yet still a low-geared steering ratio? Couldn't you get away with a smaller wheel, in which case you could dispense with the slight vertical adjustment to the column?

Hart: The obvious answer is to make parking effort as light as possible without the expense of having to have power steering. But the wheel is ½in. smaller than the Mark III's, you know.

Barker: Is this part of the penalty for having fat tyres? Because I can remember big cars that were very little heavier to steer with much higher gearing.

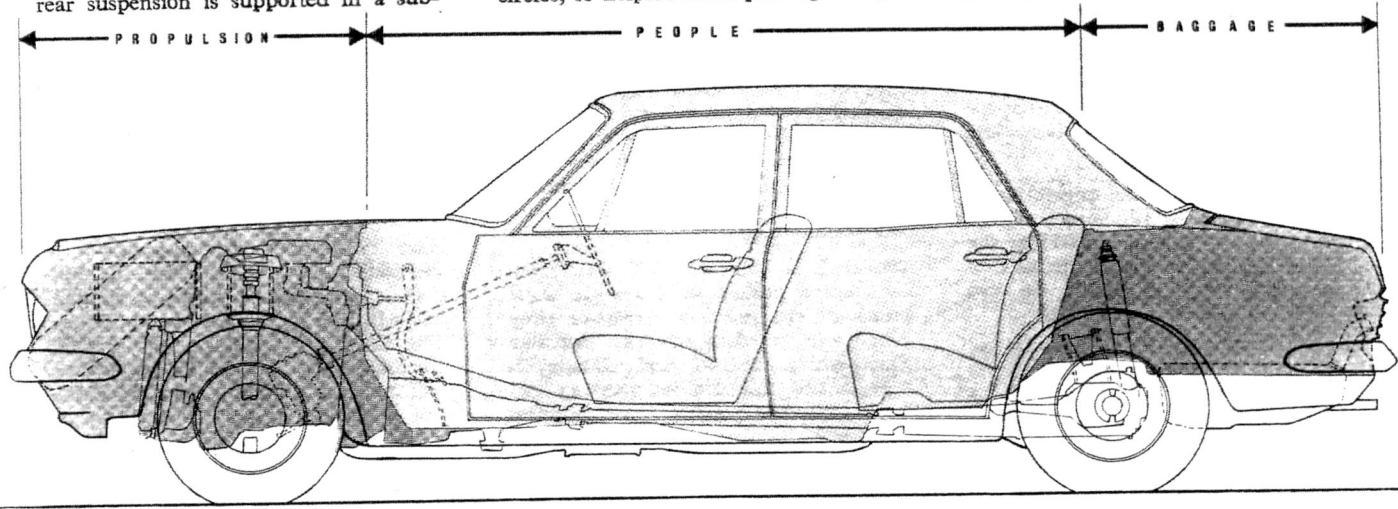

How the body volume is divided between engine, passengers and baggage

frame with two independent cross-members supported on fairly soft rubber mountings that absorb noise coming through the system.

Barker: But neither of them has any fore-and-aft compliance?

Hart: There's compliance in the wishbone bushes. We've spread the cross-members very widely, which allows fairly soft mounts without having the diff unit bouncing up and down. Moreover we've tuned the whole suspension system to the body frequency, so that road noises are not transmitted through the hull. We had noise problems at first, through trying to mount the rear suspension unit on the floor panel, well forward of the nose of the pinion. We then found a noise path coming through the floor, so brought this cross-member back, extended it out to the rocker panels and mounted the wishbone arms directly on the cross-member.

Barker: Which are the rocker panels?

Hart: They are the outer skin panels on the very outside of the car below the door.

Barker: Are you content with the standard of road noise?

Hart: Well, one is never content with the standard of road noise in any car, if it can be heard at all; but I think the

car. How have you achieved this despite the longer wheelbase?

Hart: It's quite a problem to get the back lock angle. We kept it to 40 deg to avoid any over-toggling action; with the front lock angle we went considerably sharper than Ackermann. This only affects the maximum lock condition, and a bit of scrubbing occasionally will not materially add to wear when turning into a garage or doing a U-turn.

Barker: Because you'd be going so slowly.

Hart: Yes, in other words it's only the last bit of the lock which has been modified to improve the turning circle. And, of course, the width of the track helps us to get the wheel round sharp before fouling the frame.

Barker: Did you consider front-wheel drive?

Hart: Yes, we considered front-wheel drive, but only very superficially, because of the disadvantages for a vehicle of this size. In particular, the effect of the extra weight on the front end on manoeuvrability and braking. Weight transfer from rear to front calls for some restrictive means in the braking system, which are not always functionally good. Then there is its effect on the turning circle.

Hart: It's just a penalty you pay in larger cars. Nearly all heavy modern cars have either a high steering effort or power assistance. But a large tyre footprint does make matters worse.

Barker: Do you yourself like power steering?

Hart: I don't really drive cars with power steering frequently enough to get used to its rather insensitive feel. However it is a great boon to women drivers, particularly in town. This is, incidentally, the first English Ford for which power steering has been optional. It's a Hydrosteer mechanism with a Mustang-type pump by Thompson.

Barker: Were the new vee-engines designed and developed entirely by Ford of Great Britain, or partly in Dearborn and Cologne?

Hart: Naturally we did co-operate with Dearborn and Cologne, because we couldn't ignore the many design requirements of vee-engines of which they have experience, but the designs themselves are entirely British. We looked over the shoulders of Cologne and America to see what to do, as well as what not to do, before setting about designing these 60 deg. vee-4 and vee-6 engines. ▶

Mk IV Fords...

Barker: Any comments on their production costs?

Hart: A vee-engine with separate cylinder heads and so on could never be as cheap as an in-line.

Barker: How important do you rate fuel consumption these days, as a selling feature?

Hart: Very highly; yet with this class of car economy is less important to most customers than other features such as performance—and so the accent tends to go more towards performance than economy. I think we have hit a good compromise with the Mark IV.

Barker: Safety is currently said not to sell cars; the general public tends to shun discussion of the matter. But what special safety features are incorporated in the new range?

Hart: The long nose, short engine and forward mounted spare wheel accord with the established principle that space is required for crash energy absorption.

Barker: Like a concertina?

Hart: Yes, and with the engine-transmission mass to absorb some of the shock and the spare as a cushion, the final deceleration on the occupants in a given crash situation should be less violent than in previous models.

Barker: What other safety features are there?

Hart: Well, what I've always considered to be one of the best safety features—effective face level ventilation and a controlled flow of fresh air through the car to keep the occupants fresh and comfortable at all times.

Barker: I entirely agree with that.

Hart: Others are the recessed door release triggers inside the car, and the mirror with the base of the stem designed to snap if you hit it. Then the door locks have a longitudinal burst strength of 4,000lb, there are seat belt anchorages for the front and provision for fitting these in the back, too. Crash padding and deep recess steering-wheels are standard safety items, and on our fastest car, the Zodiac, we've provided the most advanced dual headlamp lighting system available.

Barker: Why do you not fit duplicated brake lines in cars for the U.K., when you have to for certain overseas markets?

Hart: No, duplicated brake lines are not yet obligatory anywhere. But in some states of the U.S.A. this may be so within the next 12 months. The G.S.A. are demanding the duplicated or dual brake system.

Barker: What's the G.S.A.?

Hart: The General Services Administration, which buys cars for the American government. They will not buy vehicles that have not got their requirements incorporated; these now include 26 safety features. This has its influence on manufacturers, and also in certain states legislation will insist on some of the safety features required by the G.S.A. One of them is the dual brake system, so we are busy engineering these for the future.

Barker: Do you use the SAE Oscar to establish seating profiles, and do you supplement him by any other means?

Hart: We now use an SAE Manikin, which is a modified Oscar with better "comfort angles," as the minimum requirement. You can consider Manikin as a man fixed in a particular driving position with his best comfort angles—between leg and thigh, and hip and torso. If you tried to put him into the Anglia which was designed to an Oscar standard you wouldn't get him in. You would have to put the seat so far back, it would come off its runner, and this applies to most of our competition.

Barker: How do you determine the rate of the seat springs in relation to the road springs?

Hart: Basically seats must be as dead as possible, compatible with support and comfort. Suspension springs and damper settings are tailored initially to give good ride and handling using solid seats. We next put the seats in and the best seat relationship is then determined by appraisal with all types of persons and vehicle usage.

Barker: Now you have some adjustment for steering column rake, and the angle attack on the pedals is improved compared with previous models. But with Dagenham's facilities and abilities, is enough new thinking yet given to controls, driving position and comfort variables?

Hart: I don't think we in Dagenham shall ever be satisfied until there is a common control system standardized throughout the world. But every individual driver has his own preferences—some like one control on the left, others like it on the right, and so on. Until there's an international law governing this we just have to try to place our controls in positions that satisfy most people. For this reason we now employ an ergonomist, whose sole job in life is to find the best compromise for all forms of control, particularly those affecting the vehicle's safety.

Barker: I wonder how long he'll stay on speaking terms with the interior body stylist!

Hart: He may find himself in conflict with Manikin for example, but this is something that's got to be worked out, and I think it's an important issue. Some people have very peculiar driving habits, like sitting right up to the wheel, for example, and it is extremely difficult to get them away from these habits.

Barker: Why have you added this adjustment to the steering column rake, because it seems to be so little?

Hart: Well it's 1½in. and we have found this small dimension adequate and a very big advantage. When we took the smallest woman that we have in engineering here, and also our tallest man, and put them in the Mark IV, they were both able to see well over the steering-wheel; the small woman will find the lowest position on this adjustment extremely comfortable. The tall man can raise it right up to clear his thighs, for example, and this situation can occur in one family.

Barker: Do you do any wind tunnel testing?

Hart: Yes, with quarter-scale models at the initial styling stage; but the full-scale aerodynamics have to be compatible with the type of styling we require. The C_D factor (coefficient of drag) of our models for the Mark IV ranged from 0·41 to 0·51. While a low-drag design would naturally raise maximum speed a few m.p.h. and reduce fuel consumption, one has to make a compromise with practicality and fashion. For the style we chose the figure is 0·47 that's 8 per cent better than the Mark III, incidentally.

Barker: Finally, Mr. Hart, I understand that the team behind these new cars has a pretty impressive record of engineering experience.

Hart: Well, between us my four assistants and I alone have amassed 160 years of it—and all with the Ford Motor Company!

NEW BIG FORDS

ZODIAC
Zephyr V-6/V-4

Mark IV Range

design is always of interest. Ford use a machined combustion space to hold accurately a compression ratio of 9·1-to-1 with the 2·5-litre and 8·9-to-1 for the 3-litre Zodiac. A slight crown is formed in the base of the combustion bowl, and the piston crown is of adequate thickness to provide good heat transfer to the ring belt. In the interest of saving weight with a diameter-to-length ratio of 0·9 to 1, slipper type skirts are used and circumferential slots are cut between the ring belt and the thrust faces to prevent heat transfer to them. Two compression and one scraper ring are used. The upper ring is chromium plated and the second one molybdenum faced. Common connecting rods are used for both sizes of engine, the compression height of the pistons being adjusted accordingly. The rods themselves are nickel-chrome stampings, split horizontally on the centreline with pressed-in gudgeon pins.

Although the flat deck cylinder head is described as being of the crossflow type, in that the exhaust ports are on the opposite side of the head to the inlets, this is not an exact description, since the valves are in-line with the crankshaft. However, this arrangement, dictated by the vee-cylinder arrangement, does permit a good flow of water round the exhaust ports.

The Ford K-iron camshaft, running in steel-backed white metal bearings, is induction hardened and phosphate coated to ensure long life and freedom from scuffing during the break-in period. It is driven by cast-iron helical tooth gears and operates the valves by way of chilled iron tappets and short tubular pushrods. These are positively lubricated from the oil system through restrictor holes in the tappets. Following American practice, the rockers operate on individual, hemispherical mountings carried on posts pressed into the heads; they are in cast iron, the three seatings for the rocker pivot, pushrod end and valve contact face being formed in a single coining operation. Single valve springs are used, while the bi-metal valves run directly in the head. Exhaust valve head material is EN18D with an addition of columbium.

Water is circulated by a separate, belt-driven pump mounted under the right-hand bank of cylinders. It is easily detachable for renewal as a service unit. Reversing normal practice, water is fed first into the cylinder jackets—there is a cross-over pipe between the blocks at the back of the engine—and then through metering holes in the cylinder faces into the cylinder heads and induction pipe water jacket. A wax capsule thermostat ensures quick warm-up. A feature of the cooling system is the high operating pressure, 13 p.s.i., adopted to keep down the size, and cost, of the radiator.

Oil is circulated by either a Burman or Hobourn Eaton pump driven off the bottom end of the skew-driven distributor drive shaft. A throw-away "full-flow" oil filter is incorporated in the system. Mounted high up on the engine for ease of accessibility, it incorporates a weir to keep the system primed in the event of oil drain-away after long standing.

Depending on engine type, mixture is supplied by a single-choke 29mm Zenith 381VT carburettor for the 2·5-litre Zephyr, or 2-choke, vertical Weber 40DFA instrument for the 3-litre Zodiac. Individual, water-heated manifolds are fitted in each case. The single-choke unit is divided by a longitudinal partition, and the requirements of good distribution have necessitated mounting the carburettor at the front end of the manifold. The twin-choke manifold is, in effect, two separate manifolds cast as one; it has ribbed floors to assist heat dissipation from the water jacket. As with the V4, a return fuel system is employed, to prevent fuel vaporization. An AC camshaft-driven pump supplies the fuel, surplus being returned to the tank. A metering block in the system ensures a steady pressure at the carburettor.

The 12-volt electrical system is quite conventional, except that a Lucas 11AC alternator, driven at 2·12 times engine speed, is fitted on Zodiac models. All models have negative earth. ■

Gearbox

Both the manual and automatic transmissions of the V-6 Fords are new. In the case of the 4-speed manual gearbox the general dimensions have been in-

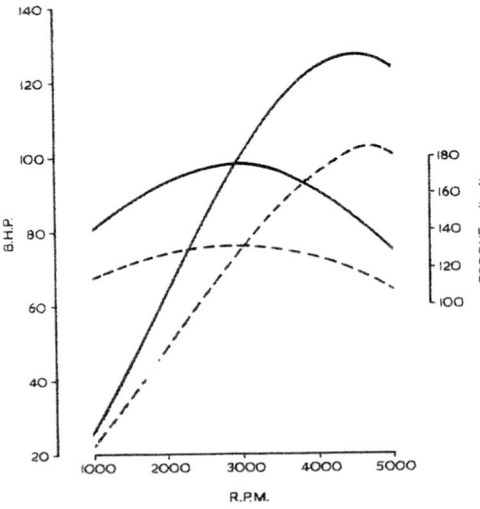

creased to take care of the extra torque of the 3-litre. The casing is a one-piece iron casting with a detachable top plate for access to the selectors. Power is taken to it through a 9-in. Borg and Beck diaphragm spring clutch.

Ford take the trouble to import their own, American made, C4 automatic transmission. It follows conventional lines with a 3-element torque converter, using a freewheel stator and epicyclic gears with hydraulically operated clutches. However, it differs from equivalent British-made transmissions in the design of the governor, which incorporates extra valves to simplify matching the gearbox and to permit the use of a vacuum-operated throttle-sensing device. Extra efficiency is obtained by omitting the push-start oil pump and there are external adjusters for the brake bands. From the driver's point of view there is a manual low hold, useful when hauling caravans or climbing steep gradients; it retains bottom gear. Also there are D1 and D2 positions for the control. The D2 setting blocks out bottom gear and the transmission does all its work in the upper two ratios.

KEY TO DRAWING: 1: Intermediate band. 2: Input shaft. 3: Forward clutch hub and gear annulus. 4: Low gear and reverse drum. 5: Reverse gear annulus. 6: Low reverse band. 7: One-way clutch. 8: Reverse planet carrier. 9: Front planet carrier. 10: Low and reverse servo. 11: Forward clutch. 12: Control levers. 13: High gear clutch

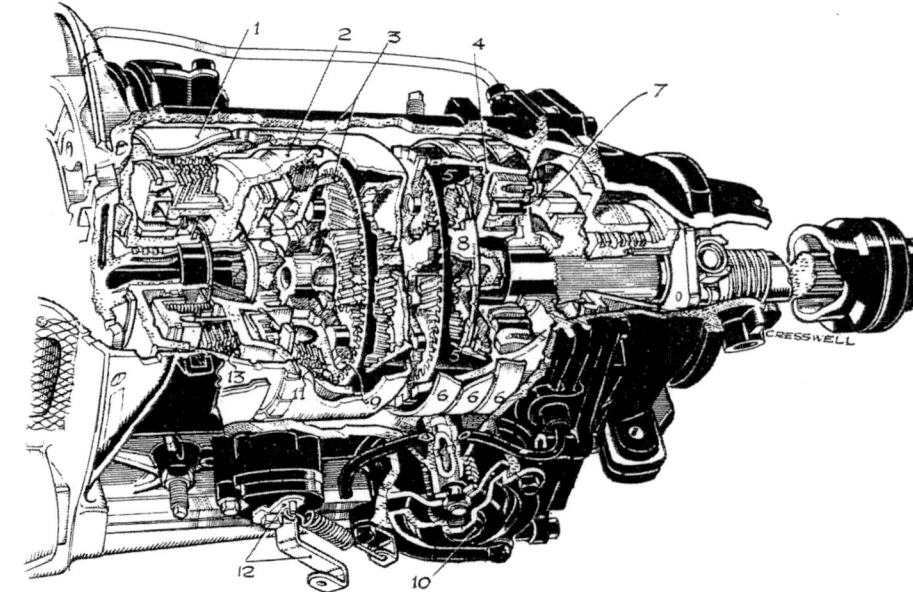